Uncommon Courage

RANDALL J. BREWER

UNCOMMON COURAGE

CONTENTS

INTRODUCTION

Courage is not a rare quality reserved for heroes in history books or warriors on distant battlefields. Courage is the quiet, daily decision to rise when fear whispers that you should retreat. It is the inner resolve to move forward when comfort invites you to stay still. At its core, courage is not the absence of fear - it is the mastery of it. And more than any other trait, courage is the decision to trust God and step forward even when fear tries to hold you back. When you choose courage, you unlock the life you were created to live, walking boldly into purpose, calling, and destiny.

Every meaningful pursuit in life demands courage. It takes courage to believe when doubt surrounds you. It takes courage to begin when the outcome is uncertain. It takes courage to endure when the journey grows long and the cost becomes clear. Success is never accidental; it is always preceded by courageous choices. Dreams do not come alive through intention alone - they are birthed through bold, decisive action. Destiny does not unfold by chance; it responds to the brave who step forward in faith and purpose. Those willing to act with courage discover that destiny meets movement with direction and sacrifice with reward.

Too many people live beneath their potential not because they lack talent, intelligence, or opportunity, but because they lack courage. Fear becomes a silent prison, shaping decisions, limiting vision, and shrinking possibilities. Fear convinces people to settle for what is safe instead of pursuing what is significant. Yet courage disrupts this pattern. Courage challenges the familiar, confronts resistance, and refuses to bow to intimidation. It dares to stand where others withdraw and to speak when silence feels easier.

Uncommon courage is different from ordinary bravery. Ordinary courage appears when circumstances demand it; uncommon courage is a lifestyle. It is the discipline of choosing faith over fear, obedience over hesitation, and purpose over comfort. It is the resolve to stand firm when pressure mounts and to move forward even when confidence feels fragile. Uncommon courage is not loud or reckless - it is steady, intentional, and deeply rooted in conviction. It stands firm when no one is watching, choosing faithfulness over applause and obedience over fear.

Life itself is a series of courageous moments strung together, each choice requiring faith to step forward despite uncertainty. It takes courage to grow, because growth requires change. It takes courage to lead, because leadership invites resistance. It takes courage to love, because love risks rejection. It takes courage to stand for truth, because truth is often unpopular. And it takes courage to finish strong, because endurance demands more than excitement - it requires resolve.

This book is written for those who sense there is more within them than what has been expressed so far. It is for the dreamer who feels the pull of purpose but wrestles with fear. It is for the leader who knows the right direction but feels the weight of responsibility. It is for anyone who has ever stood at the edge of a decision and wondered if they were strong enough to step forward. Within these pages, you will discover that courage is not something you wait for - it is something you build. Courage is strengthened through obedience, sharpened through discipline, and sustained through faith.

As you learn to confront fear rather than accommodate it, you will find that courage becomes a guiding force in every area of life—your work, your relationships, your calling, and your legacy. Uncommon courage changes the trajectory of a life. It transforms hesitation into action, potential into achievement, and vision into reality. When courage becomes your companion, obstacles lose their power, setbacks become teachers, and adversity becomes a proving ground. The life you desire - successful, fulfilled, and purpose-driven - lies on the other side of courageous decisions.

This is an invitation to rise above the ordinary - rejecting fear's limitations and stepping into courage with unwavering resolve. It is a call to embrace the bold, purpose-driven life you were created to live, marked by faith, strength, and forward motion. Courage is not optional for destiny - it is the essential decision that moves you from intention to action. Without courage, purpose remains a promise unfulfilled; with it, destiny begins to take shape. And as you turn the pages ahead, may you discover that the courage you have been searching for has been within you all along waiting to be awakened, strengthened, and unleashed.

| 1 |

"THE KEY TO LIFE"

Courage is the key to life. It takes courage to be successful, to achieve your goals, to fulfill your destiny. Aristotle said, "You will never do anything in this world without courage. It is the greatest quality of the mind next to honor." Courage makes you unbeatable. It takes courage to win. It takes courage to fight back against the forces that try to take you down. Without courage all you'll do is live a life of mediocrity. You'll go nowhere in life and will accomplish nothing of significance. Muhammad Ali said, "He who is not courageous enough to take risks will accomplish nothing in life." You need courage to change your life. You need courage to push through the barriers that try to hinder your forward progress. David Viscott said, "If you could get up the courage to begin, you have the courage to succeed." It takes true courage to master life by choosing responsibility, faith, and resilience, refusing to live as a victim of circumstances and instead rising with purpose and strength.

Without courage, nothing meaningful ever truly begins. It is courage that compels us to step beyond fear, confront uncertainty, and move forward when comfort would keep us still. Every purpose discovered, every calling answered, and every transformation achieved starts with a brave decision to act despite the risk. Courage does not eliminate fear; it masters it, turning hesitation into obedience and potential into progress. Without courage, dreams remain ideas and faith goes untested. But with it, life is unlocked and destiny is set in motion. Every step forward begins with a decision to trust God more than your fear, choosing obedience even when the path ahead is unclear. Faith is not the absence of uncertainty, but the courage to move forward knowing the Lord goes before you. Courage is not the absence of fear; it is the resolve to move forward despite it, the determination to act even when fear is present. True bravery is found in choosing faith-filled action when fear whispers retreat.

From the moment you choose to pursue purpose, courage becomes your constant companion. It rises within you when fear whispers retreat, reminding you that obedience and faith are never passive - they are bold, decisive steps forward. With every act of courage, you align your life with God's calling and discover the strength to endure, advance, and overcome. Dreams demand bravery because they pull us beyond what is comfortable or familiar, calling us to grow into who we are meant to become. They challenge our fears, test our faith, and require us to step forward even when the path is uncertain. Yet it is in that courageous pursuit that purpose is awakened and true transformation begins. A life of significance is always found on the other side of courage, where fear is faced instead of avoided. Courage moves you from comfort into calling, from intention into action. When you dare to step forward in faith, you discover that purpose has been waiting just beyond your willingness to be brave.

It takes courage to believe you were created for more, especially when fear and doubt try to define your limits. Faith rises when you choose to trust God's purpose over your present circumstances. When you step forward in courage, you align your life with the greater calling He placed within you from the very beginning. Many people settle for less, not because they lack ability, but because they lack the boldness to trust their calling. When fear is allowed to speak louder than faith, potential remains buried and purpose goes unfulfilled. Bold trust unlocks the courage to step forward and become everything you were created to be. Courage awakens faith and gives permission for potential to rise, breaking the grip of fear that keeps purpose dormant. When faith is stirred by courage, the heart dares to believe God for more than what is seen or felt. In that bold trust, hidden potential is released and destiny begins to move forward.

Success is not an accident but the result of courageous choices made again and again, even when fear and uncertainty try to hold you back. Each bold decision, no matter how small, compounds over time into growth, strength, and forward momentum. In the end, success belongs to those who choose faith over fear and persistence over comfort, day after day. Behind every achievement stands a person who refused to quit when quitting seemed easier. They pressed forward through doubt, fatigue, and opposition, choosing perseverance over comfort. Victory is often claimed not by the most gifted, but by the most faithful to endure. Courage fuels perseverance when progress feels slow and obstacles feel heavy. It empowers you to take the next step even when the path ahead is unclear and the burden feels overwhelming. With courage, perseverance becomes more than endurance - it becomes a quiet declaration that you will not give up.

To achieve your goals, you must have the courage to begin, because every meaningful victory starts with a single, decisive step. Fear, doubt, and uncertainty often stand guard at the entrance to purpose, but they lose their power the moment you move forward. Beginning turns dreams into direction, faith into action, and hope into progress. When you choose to start, you activate momentum, build confidence, and invite growth along the journey. Courage is not the absence of fear - it is the decision that your calling is greater than your hesitation. Starting is often the hardest part because it exposes you to risk, uncertainty, and criticism from others. Fear magnifies the cost of failure, making delay feel safer than action. Yet nothing truly changes while potential remains trapped in hesitation. Breakthrough begins when courage speaks louder than fear and calls you forward. Transformation begins the moment courage rises and declares, "Now."

Courage also requires discipline, because staying the course is just as demanding as starting the journey. It is one thing to step forward in a moment of inspiration, but it is another to remain faithful when progress feels slow, opposition rises, or the path grows weary. Discipline anchors courage in consistency, turning bold beginnings into steadfast endurance, and momentary bravery into a lifelong commitment to finish what was started. When motivation fades, courage steps in and carries you forward, refusing to let wavering emotions dictate your direction. It becomes the steady anchor when strength feels low, reminding you that progress is not sustained by feelings alone but by conviction and resolve. Courage chooses faith over fear, obedience over comfort, and perseverance over retreat. In those quiet moments when inspiration is absent, courage rises as a disciplined commitment to keep moving, trusting that consistency will eventually restore strength and renew purpose.

Fulfilling your destiny demands a higher level of courage because it calls you to step beyond comfort and familiarity into the unknown. True courage is choosing obedience and faith even when the path is uncertain and the cost feels high. When you rise to that call, you discover that God's strength meets you at every step, empowering you to become who you were created to be. Destiny is rarely convenient; it disrupts comfort and summons you into arenas of responsibility where growth is demanded. It calls you to rise beyond ease, embrace courage, and shoulder purpose even when the cost feels heavy. In answering that call, you will discover that true fulfillment is found not in comfort, but in obedience to what you were created to become. When courage speaks, it silences every excuse as it pushes you forward into purpose despite every reason to hold back. It rises within you, reminding your heart that obedience is stronger than comfort and faith is greater than doubt.

There will be moments when fear whispers lies about your ability, worth, or future, but those voices are not the truth that defines you. Courage confronts those lies with truth and refuses to retreat, standing unmoved when fear tries to distort reality. It holds fast when doubt presses in, strengthening resolve rather than surrendering ground. True courage chooses faith over fear and moves forward with confidence, even when the path is uncertain. Courage is required when failure confronts you, because it gives you the strength to rise instead of retreat. It transforms setbacks into steppingstones, reminding you that growth is forged by pressing forward despite fear. Every meaningful pursuit includes setbacks, but failure is not the end - it is instruction shaping wisdom and resolve. Courage refuses to quit; it learns from the fall, adjusts its course, and presses forward with clarity. Each time it rises again, it stands stronger, wiser, and more determined than before.

It also takes courage to stand alone when obedience sets you apart from the crowd. True faith is proven when you choose God's approval over human applause, trusting that His path - though lonely at times - always leads to purpose and victory. True faith is often proven in the quiet moments when no one else is standing with you. In those moments, God honors the courage that trusts Him above approval, comfort, or compromise. Sometimes obedience to purpose means walking a road few will understand and even fewer will support. It requires courage to trust the calling within when affirmation is absent and the way feels lonely. Yet faithfulness to that purpose produces strength, clarity, and fulfillment that approval from others could never give. Courage reminds you that approval is not the measure of alignment. True alignment is standing firm in truth even when applause is absent and resistance is loud. It chooses obedience over popularity and conviction over comfort.

Relationships require courage because they ask us to be vulnerable, honest, and willing to risk our hearts for genuine connection. True strength is shown not by guarding ourselves, but by choosing love, commitment, and growth even when it feels uncomfortable. It takes bravery to love deeply in a world that often wounds the heart, to forgive freely when holding on to pain feels easier, and to speak truthfully when silence seems safer. True courage is not found in hardness or retreat, but in choosing vulnerability, grace, and honesty even when the cost is high. Those who walk this path reflect strength of character, because they dare to live with an open heart, a clear voice, and a spirit anchored in purpose rather than fear. Courage builds connections that are real because it risks honesty, vulnerability, and truth instead of hiding behind comfort. Real connection is never shallow or safe - it is forged when you dare to show up fully and authentically.

Spiritual growth is rooted in the courage to surrender comfort, confront truth, and obey God even when the path is uncertain. It requires a willing heart that chooses faith over fear, trusting that every step of obedience, though sometimes costly, leads to deeper maturity and stronger intimacy with the Lord. True growth happens when we dare to follow His voice, allowing Him to refine us, stretch us, and shape us into who we were created to become. Trusting God, obeying His voice, and stepping out in faith often defy logic and comfort, requiring us to surrender our need for certainty and control. Faith calls us to move forward even when the path is unclear, believing that God sees what we cannot and knows the end from the beginning. As you respond to His voice with courage, trust becomes an act of worship, declaring that His wisdom is greater than your understanding. God meets your obedience with His presence, power, and purpose, leading you into growth, maturity, and deeper dependence on Him.

Courage strengthens character by calling us to stand firm when fear, pressure, or uncertainty demand that we retreat. Each courageous choice - whether spoken in truth, shown through integrity, or lived out in perseverance - shapes the inner foundation of who we are. Over time, courage forges resilience, deepens conviction, and builds a steady confidence rooted not in ease, but in faithfulness to what is right, even when the cost is high. Each brave decision shapes integrity, resilience, and confidence by forging character in moments where comfort must be exchanged for conviction. When you choose courage over fear, you align your actions with your values, strengthening integrity and building the resilience needed to stand firm under pressure. Over time, these choices cultivate confidence - not rooted in pride, but in the quiet assurance that you can be trusted to do what is right, even when it is difficult. Over time, courage becomes a habit rather than a moment.

Life's battles are not won by strength alone, but by the courage to remain standing when everything within you wants to fall. True victory is found in perseverance, in the quiet resolve to rise up again after failure, to endure pain without surrendering purpose, and to trust that endurance itself is shaping you. In the moments when strength fades, courage carries you forward, teaching you that resilience, faith, and unwavering commitment are often more powerful than force. When pressure mounts and storms rage, courage holds the line not because the battle is easy, but because the heart is anchored in truth. Courage stands firm when fear shouts loudest, choosing faith over retreat and resolve over surrender. It is the quiet strength that refuses to bend, trusting that endurance in the storm forges character, sharpens purpose, and proves that what stands within you is stronger than what rises against you. It refuses to surrender ground meant for victory, standing firm in faith until every promise is fulfilled.

Courage transforms fear into fuel by refusing to let uncertainty dictate the outcome. Instead of running from fear, courage harnesses it, turning tension into determination and resistance into resolve. What once threatened to stop you becomes the very force that sharpens your focus, strengthens your faith, and propels you forward with bold purpose. Instead of running from fear, courage leans into it, recognizing that fear often stands as a marker on the edge of transformation. When you feel afraid, it is usually because you are stepping beyond what is familiar and comfortable, pressing into territory that demands growth, trust, and strength. Courage does not deny fear's presence; it interprets it as confirmation that something meaningful is unfolding. In this way, fear becomes not a signal to retreat, but an invitation to advance forward in pursuit of your dreams. Fear often guards the doorway to your next breakthrough, and courage is the key that unlocks the promise waiting on the other side.

Leadership is impossible without courage, because true leadership demands the strength to stand firm when pressure rises and clarity fades. Courage empowers leaders to make difficult decisions, speak truth when silence is safer, and move forward even when the outcome is uncertain. It is the force that enables a leader to take responsibility, face opposition, and remain faithful to their convictions rather than retreating into comfort. Without courage, leadership becomes passive and reactive but with it, leaders inspire confidence, ignite vision, and guide others through challenge toward growth and purpose. True leaders move forward first, stepping into uncertainty so others have the courage to follow. They take responsibility not only for success, but for mistakes, understanding that accountability builds trust. When hard decisions must be made, they choose what is right over what is easy, knowing leadership is proven in moments of cost. Courage gives them the backbone to lead with conviction and humility.

Your future is shaped by courageous moments that often seem small at the time, those quiet decisions made when no one is watching, faithful steps taken without applause, and choices to obey what is right even when it feels uncomfortable. These moments may not feel heroic, but they carry the weight of destiny, because courage is rarely loud at first; it is steady, intentional, and rooted in conviction. Over time, those small acts of bravery compound, forming character, strengthening faith, and opening doors that fear would have kept closed. What feels like a simple "yes" today can become the foundation for a transformed tomorrow. One brave choice, made in faith and obedience, can redirect the entire course of a life. Courage creates outcomes greater than imagined. In a single moment of courage, God can turn fear into purpose and uncertainty into divine direction. When you step forward trusting Him, that one decision can become the doorway to everything He has prepared for you.

In the end, courage is the key that unlocks purpose, progress, and destiny. It is the quiet resolve to move forward when fear is loud, the strength to obey conviction even when the path is uncertain, and the faith to believe that what lies ahead is greater than what stands in the way. Courage awakens purpose by calling us out of comfort, fuels progress by pushing us beyond hesitation, and shapes destiny by aligning our steps with what we were created to become. Without courage, purpose remains dormant, progress stalls, and destiny is delayed but with it, ordinary lives are transformed into testimonies of faith, growth, and fulfillment. Those who live courageously live fully, embracing each day with purpose rather than fear. They live faithfully, trusting God's direction even when the path requires bold obedience. As a result, their lives become fruitful bearing lasting impact, strong character, and blessings that extend far beyond themselves. Choose courage, and life will open doors no fear ever could.

| 2 |

"STRONG AND COURAGEOUS"

To succeed or fail is a choice you have to make, long before results ever appear. It is decided in the quiet moments when you choose discipline over comfort, faith over fear, and perseverance over excuses. Success is not reserved for the lucky it belongs to those who consistently decide to stand, act, and move forward even when quitting feels easier. Failure, likewise, is rarely sudden; it is the outcome of repeatedly choosing delay, doubt, and surrender instead of resolve. The only enemy that can truly destroy you is the one that convinces you to stop moving forward. Fear, doubt, and complacency gain power only when they paralyze your progress. Keep pressing ahead, because forward motion is where growth, victory, and purpose are found. So be strong! Be courageous! Never give up! Press on! Napoleon Bonaparte said, "Courage isn't having the strength to go on, it is going on when you don't have strength."

Begin your day with courage by choosing faith over fear before the first challenge ever appears. When you rise with courage, you set the tone for victory speaking life, walking in obedience, and facing each moment with confidence that the Lord goes before you and strengthens you for whatever the day holds. When you wake up each morning, start your day by meditating on what God said in Josh. 1:9, "Have I not commanded you? Be strong and of good courage; do not be afraid, nor be dismayed, for the Lord your God is with you wherever you go." Notice that you are commanded to be strong and courageous. This is not an option. Why? "Because your adversary the devil walks about like a roaring lion seeking whom he may devour" (1 Peter 5:8). When you meditate on this command, positive changes will take place in your life. Your attitude will change, your character will change, your words and actions will change.

What you choose to think about when you first wake up sets the direction for your entire day. If your mind begins with gratitude, faith, and purpose, your actions will naturally follow that path. Start your morning with the right thoughts, and you position yourself to walk in strength, clarity, and peace no matter what comes. Be aware that the enemy is poised and ready to attack you before you ever put your feet on the floor. As soon as your eyes open in the morning you need to confess that you are "strong in the Lord and in the power of His might" (Eph. 6:10). Beginning your day with this declaration aligns your heart and mind with God's strength, reminding you that you do not face the day in your own power, but in His. When you start the day aligned with God, you stand prepared, unshaken, and victorious no matter what comes. If you think you're strong, you'll be strong. If you think you're courageous, you'll be courageous. "As a man thinks in his heart, so is he" (Prov. 23:7).

You draw strength from God when you choose to spend time with Him on a daily basis, especially in the early hours of the day when distractions are few and your heart is most receptive. In those quiet moments, His presence renews your spirit, sharpens your focus, and anchors your faith before the demands of life begin to press in. Morning communion with God sets the tone for obedience, clarity, and peace, allowing His wisdom to guide your decisions and His strength to carry you through every challenge you face. You need His strength most at the beginning of the day, before the pressures, decisions, and distractions begin to weigh on your heart and mind. When you start your day in His presence, you are equipped with divine power, clarity, and peace that carries you through every challenge that follows. David wrote in Ps. 63:1, "O God, You are my God; Early will I seek You; My soul thirsts for You." Get up and before you do anything else, spend time with God. Draw your strength from Him.

The basis of courage is not how strong you are, nor how confident you feel in the moment. The basis of courage is God Himself. True courage is born when you recognize that your strength is limited but His is limitless. When God is the foundation, courage becomes a steady resolve rather than a fleeting emotion, anchored in faith instead of fear. You move forward not because you trust your own ability to overcome every obstacle, but because you trust the One who goes before you, stands with you, and empowers you to face whatever lies ahead. Depending on God means recognizing that true strength and lasting courage do not come from within ourselves, but from His presence working in us. When you lean fully on Him, you invite His power to carry you through moments of weakness, and uncertainty. As you trust Him to be strong through you, He enables you to stand firm, move forward in faith, and face every challenge with confidence rooted in His unfailing strength.

Don't just ask God to give you strength but say to Him, "God, you are my strength." In Christ, you are stronger than you think you are, because your strength does not come from your own ability but from His unfailing power. When you feel weak, uncertain, or overwhelmed, He becomes your steady foundation, supplying courage where fear once lived and endurance where you thought you had none. Christ strengthens your heart to stand firm, to move forward in faith, and to rise above every challenge. He is your strength in every season and the living source of all courage that enables you to overcome. Don't measure your circumstances by the size of the problem in front of you; measure them by the greatness of the God who stands with you. When you fix your eyes on how big God is, even the largest challenges shrink in the light of His power and faithfulness. In Him, there is no challenge you can't overcome, no hurdle you can't jump over, no roadblock to hold you back.

God gave His people the Promised Land, but they still had to step forward in faith and fight the battles required to possess it. The promise was certain, yet obedience, courage, and perseverance were demanded along the way. This is why God told them to be strong and courageous. He knew the journey ahead would demand unwavering faith, steadfast obedience, and trust in His promises. Strength and courage were not rooted in their own ability, but in the assurance that the Lord Himself would go before them and never leave their side. So where is courage found? Where does courage come from? It abides with those who have been with Jesus (Acts 4:13). The more time you spend with Him, the more courage you will have. This is why you need to be in the presence of God all day, every day, and not just on Sunday. When you spend quality time with God, His greatness fills your vision so completely that every problem you face becomes smaller than your faith in Him.

To David, God was bigger than Goliath because he had spent quality time in God's presence, learning to trust His power and faithfulness. Those private moments with the Lord shaped David's confidence, so the giant before him looked small compared to the God within him. When you truly know God through daily fellowship, every obstacle shrinks in the light of His greatness. Being with God opens your eyes to the vastness of who He truly is, that He is far greater than your fears, limits, or circumstances. In His presence, your perspective shifts, and what once seemed overwhelming becomes small when compared to His power and faithfulness. The closer you walk with Him, the more clearly you see that nothing is too great for God. You'll begin to say, "Greater is He who is in me than he who is in the world" (1 John 4:4). Courage that comes from being with God will cause you to "run through a troop and leap over a wall" (Ps. 18:29). Always seek the face of God. When you find Him, you'll find courage.

You are called to live boldly and without fear, knowing that your life is anchored in a strength far greater than your own. When doubt or opposition rises, remember that through Christ you are empowered to stand firm, move forward, and accomplish whatever He has placed before you. His strength fills every weakness, His presence drives out fear, and His power enables you to walk with confidence, courage, and unwavering faith in every season of your journey. Jesus is in you, He's for you, He's with you. He said He'll never leave you or forsake you. What more do you need? Have the freedom to live boldly, unchained by the fear of failure, knowing that every step forward is part of your growth. You are fully capable of accomplishing amazing things with your life when you choose courage, purpose, and belief over doubt. Obey God and do the things He tells you to do with strength and confidence and joy in your heart. Trust God and believe He'll do what He said He would do. That is where courage comes from.

There is God-given ability placed deep on the inside of you, crafted by the Creator with purpose and intention. What you see as limitation, God sees as untapped potential waiting to be awakened through faith and obedience. When you trust Him and step forward boldly, you will discover you can do far more with your life than you ever thought possible. Grasp the truth that in Christ you are strong and courageous, equipped with everything you need to face whatever stands before you. His strength flows through your obedience, and His courage steadies your heart when fear tries to rise. Because He goes with you, you can do whatever you need to do - confident, unshaken, and victorious. You have uncommon courage and you are a giant killer. You don't have to be afraid of giants if you know God is with you. You are more than a conqueror so run toward your giant and cut his stupid head off. You are strong and very courageous. Knowing that is enough to take you through anything you face in life.

Courage is also found in the company of other men because faith was never meant to be walked out alone. When men gather with a shared devotion to truth and obedience, Jesus stands in their midst. He said in Matt. 18:20, "For where two or three are gathered together in My name, I am there in the midst of them." He is present strengthening hearts, sharpening resolve, and reminding each one that they are not fighting in their own strength. In that brotherhood, fear loses its grip, courage rises, and men are empowered to stand firm because where Christ is present, courage becomes contagious. Are you looking for courage? Courage is forged when men stand shoulder to shoulder, sharpening one another through faith, truth, and accountability, so do not forsake the assembling of yourselves together as Hebrews 10:25 exhorts us. In the presence of other godly men, strength rises, fear diminishes, and bold faith is awakened. Prov. 27:17 says, "Iron sharpens iron."

Courage is needed today like never before, and it is forged in the presence of God where fear is replaced with faith. With God on your side, one can put a thousand to flight and two can put ten thousand to flight (Deut. 32:30). Jesus said in Matt. 18:19 (NLT), "If two of you agree here on earth concerning anything you ask, My Father in heaven will do it for you." When men seek the Lord together, sharpening one another through genuine fellowship, strength and resolve are renewed. Stand firm, walk boldly, and let God's presence shape you into the man of courage this generation needs. Courage abides in community because Christ abides in community. Courage is born when men speak life into one another, reminding each other who they are and what they're called to become. When men choose to walk together, encouragement multiplies and courage rises to meet every challenge. 1 Thess. 5:11, "So encourage each other and build each other up, just as you are already doing."

Where is courage found? Where does courage abide? It is found where fear is confronted rather than avoided, in the heart that chooses to stand firm. It abides in the place where resolve outweighs hesitation and conviction overrules comfort. Where determination exists, courage takes root and rises to meet every challenge. When you make up your mind that the will of God will be fulfilled in your life, courage rises to meet your obedience. What once felt impossible becomes attainable when faith moves you from intention to action. Peter and John were beaten and told to stop preaching the gospel. They prayed and asked God for the boldness to preach the Word anyway. Acts 4:29, "And now, O Lord, hear their threats, and give us, Your servants, great boldness in preaching Your word." That's determination! They were resolute in faith, fully determined to possess everything God promised and to walk in complete obedience to all He instructed them to do.

Because of their determination, courage came. Vs. 33, "And with great power the apostles gave witness to the resurrection of the Lord Jesus." Their prayer for boldness rose as a direct response to a world demanding their silence. Rather than shrinking back, they chose obedience, placing God's will above comfort, approval, and consequence. In doing so, they demonstrated that true faith speaks most clearly when it refuses to be quiet. Are you determined to be the man God called you to be? Are you determined to do what God has called you to do? Be determined! "Having done all to stand, stand therefore" (Eph. 6:13,14). Determination anchors your faith when the battle is fierce and the journey is long, empowering you to remain steadfast in the strength God supplies. Indeed, unwavering determination will carry you through every trial and take you all the way to your destiny. Where will you be in two years? Wherever you determine to be. The choice is yours.

Where does courage abide? Courage abides where the Holy Spirit is poured out, strengthening the heart and steadying the soul. When the Spirit fills a life, fear loses its voice and bold obedience rises to take its place. Acts 4:31, "After this prayer, the meeting place shook, and they were all filled with the Holy Spirit. Then they preached the word of God with boldness." Without a doubt, the world today needs an outpouring of the Holy Spirit - one that brings conviction where hearts have grown cold, wisdom where confusion reigns, and hope where despair has taken root. In an age marked by division, moral uncertainty, and restless souls searching for meaning, the Holy Spirit alone can awaken truth, restore compassion, and realign humanity with God's purpose. Such an outpouring would renew faith, heal broken lives, and empower believers to live boldly in love, humility, and obedience, becoming living witnesses of God's transforming grace in a world desperate for light.

The good news is there is a latter-day outpouring of the Holy Spirit reserved for the days in which we now live (Joel 2:23). When you get together with other men, pray for the outpouring of the Spirit of God. Acts 1:8, "But you will receive power when the Holy Spirit comes upon you. And you will be My witnesses, telling people about Me everywhere." Acts 4:30, "Stretch out Your hand with healing power; may miraculous signs and wonders be done through the name of Your holy Servant Jesus." Miracles happen when you arrive at the place where courage abides, because fear no longer governs your steps and faith is free to move. In that space, obedience replaces hesitation, and trust in God outweighs every obstacle standing in the way. When courage takes root in the heart, the impossible becomes possible, and divine power is released to accomplish what only God can do. Miraculous things happen through the hands of courageous men. Be a man with uncommon courage and watch what God will do.

Courage is the visible fruit of confidence, the inner assurance that steadies a person when fear tries to take control. You have never seen a truly courageous individual who lacked confidence, because courage is born when someone trusts what they believe, who they are, and what they stand for. Confidence doesn't mean the absence of fear; it means having enough conviction to move forward despite it. When confidence is rooted deeply - especially in faith and purpose - it empowers a person to stand firm, speak boldly, and act decisively even in uncertain moments. Courage, then, is not a sudden burst of bravery, but the natural outcome of a confident heart that refuses to be ruled by doubt. Courage is the most important of all virtues because without courage you can't practice any other virtue consistently. Your potential has no limit. You can go as far as you desire, as far as your courage will take you. Courage is not the absence of fear; it's the judgment that what you want is far more important.

It takes courage to stand strong when the wind is blowing and the storm is raging, refusing to be moved by fear or doubt. True strength is revealed in the decision to remain faithful, anchored, and unshaken when everything around you is trying to pull you apart. In those moments, perseverance becomes a testimony that storms may test you, but they will never define you. John Wayne said, "Courage is being scared to death but saddling up anyway." George Patton said, "Courage is fear holding on a minute longer." Have the courage to step out of the boat and trust God when others choose comfort in the safety of the familiar. Faith is often found beyond the comfort zone, where obedience requires risk and miracles begin. It takes uncommon courage to be a man; courage not found in comfort but forged in the decision to rise up and face your fears head-on. As Thomas Jefferson once said, "One man with courage is a majority." Be that man!

| 3 |

"THE COST OF COURAGE'

ourage has a lot to do with the unexpected. Sometimes it's the unknown that keeps people from being courageous. People don't want to walk through a door if they don't know what's on the other side. Courage says you must step out in order to find out. You must come to a place of openness and willingness. William Faulkner said, "You cannot swim for new horizons until you have courage to lose sight of the shore." The word "courageous" means 'to be not deterred by danger or pain.' Courage says, "I can do all things through Christ who strengthens me" (Phil. 4:13). Courage is not defined by how you missed the mark in the past, it's about how you're willing to step out and do the right thing today. Reach out and stretch your faith. Step into the unknown with confidence, knowing that God goes before you and stands faithful in every moment you cannot yet see. What feels uncertain to you is already held securely in His hands, where purpose, protection, and promise await.

Courage is often portrayed as strength without fear, resolve without hesitation, and confidence without doubt. We imagine courage as standing tall, chest out, ready to face anything alone. Yet biblical courage tells a very different story. True courage does not begin with self-confidence; it begins with God-confidence. When we stop relying on our own strength and fully trust in His power, fear loses its grip and faith takes the lead. Courage is born when we know that the

One who goes before us is greater than any challenge we face. The cost of courage is humility. It requires admitting that you are not enough on your own. True bravery begins when you recognize your own limitations. It takes strength to admit that you are not enough on your own and that pride cannot carry you forward. Courage bows before truth, acknowledging the need for growth, guidance, and grace. In that surrender, humility becomes the doorway through which real power and purpose are found.

That truth cuts against pride, independence, and self-reliance. It forces us to lay down the illusion that we can handle life by sheer willpower. Pride goes before a fall (Prov. 16:18) but humility leads to promotion. "Humble yourself in the sight of the Lord and He will lift you up" (James 4:10). Humility is not weakness; it is clarity. It is seeing yourself accurately in light of who God is. It is recognizing your limits while fully trusting the limitless power, wisdom, and holiness of God. In that clear perspective, dependence becomes strength, and surrender becomes the doorway to grace. When you recognize your limitations, you come face to face with the truth that you were never meant to do life on your own. In that moment of humility, God's unlimited power becomes evident, stepping in where human strength falls short. What feels like weakness is often the very doorway through which His strength is most clearly revealed. Courage grows not from denying weakness, but from surrendering it.

Many people hesitate to step out in faith because they feel unqualified, focusing more on their limitations than on God's power. They wait until they feel strong enough, prepared enough, or brave enough but that moment rarely comes. Growth begins the instant you step forward in faith, not when fear finally disappears. Courage is not the denial or absence of fear; it is the decision to obey God even when fear is present and pressing in. It rises from a heart anchored in trust, not in self-confidence or favorable circumstances, but in the unchanging faithfulness of God. True courage acknowledges the risk, feels the weight of uncertainty, and still steps forward because obedience matters more than comfort. It is faith in motion - choosing to believe God's promises over visible threats, choosing surrender over retreat, and choosing action over paralysis. In this way, courage becomes an act of worship, declaring that God is greater than what we fear and worthy of our trust, even when the outcome is unseen.

Admitting you need God is costly because pride resists dependence and insists on self-sufficiency. To acknowledge your need for Him requires laying down the illusion of control and surrendering the ego that wants credit and authority. Yet in that surrender, pride is broken and true strength is found not in ourselves, but in God. Pride says, "I've got this," standing tall on self-confidence and human strength, trusting its own wisdom to navigate life's battles. Humility, on the other hand, bows its heart and says, "Lord, I can't do this without You," fully aware that apart from God we are weak, limited, and prone to stumble. Pride isolates you by convincing you that you don't need anyone - not even God. Humility positions you for divine help by opening your heart to dependence on the Lord, where grace, strength, and guidance freely flow. Pride leans on self; humility leans on grace. Pride seeks control; humility seeks surrender. And it is in that surrender where we acknowledge our dependence on God.

God never asked His people to be strong apart from Him. Over and over in scripture, God calls ordinary, fearful, imperfect people and invites them to rely on His strength. Courage is born when faith rises to meet God's call. True courage does not deny weakness; it acknowledges it and still steps forward in obedience. When God calls, He is not looking for flawless vessels but willing men who trust His strength more than they fear their own limitations. Faith answers not with confidence in self, but with confidence in God, believing that what He initiates, He empowers. In that moment of surrender, courage takes root. It grows as faith shifts the focus from personal inadequacy to divine sufficiency. God's call often stretches us beyond what feels safe or reasonable, precisely so His power can be revealed through our dependence on Him. Courage, then, is not the absence of fear or doubt; it is the decision to move forward anyway, trusting that God's presence will fill every gap where our ability falls short.

Humility keeps your heart teachable by positioning you as a lifelong learner rather than a finished product. When you walk in humility, you remain open to correction, wisdom, and growth whether it comes from God, scripture, or the people He places in your life. A humble heart doesn't resist truth; it welcomes it. It understands that strength is not found in pretending to know everything, but in acknowledging there is always more to learn. This posture allows God to shape character, refine motives, and expand capacity without resistance. At the same time, humility anchors your spirit, keeping you steady when circumstances shift or success arrives. It guards against pride and insecurity by rooting your identity in God rather than performance or position. When storms come, a humble spirit doesn't panic - it trusts God. It knows who is in control and rests in that assurance. Humility keeps you grounded, stable, and aligned, allowing you to stand firm in faith while remaining gentle, receptive, and led.

Trusting God means releasing your grip on control and surrendering the steering wheel of your life to the One who sees the road ahead. It requires humility to admit that our vision is limited, shaped by emotion, fear, and incomplete information. God's wisdom, however, is not constrained by time or circumstance. When you trust Him, you choose faith over anxiety and obedience over understanding, believing that even when the path feels uncertain, He is guiding you with perfect clarity and purpose. Surrender does not mean passivity; it means active reliance on God's character and promises. Trusting Him is a daily decision to move forward even when explanations are absent, confident that His plans are higher and His ways are better than your own. As you let go of the need to control every outcome, you will discover peace, freedom, and strength. In yielding to God's wisdom, you find that what we lose in control, we gain in direction, assurance, and unshakable hope.

You need God's help not only to begin the journey, but to stay on it. He is the strength that carries you when your resolve fades and the guide that keeps your steps aligned when the path grows unclear. What grace starts, only steadfast reliance on Him can sustain. Each step forward requires renewed dependence, renewed prayer, and renewed trust because growth in faith is never sustained by yesterday's strength. As we move ahead, we are reminded that self-reliance fades quickly, but dependence on God anchors us in purpose and peace. Renewed prayer keeps our hearts aligned with His will, allowing us to listen as much as we speak, and to receive fresh wisdom for each new challenge. Renewed trust releases our grip on fear and uncertainty, affirming that God's guidance is sufficient for what lies ahead. Forward movement in life is not about having all the answers, but about continually returning to the Source who does - step by step, day by day, with humility, faith, and confident expectation.

Humility keeps courage from becoming arrogance. Without humility, courage turns into recklessness. Humility anchors courage in grace, ensuring boldness serves others rather than elevating self into haughtiness. God does not honor self-promotion, because self-promotion places the spotlight on human strength, ambition, and pride rather than on His power and purpose. Scripture consistently shows that when people strive to exalt themselves, they limit what God desires to do through them. In contrast, God empowers surrender. When a person humbles themselves, lays down personal agendas, and yields fully to His will, God releases grace, authority, and favor that cannot be produced by effort alone. Surrender creates space for God to move, guide, and elevate in His timing and His way. It is not weakness but an act of trust that invites divine strength to flow through a yielded life, proving that true elevation comes not from self-promotion, but from wholehearted dependence on God.

The enemy of courage is not fear; it is self-sufficiency, the quiet confidence that says, "I don't need any help." Fear, when faced honestly, can drive a person to seek strength beyond themselves, to lean into faith, wisdom, and truth that steadies the heart. Self-sufficiency, however, convinces the soul it needs nothing and no one, quietly eroding humility and dependence on God. It replaces bold trust with guarded control and surrender with stubborn pride. True courage is not born from believing you are strong enough on your own, but from recognizing your need for God's power working through your weakness. When self-sufficiency is laid down, courage rises not as reckless confidence, but as resolute faith that steps forward knowing the outcome rests in His hands. When you believe you must stand strong alone, fear quietly takes control of your heart. When you believe God is with you, fear loses its grip and its voice grows weak. Courage rises where trust in Him is planted and allowed to grow.

God's strength is most visible when your weakness is acknowledged. He does His greatest work in hearts fully surrendered where His power, purpose, and grace are free to move unhindered. When you say, "Lord, I need You," you are opening the door for God's power to move in your situation. That simple, sincere confession shifts the burden from your own limited strength to His limitless ability. It is an act of humility that acknowledges you cannot do life alone and an act of faith that declares God is both willing and able to intervene. In that moment, pride gives way to dependence, fear bows to trust, and chaos begins to yield to divine order. God responds to hearts that lean on Him, because dependence invites His presence, and His presence carries power, wisdom, and peace. When you admit your need, you position yourself to receive His guidance, His strength, and His supernatural help transforming desperation into expectation and turning impossibility into an opportunity for Him to be glorified.

Humility opens the door for grace. Grace does not flow to the proud, but to the dependent. Courage fueled by grace endures long after the rush of adrenaline fades and the applause of ego grows silent. Adrenaline-driven courage burns hot but briefly, rising in moments of excitement, fear, or pride, only to collapse when the pressure becomes steady and the cost becomes real. Ego-based courage seeks recognition and validation, but it weakens when sacrifice goes unnoticed or when failure threatens identity. Grace-fueled courage, however, is sustained by humility, purpose, and trust in something greater than self. It does not depend on emotion, recognition, or immediate victory. Instead, it draws strength from conviction, perseverance, and the quiet assurance that obedience and faithfulness matter even when no one is watching. This kind of courage remains standing in long seasons, heavy trials, and unseen battles because grace supplies what adrenaline and ego never can: lasting strength.

You were never meant to carry the full weight of God's call on your own. God never intended courage to be a solitary act of willpower, but a shared exchange between divine strength and human obedience. When you attempt to shoulder the assignment alone, courage turns heavy and purpose feels exhausting. But when you lean into God's presence, courage becomes sustainable. His strength was always meant to undergird your yes, filling the gap where your ability ends and His faithfulness begins. The burden lifts the moment you stop pretending you can do it all. Relational courage invites humility - the willingness to depend, to listen, and to receive help from God and others He places around you. In that surrender, obedience no longer feels like strain but alignment. You discover that you are not weak for needing support; you are walking as designed. Courage flourishes not in isolation, but in communion, where God carries what you were never meant to bear alone.

Courage that honors God begins where self-confidence ends. It does not deny your weakness; it acknowledges it and then places full weight on the faithfulness of God. When you trust God's character, His goodness, wisdom, power, and faithfulness you stop measuring the moment by your limitations and start measuring it by His promises. That shift lifts the burden of performance and replaces it with the confidence that obedience, not ability, is what God requires. When courage moves from capability to trust, everything changes. Fear loses its authority because the outcome no longer rests on your strength alone. Faith steps forward even when the path is unclear, because God's character has already proven trustworthy. This kind of courage doesn't rush ahead in arrogance or shrink back in insecurity - it walks forward in surrender. It knows that if God has called you, He will sustain you, and that trusting Him fully is the bravest step you can take, the boldest choice you'll ever make.

When you admit you need God, you stop striving in your own strength and start standing in His. Striving depends on human effort, limited understanding, and fragile resolve. Standing, however, is an act of trust. It is the decision to rest your weight on God's promises, to believe that what He has spoken is enough, and to anchor your heart in His unchanging faithfulness. In that posture, fear loses its grip because your confidence is no longer built on what you can control, but on who He is. This is where true courage finds its footing. Courage is not the absence of weakness; it is the willingness to rely fully on God's power in the midst of it. When you stand on His promises, you discover that His strength sustains you, His presence steadies you, and His power carries you forward. You may not always know the next step, but you know the One who holds the path. And when God is your foundation, you can stand firm, unshaken, and bold because your courage is rooted in Him, not in yourself.

The cost of courage will always be humility, but the reward is God's presence. You gain peace instead of pressure, strength instead of striving, and confidence rooted in Him rather than yourself. To walk courageously is to lay down the need to be seen, applauded, or proven right, and instead trust God with the outcome. Doing that creates space for God's presence to dwell richly in your life. The reward for this courage is a life anchored in God's presence, strengthened by His peace, and sustained by a confidence that no circumstance can shake. In God's presence, peace replaces pressure because the burden of performance is lifted. Strength replaces striving because we are no longer powered by exhaustion but by His Spirit. Confidence takes on a new foundation - no longer rooted in your abilities, titles, or achievements, but anchored in who God is and who you are in Him. This kind of courage stands quietly, assured that when we humble ourselves before God, He supplies everything we need.

True courage is not stepping out alone; it is stepping out with God. It is the quiet, unshakable resolve to move ahead with God, fully aware of your limitations and fully trusting His strength. Courage begins where pride ends - when you acknowledge that your wisdom is insufficient and your power incomplete. To say, "I cannot do this without You and I don't want to," is not weakness; it is spiritual clarity. It is the recognition that your best steps are taken when they are guided, supported, and sustained by a faithful God. There is a deeper boldness found in surrender than in striving. By seeking God's help you are choosing dependence over independence, partnership over performance. In that moment, fear loses its grip because the outcome is no longer resting on you alone. Surrender invites God's power into your obedience, transforming human courage into something unstoppable. When you step forward with God, humility becomes strength, faith becomes fuel, and courage becomes a force that cannot be shaken.

| 4 |

"ACTIVATE YOUR COURAGE"

Activate your courage by having a one-on-one encounter with God. Do that and He will give you the courage to do what He has called you to do. Courage is not something you manufacture through willpower or motivational speeches. True courage is awakened when you encounter God personally, not merely as an idea or tradition, but as a living, holy presence that transforms us from the inside out. In His presence, fear begins to lose its grip, because we realize we are not standing alone - we are standing before the One who is greater than every obstacle we face. When God reveals Himself to us, He replaces our uncertainty with assurance and our weakness with divine strength. Courage rises not from self-confidence, but from God-confidence, born in moments of surrender, reverence, and intimacy with Him. It is there, in His presence, that our hearts are steadied, our vision is clarified, and we are empowered to step forward in obedience, faith, and bold trust.

A one-on-one encounter with God strips away the noise of expectations, fears, and comparisons that so often shape how we live and how we see ourselves. In that sacred space, there is no audience to perform for and no standard to measure up to except truth itself. The pressure to impress dissolves, and the exhausting effort of pretending fades. What remains is a quiet, honest meeting where the soul is laid bare, and the heart can finally speak without interruption or disguise. In that moment, it is just you and the One who knows you completely - every strength, every wound, every hidden thought. God does not meet you with condemnation or surprise, but with clarity, mercy, and love. There, you are not reduced to your failures or elevated by your successes; you are simply known. And in being fully known, you are invited to be fully healed, reshaped, and restored, discovering that true freedom is found not in comparison or approval, but in His presence alone.

God does not demand perfection, but He does require surrender. He is not searching for flawless performance, but for a willing heart. Surrender becomes the doorway through which peace enters, because you are no longer striving to be enough - you are trusting the One who already is. Courage is not birthed by pretending to be strong, but by admitting where we are weak. It takes far more bravery to say, "I can't do this on my own," than to hide behind confidence we don't truly have. In acknowledging your limitations, you make room for God's strength to move. Weakness becomes an invitation for His power to be revealed. When you allow Him to meet you in your weakness, transformation begins. God does His deepest work in the surrendered places, turning brokenness into testimony and fear into faith. As you yield control, He replaces anxiety with assurance and uncertainty with hope. In that sacred exchange, you discover that true courage is not found in self-reliance, but in wholehearted dependence on Him.

Many people want courage without communion. They long for boldness but resist intimacy, hoping strength will rise from sheer determination or ambition alone. Courage is not manufactured by sheer willpower or personal resolve; it is cultivated through relationship with God. Strength is born from nearness to Him, rising naturally through intimacy rather than effort. When the heart remains distant from God, confidence becomes fragile and easily shaken. True courage cannot survive on hype or self-motivation - it must be rooted in something deeper and eternal. As you draw closer to God, strength rises within you. In His presence, fear loses its grip and clarity replaces confusion. Communion aligns your heart with His, and from that alignment flows a quiet, unshakable boldness. This courage is not loud or boastful; it is steady, grounded, and enduring. It rises not because you strive harder, but because you are standing closer anchored in intimacy, sustained by relationship, and empowered by His nearness.

Throughout scripture, men and women were profoundly changed in moments alone with God. It was not in the noise of the crowd or the safety of routine that their lives were reshaped, but in quiet encounters where heaven met the human heart. Moses was transformed on the mountain, David in the fields, Elijah in the cave, and Mary in stillness and surrender. Their courage did not rise from strategy, influence, or position, but from an undeniable encounter with the living God that redefined who they were and what they were called to do. God still speaks in this way today. When distractions are stripped away and we intentionally listen, His voice becomes clear and personal. In solitude, fear gives way to faith, confusion to clarity, and weakness to strength. These sacred moments recalibrate our hearts, reminding us that true courage is not manufactured - it is imparted. When we step away from the noise and draw near to God, we discover that His presence alone is enough to change everything.

A personal encounter with God has a way of realigning everything we thought we understood. In His presence, our perspective shifts from limitation to possibility, from self-reliance to surrender. Fear that once shouted over our thoughts grows quiet when God speaks with clarity and authority. His voice cuts through confusion, not with condemnation, but with purpose that reminds us of who He is and who we are in Him. When His truth fills the silence, doubt has no room to grow. What once felt overwhelming and unreachable begins to take on a new shape not as something we must conquer, but something we are called to obey. The impossible becomes an invitation to trust, and obedience no longer feels like loss, but an alignment with His will and purpose. In that encounter, we discover that God never asks us to move without first reshaping our hearts to trust that He will meet us there. Before He changes our direction, He transforms our belief preparing us inwardly for the step of faith ahead.

God does not call us because we are courageous; He gives us courage because He has called us. The order matters. God's calling always precedes our confidence. He does not wait for us to be ready or fully equipped before He speaks our name. Instead, He calls us in our weakness and meets us there with His presence. Courage is not the qualification for the call - it is the result of responding to it. When God speaks, He is already accounting for everything we lack and promising to supply it through Himself. When you encounter Him, you receive more than direction -you receive divine empowerment. What once felt impossible becomes achievable because His strength now fuels your steps. God never sends you forward empty-handed; He sends you empowered by His Spirit. The calling releases the courage, and obedience unlocks the strength. Step forward knowing that if He has called you, He has already placed within you everything you need to walk it out.

Courage is activated the moment you learn to recognize and respond to God's voice above the noise of your own insecurity. In His presence you'll stop asking, "Am I capable?" and start trusting that He is forever faithful. When you quiet your doubts and lean in to hear Him, courage rises not because you suddenly feel strong, but because you are anchored to His word. His voice doesn't deny our weakness; it transcends it, reminding us that obedience is not fueled by self-confidence, but by trust in the One who calls us. In His presence, identity becomes clear and confusion loses its grip. We stop measuring ourselves by limitations, past mistakes, or human expectations, and we begin to see ourselves through the lens of His purpose. When you trust His faithfulness, courage becomes a response, not a struggle. You will move forward not because you are certain of yourself, but because you are certain of Him. When your trust rests in Him, uncertainty loses its power and obedience becomes your strength.

One-on-one moments with God are where spiritual confidence is formed. In the quiet places away from applause, pressure, and opinions God strengthens your heart through His presence and His Word. These moments don't inflate self-belief; they deepen trust. Confidence grows not from knowing your own ability, but from knowing His voice and choosing to obey it. When you walk closely with Him, obedience becomes less about fear of failure and more about faith in His faithfulness. As that confidence takes root, forward movement follows. You don't step out because everything feels safe or because you feel fully prepared - you step out because you know He is with you. His presence becomes your assurance, His promise your anchor. Even when the path is unfamiliar, obedience becomes possible because you're no longer relying on your readiness, but on His companionship. With God beside you, obedience turns uncertainty into courage and faith into action.

God often chooses the quiet, hidden places to speak His clearest words. It's in the secret place where it's just you and Him that He forms convictions, calls, and directions that are meant to shape your life. What He births in private is not fragile; it is deeply rooted, tested in stillness, and anchored in intimacy with Him. When the season comes for that word to be revealed publicly, it carries weight and endurance because it was first sustained by His presence, not by human approval. Private encounters with God always lead to public obedience. When you have learned to hear His voice in solitude, you are not easily swayed by noise, fear, or opposition when obedience requires visibility. The strength to stand, speak, and act openly comes from time spent listening, surrendering, and aligning your heart with Him in secret. What is formed in private becomes the foundation for faithful obedience in public, proving that intimacy with God always precedes impact for God.

When you meet God personally, fear is confronted at the root - not just managed but exposed openly. In His presence, fear loses its authority because you discover it was never meant to lead you. What once felt like a warning to retreat becomes an invitation to lean in, to trust Him where your understanding runs out. A personal encounter with God reframes fear from a threat into a doorway, revealing that He is already present on the other side of what you're afraid to face. When you meet God personally, fear is confronted at the root. You realize fear is not a signal to stop - it is an invitation to trust God deeper. Trust anchors your heart in who God is rather than what you can manage, and that confidence empowers you to move forward despite uncertainty. You'll have the strength to walk boldly where fear once tried to stop you, transforming hesitation into holy confidence. When you trust God, the very place that once intimidated you becomes the ground where courage rises and purpose moves forward.

Encountering God reminds us that we are never stepping out alone. When He calls us forward, He goes before us, clearing the way and aligning each step with His purpose. In seasons of uncertainty or transition, this truth anchors our hearts knowing that God is already present in the place we are heading. Not only does He go before us, but He also stands beside us. His presence is constant, not distant, offering guidance, comfort, and reassurance along the journey. God walks with us in every moment, strengthening our resolve and reminding us that His companionship is our confidence. As we encounter Him daily, courage begins to flow from within rather than being forced from without. Faith becomes a calm, confident response to His nearness, not a fearful reaction to changing circumstances. Because He strengthens us from the inside out, we can move forward with boldness and trust knowing that no matter what lies ahead, His presence is enough to sustain us.

In that sacred one-on-one place with God, your motives are reshaped. In the quiet, without an audience, He refines the intentions of your heart. You begin to realize that obedience carries more weight than approval, and faithfulness matters more than fame. In that intimate space, He aligns your desires with His will, teaching you that true significance is found not in being seen by people, but in being known by Him. As your motives shift, so does your courage. It no longer rises from pride or the need to prove yourself; it flows from a sincere longing to honor God alone. This kind of courage is steady, humble, and unshakable because it is rooted in devotion rather than performance. When your heart is set on pleasing Him, boldness becomes pure and conviction becomes clear. You stand firm not for applause, but for obedience. And in that purified courage, you discover a strength that cannot be manipulated by praise or diminished by criticism because it was born in the presence of God.

God does not reveal the entire path before you move. Instead, He places a single step in front of you - clear enough to obey, but small enough to require trust. We often want guarantees and visible outcomes, but faith does not grow in full visibility; it grows in partial light. The Lord teaches us to walk by trust, not by sight. When He gives you the next step, He is inviting you into a deeper relationship where obedience matters more than understanding. Courage is activated the moment you step forward without seeing the end of the journey. When you move in faith, you declare that His character is more reliable than your fear. You may not see what's around the bend, but you trust the One who does. Each faithful step builds spiritual strength, clarity, and confidence. And as you walk, what once felt uncertain becomes testimony. God doesn't show you the entire path because He wants you listening, trusting, and moving with Him one courageous step at a time.

The more you encounter God; the more courage becomes less of a struggle and more of a reflex. In His presence, fear begins to lose its grip because you are reminded of Who walks with you and Who goes before you. What once demanded extraordinary effort slowly transforms into a steady confidence rooted in trust. When you have seen His faithfulness again and again, bravery is no longer something you manufacture - it becomes something you carry. Courage stops being an event and starts becoming your posture. As your relationship with Him deepens, obedience shifts from feeling dangerous to feeling natural. What once seemed risky now feels right, because your heart has been aligned with His will. The unknown is no longer threatening when you trust the One who knows all things. Each encounter builds spiritual memory, and that memory strengthens your resolve. You begin to move not out of pressure, but out of knowing that wherever He leads, grace will meet you there.

God's presence has a way of silencing the internal debate that once kept you stuck between fear and faith. When you truly encounter Him, hesitation begins to lose its voice. The doubts that once seemed loud and convincing are overshadowed by the steady assurance of His nearness. In His presence, you begin to see that obedience is not a reckless leap into the unknown, but a confident step with the One who knows the end from the beginning. As His presence surrounds you, a quiet strength settles deep within your spirit. It is not loud or boastful; it is calm, steady, and unshakable. You move forward not because you have figured everything out, but because you trust the One who called you. The God who summoned you into purpose is the same God who sustains you along the way. His calling always comes with His carrying. And when you realize that He goes before you, walks beside you, and stands behind you, hesitation gives way to holy resolve, and you advance forward with peace.

Courage rooted in an encounter with God is not manufactured by emotion or sustained by favorable circumstances - it is born in His presence. When you have truly met Him, when His voice has steadied your heart and His Spirit has affirmed your calling, something unshakable is established within you. This kind of courage does not depend on applause, visible progress, or guaranteed outcomes. It flows from relationship. It stands firm because it knows Who stands behind it. Pressure may rise, doors may close, and uncertainty may linger, but the soul that has encountered God remembers His faithfulness and refuses to retreat. Sustainable courage is anchored in intimacy with Him. It endures because it is not fueled by hype but by revelation. Your boldness is not rooted in your strength, but in His character. And because He does not change, the courage He births in you does not fade. It perseveres, it presses forward, and it remains steady because your relationship with Him is secure.

Activate your courage by stepping into the presence of God and meeting Him face to face. True courage is not born from self-confidence, talent, or willpower but is ignited in an encounter with the living God. When you draw near to Him in prayer, worship, and surrender, fear begins to lose its grip. In His presence, you gain clarity about who He is and who you are. You begin to see that the battles before you are not yours alone to fight. Courage awakens when you realize you are standing with the Almighty, and nothing is impossible for Him. In that sacred encounter, God will give you the strength to do what He has called you to do not in your power, but in His. His Spirit empowers, equips, and emboldens you to step forward even when the path looks uncertain. When God goes with you, courage becomes unstoppable because it is anchored in His faithfulness, not your feelings. You speak boldly, act confidently, and stand firmly not because you are strong, but because He is.

| 5 |

"THE BENEFITS OF COURAGE"

The spiritual benefits of courage are profound and life-shaping. It develops within you a deeper trust in God for it forces you to step beyond comfort and lean fully on God's promises rather than your own strength. When you confront fear instead of avoiding it, your faith muscles develop. Trials become training grounds. Courage empowers you to follow God's calling even when it's unpopular, uncertain, or costly. Courage breaks the bondage of fear and releases you into peace and confidence. A man who is strong and courageous stands firm in truth, inspiring others and reflecting Christ boldly. Courage under pressure produces perseverance, maturity, and integrity. When you step into the valley of the shadow of death, you will experience His presence, power, and faithfulness in deeper ways. In short, courage is not just bravery - it is faith in action. Spiritually, it transforms believers from spectators into warriors, from hesitant followers into bold ambassadors of the Kingdom.

Courage is not the absence of fear; it is the decision to move forward in spite of it. Fear is a natural response to the unknown, but it does not have to dictate your direction. True courage rises when your faith becomes louder than your fear. It is the quiet resolve that says, "I will trust God anyway. I will step out anyway. I will believe anyway." Every great calling, every divine assignment, and every meaningful breakthrough begins with a courageous step into territory that feels uncomfortable, uncertain, and even intimidating. Fear may knock at the door, but courage answers it with faith. When you choose to move forward, you declare that your confidence is not in your own strength, but in the One who called you. The path to purpose is rarely free of obstacles, yet it is always paved with opportunity for growth. Courage transforms hesitation into action and doubt into determination. Take the step. Speak the word. Make the move. On the other side of your obedience is the breakthrough you have been praying for.

One of the greatest benefits of courage is clarity. When you choose courage, confusion begins to fade and the fog of hesitation starts to lift. Fear has a way of clouding the mind, distorting perspective, and magnifying obstacles until they seem insurmountable. But courage cuts through that noise. It steadies your thoughts, strengthens your focus, and sharpens your vision. Instead of reacting emotionally, you begin responding intentionally. Courage aligns you with purpose and helps you see what truly matters. When you step forward boldly, distractions lose their grip and priorities come into focus. You stop fearing loss and start valuing growth. Clarity comes not because every answer is revealed, but because your heart is settled in conviction. With courage, you gain the confidence to move decisively, trusting that each faithful step will reveal the next. And in that alignment between faith, purpose, and action you discover a clearer path forward than fear could ever provide.

Courage strengthens your faith because it moves belief from theory into action. Faith is not passive agreement with truth; it is active trust in the One who spoke the truth. When you step forward despite fear, uncertainty, or opposition, you demonstrate that your confidence rests in God and not in circumstances. Courage forces faith to stretch, to grow, and to mature. Every courageous decision becomes living evidence that your faith is real and resilient. When you act courageously, you prove that your faith is alive. Courage becomes the bridge between what you believe and how you live. It closes the gap between confession and conduct, between prayer and practice. Without courage, faith remains a concept; with courage, faith becomes a testimony. Each bold step builds spiritual strength, deepens trust, and reinforces your dependence on God's promises rather than your own comfort. In choosing courage, you are not denying fear - you are declaring that your faith is greater than it.

Courage builds character by calling you to rise when everything in you wants to shrink back. It demands that you face uncertainty, endure discomfort, and press forward despite fear. In those moments when the pressure is heavy and the outcome is unclear; you are given a choice to either retreat or to stand firm. Choosing courage, even in small decisions, begins shaping the kind of person you are becoming. Character is not developed in ease; it is forged in resistance. Courage stretches you beyond convenience and pushes you toward integrity. It teaches you discipline, conviction, and the power of standing by your values no matter the cost. Over time, those brave choices build resilience within you, forming a steady confidence that cannot be easily shaken. Courage becomes more than an occasional act - it becomes part of your identity. And when courage defines you, your character stands strong in adversity, unwavering in purpose, and prepared for whatever challenges lie ahead.

Courage produces growth. Comfort zones feel safe, predictable, and manageable but they are rarely transformative. Nothing stretches in an environment where nothing is challenged. The very things that feel uncomfortable, things like new responsibilities, difficult conversations, bold decisions, unfamiliar territory are the very tools that enlarge your character. When you step outside of comfort, you expand your capacity. You discover strength you didn't know you had, resilience you hadn't yet needed, and faith that only awakens when risk is required. Growth lives on the other side of brave obedience. When you obey the call to move forward despite fear, you partner with progress. Courage is not the absence of fear; it is the decision to move anyway. Every step taken in faith builds confidence for the next. The boundaries of your life widen each time you choose boldness over safety. If you want transformation, choose courage because what stretches you ultimately strengthens you.

Courage releases potential. So many people carry divine gifts, callings, and abilities that never fully see the light of day because fear whispers that it's safer to stay small. Fear convinces them to shrink back, to wait for the "right time," or to let someone else step forward. But potential cannot flourish in the shadows of hesitation. It is activated the moment you choose to trust God more than your insecurities. Every step of faith stretches your capacity and awakens what has been dormant inside you. When you walk in courage, you give God permission to use what He placed within you for His glory. Courage breaks the lock that fear tries to place on your future. It unlocks vision, creativity, leadership, and influence that were always there but waiting for bold obedience. The world is changed not by those who feel ready, but by those who are willing. Step forward. Speak up. Build it. Start it. Obey. On the other side of courage is the release of your true potential and the impact God designed your life to make.

Courage inspires others because boldness is contagious. When one person chooses to stand firm in faith, integrity, and conviction, it breaks the invisible barrier of fear that holds others back. Your willingness to step forward and pursue what God has placed in your heart silently declares to those watching, "It's possible." You may never fully realize who is observing your journey, but your obedience becomes a living testimony. Your bravery becomes a catalyst for transformation far beyond your own life. Someone is waiting for your example to give them strength. Someone is watching to see if faith can truly overcome fear. When you move forward with courage, you light a path for others to follow. What feels like a personal decision to trust God in your circumstances can become the spark that ignites confidence, hope, and action in someone else. Courage doesn't just change you - it creates a ripple effect that empowers others to step into their own calling.

Courage silences regret. Too many people reach the later chapters of their lives haunted not by their failures, but by their inaction. The words "What if?" can echo louder than any mistake ever could. What if I had tried? What if I had spoken up? What if I had trusted God and taken the step? Failure may bruise your pride but regret wounds your spirit. It is far better to fall while moving forward than to sit safely on the sidelines, forever wondering what might have been. Courage gives you the peace of knowing you showed up when it mattered most. It allows you to look back over your life and say, "I stepped forward. I trusted. I obeyed." Even if the outcome wasn't perfect, your obedience was powerful. When you choose courage, you step beyond the comfort of certainty and into the promise of growth, trusting that every challenge is shaping you for something greater. In that bold decision, fear loses its grip and faith rises, turning the unknown into an opportunity for transformation.

Courage strengthens leadership because it calls a leader to stand firm when comfort would suggest retreat. True leaders are not fearless; they are faithful. When the road ahead is unclear and the outcome uncertain, courageous leaders step forward anyway, not because they have all the answers, but because they are anchored in conviction. Their willingness to move despite uncertainty becomes a steady light for others who are watching and wondering which way to go. Courage earns trust and establishes authority rooted in integrity rather than intimidation. People do not follow titles; they follow conviction. When a leader consistently chooses faith over fear, action over hesitation, and principle over popularity, trust is built brick by brick. Authority that grows from courage carries weight because it is proven in adversity. In the face of challenge, courageous leadership does more than survive - it inspires, strengthens, and sets the tone for others to rise up and become all that God created them to be.

Courage deepens trust in God because it calls you to move beyond the limits of your own understanding and strength. When you take a step you cannot manage on your own, you are forced to rely on something greater than yourself. In that sacred space between fear and faith, you discover that God is faithful. Courage is not the absence of fear - it is the decision to trust God more than you trust your doubts. Every bold step becomes a testimony that His strength is made perfect in your weakness. Courage also reminds you that you were never meant to carry everything alone. The weight of life was never designed to rest solely on your shoulders. When you step forward in faith, you lean into divine strength, and in doing so, you exchange anxiety for assurance. Courage shifts your focus from your limitations to His limitless power. It teaches you that partnership with God is the pathway to victory, and that when you trust Him fully, He will carry what you cannot.

Courage creates breakthrough. The walls that block your path may look permanent but, in reality, they are nothing more than barriers waiting for someone bold enough to confront them. What appears immovable begins to crack the moment you refuse to retreat. When bold persistence meets opposition, pressure builds, momentum shifts, and what once seemed impossible begins to give way. Every defining moment in history was preceded by someone choosing bravery over comfort. Many victories are just one brave decision away. One phone call. One conversation. One step of faith. One act of obedience. The breakthrough you're praying for may be waiting on the other side of your willingness to act. Courage unlocks doors hesitation keeps closed. When you stand firm and take that decisive step, you position yourself for the miracle, the promotion, the healing, the restoration. Choose boldness today. The wall is not as strong as it looks, and your courage is stronger than you think.

Courage strengthens your voice by reminding you that what you carry inside is worth expressing. Fear whispers that silence is safer, that speaking up will cost too much, or that your words will not matter. But courage interrupts that lie. It rises within you and says that truth deserves to be heard, and conviction deserves to be spoken. When you choose courage, your voice gains clarity and confidence. You no longer speak to please the crowd or avoid criticism - you speak because what is right must be declared. Fear keeps people silent when they should speak, but courage empowers you to stand firm. It gives you the strength to defend what is right even when opposition is loud and pressure is intense. Courage does not mean the absence of fear; it means you refuse to let fear control your voice. When you speak with courage, you become a light in dark places and a steady sound in moments of confusion. One brave decision to speak truth can inspire others that echoes far beyond the moment.

Courage builds endurance. Every time you choose bravery over fear, you are strengthening your spirit. Battles are not sent to break you; they are opportunities to train you. When you stand firm in the face of opposition, disappointment, or uncertainty, something powerful happens within you. Your faith stretches, your character deepens, and your confidence in God grows. What once felt overwhelming begins to feel manageable because you have proof that you can endure. With each storm you survive, your spiritual stamina increases. You become less reactive to pressure and more rooted in truth. Instead of being shaken by every gust of adversity, you stand steady, knowing that the same God who brought you through before will bring you through again. Storms no longer intimidate you the way they once did, because endurance has replaced anxiety and resilience has replaced fear. Courage doesn't remove the battle; it transforms you into someone who can outlast it.

Courage transforms your identity from the inside out. Every time you choose boldness over fear, action over hesitation, and faith over doubt, you are reshaping the way you see yourself. With each bold step, you chip away at the old labels of weakness, insecurity, and uncertainty. You begin to realize that fear does not define you; your response to it does. Courage becomes the lens through which you interpret challenges, and instead of seeing obstacles as threats, you see them as opportunities to grow stronger. When you repeatedly choose boldness, you begin to see yourself differently. The hesitant version of you fades, replaced by someone who trusts their convictions and moves with purpose. You no longer identify as weak or unsure - you recognize resilience rising within you. There is a warrior spirit forged in the fires of consistent bravery, and it awakens when you refuse to back down. The more consistently you choose courage, the more natural it feels until boldness becomes part of your very identity.

Courage cultivates peace. At first glance, that may sound contradictory. After all, courage often requires stepping into conflict, discomfort, or uncertainty. Yet true peace is not the absence of pressure; it is the presence of steadiness within it. When you confront what you fear instead of running from it, the storm inside begins to quiet. What once seemed overwhelming becomes manageable, and what once stirred turmoil begins to settle. Courage transforms anxiety into assurance. Avoidance, on the other hand, feeds unrest. The more you delay difficult conversations, decisions, or responsibilities, the louder your fears grow. Anxiety thrives in hesitation, but confidence is born in action. Each courageous step you take builds strength, clarity, and self-trust. You begin to realize that you are capable, resilient, and equipped to handle what stands before you. In choosing courage, you cultivate an inner calm rooted in conviction. And from that calm comes a peace that circumstances cannot steal.

Courage positions you for destiny because it moves you from intention to action. Destiny is never fulfilled by comfort; it is discovered in the moments when fear whispers "stay" but faith says "go." Every significant calling requires a step beyond what is familiar. Courage is not the absence of fear - it is the decision that purpose matters more than fear. When you choose to move forward in spite of uncertainty, you align yourself with the path prepared for you long before you ever saw it. Opportunities often appear disguised as risk. They rarely announce themselves with guarantees or applause. Instead, they come wrapped in challenge, stretching your confidence and demanding trust. Those who step forward inherit ground others were too afraid to claim. While some shrink back and protect what they have, the courageous advance and gain what could be. The difference between regret and reward is often one bold step taken when others hesitated.

In the end, courage is a decision made daily. It is waking up each morning and choosing faith over fear, obedience over hesitation, and purpose over comfort. Courage does not always roar; sometimes it whispers, "Trust God again today." It means standing firm when doubt presses in, stepping forward when the path is uncertain, and believing that what God has spoken is greater than what you currently see. Every day presents a choice, and every courageous choice strengthens your spirit, sharpens your character, and deepens your trust in the One who called you. The benefits of courage ripple far beyond the moment. They flow into your family through your example, into your leadership through your integrity, and into your legacy through your consistency. When you walk in courage, you do more than survive trials - you advance through them. Courage positions you to fulfill the purpose placed upon your life, not by accident, but by intentional, faithful decisions made one day at a time.

| 6 |

"THE CALL TO COURAGE"

From the very beginning, God has called His men to rise above fear and stand firm in faith. He never intended for them to rely solely on their own strength or ability, but to anchor their confidence in Him. Throughout scripture, the pattern is clear: when men trusted in their own power, they faltered; but when they leaned fully on God, they prevailed. True boldness is not arrogance or bravado - it is the quiet, unshakable assurance that the Lord goes before you, stands beside you, and secures your steps. Courage is the heartbeat of godly manhood, forged in the fires of faith and obedience. It is strengthened in moments of testing, refined in seasons of waiting, and proven through decisive action. When a man chooses integrity over compromise, conviction over comfort, and obedience over convenience, he reflects the very character of Christ. This kind of courage shapes leaders, strengthens families, and transforms communities. It is not the absence of fear, but the resolve to trust God in spite of it.

Every godly man receives a call to courage, whether he recognizes it or not. This call does not promise comfort or ease, but it does promise purpose. God never wastes a battle, a burden, or a season of pressure. The very places that stretch a man are the places that shape him. When a man answers that call, he steps into the identity God designed for him from the beginning. God shapes men through challenges so their faith will rise stronger than their circumstances. Trials are not meant to break him - they are meant to build him. Pressure refines character. Obstacles develop endurance. Opposition deepens dependence on the Lord. The fire that feels intense today is forging strength for tomorrow. When a man chooses obedience over ease and faith over frustration, he becomes steady, grounded, and unshakable. His courage begins to inspire others. His faith becomes a covering for his family. And his life becomes living proof that when a man trusts God fully, no circumstance can define him.

The courage God desires is holy confidence anchored in His unchanging Word. It kneels before it stands. It listens before it speaks. It seeks God's direction before it takes a single step. This kind of courage understands that obedience is greater than impulse and that waiting on the Lord is not weakness but wisdom. When the path ahead is unclear and the outcome uncertain, holy courage chooses trust over control, surrender over self-reliance, and faithfulness over fear. True courage begins on the inside, where faith confronts doubt and refuses to bow to it. It is forged in quiet moments of prayer, strengthened in the study of Scripture, and tested in the unseen battles of the heart. Before it is ever displayed outwardly, it is settled inwardly. A man who walks in this courage does not deny fear - he overcomes it through confidence in who God is. His boldness flows not from ego, but from assurance that God goes before him, stands beside him, and upholds him.

Throughout Scripture, we see a consistent pattern: God delights in choosing ordinary men and entrusting them with extraordinary assignments. Shepherds become kings, fishermen become apostles, and reluctant leaders become deliverers. God has never been searching for perfection; He has always been searching for availability. He is not intimidated by weakness, insecurity, or past mistakes. In fact, He often calls men precisely in those moments when they feel the least prepared, so that His power and not their ability receives the glory. A courageous man does not wait until he feels fully equipped, fully confident, or fully worthy. He simply says yes. He steps forward in faith when doubt whispers and obedience feels costly. He trusts that the God who calls also equips, strengthens, and sustains. When a man yields his willingness to God, heaven meets his obedience with divine empowerment and ordinary lives become extraordinary testimonies.

Godly courage often requires standing alone. There are moments when truth is unpopular, when compromise is applauded, and when righteousness is resisted by the very culture that claims to value integrity. In those defining hours, the courageous man does not bend to the pressure of applause or the fear of rejection. He stands anchored in conviction, rooted in the unchanging Word of God. His strength is drawn from the depth of his surrender. Even if he must walk a narrow road by himself, he knows that obedience is never lonely when the Lord walks beside him. The courageous man understands that pleasing God is far more important than gaining the approval of people. He measures success not by popularity but by faithfulness. He is willing to be misunderstood, criticized, or even isolated if it means remaining true to his calling. For he knows that applause fades, opinions shift, and crowds scatter but the favor of God endures forever.

Courage is tested most intensely in seasons of adversity. When the winds rise and the ground beneath him feels uncertain, a man discovers what truly anchors his soul. The courageous man does not deny the storm, but he refuses to be ruled by it. He understands that adversity is not an interruption to his calling; it is often the proving ground where God strengthens his resolve and refines his spirit. When hardship comes, the courageous man leans into God rather than retreating from Him. Instead of isolating himself, he seeks the Lord in prayer, stands firmly on His promises, and walks forward in obedience even when the outcome is unclear. In leaning closer to God, he finds supernatural strength, steady peace, and renewed perspective. Through adversity, his faith is deepened, his leadership is sharpened, and his life becomes a testimony that true courage is born from unwavering dependence on the One who never fails.

A godly man is not merely called to possess faith, love his family, or value integrity - he is called to protect them. What God entrusts to a man is sacred. His faith must be guarded against doubt, distraction, and deception. His family must be shielded with prayer, leadership, and sacrificial love. His integrity must be defended in private long before it is ever tested in public. This protection requires courage. It requires a watchful heart and a disciplined spirit. A man who stands guard over what God has placed in his care understands that these are not casual responsibilities - they are divine assignments. In a world that constantly pressures compromise, courage becomes essential. A godly man does not bow to moral surrender. He stands tall. He draws a line. Every time he chooses obedience over ease and righteousness over reputation, he honors God. Standing guard over these sacred trusts is how a man declares with his life, "As for me and my house, we will serve the Lord."

Courage also means taking responsibility. It is easy to be bold when the battle is external, but true courage is revealed when the battle is within. Godly men do not shift blame, make excuses, or hide behind pride when they fall short. They stand in the light of truth, own their decisions, and accept the consequences of their actions. It takes far more bravery to say, "I was wrong," than to defend a mistake. A man of God understands that accountability is not an attack on his identity, but a refining fire that shapes his character. Godly men face their failures honestly, repent quickly, and rise again with renewed determination. Repentance is not retreat - it is a strategic reset of the heart. Courageous men learn, grow, and press on. They understand that falling is not the end; refusing to get back up is. With every honest confession and renewed commitment, they become more steadfast, more faithful, and more aligned with the purpose God has placed on their lives.

The call to courage extends far beyond personal strength; it is a summons to spiritual leadership. Godly men are called to lead by example - demonstrating integrity when no one is watching, humility when success could breed pride, and perseverance when trials press hard. Their lives become living testimonies that strength is found not in self-reliance, but in surrender to God's will. Through consistency and unwavering trust, they establish a standard that reflects Christ's character in both word and deed. When a man walks courageously with God, his influence reaches far beyond himself. His faith steadies his family, strengthens his community, and inspires others to trust God more deeply. Spiritual leadership is not about dominance, but about devotion - modeling what it means to follow God wholeheartedly. In doing so, godly men become pillars of strength, lighting the way for others to rise, believe, and walk boldly in their own calling.

Prayer is a hidden source of courage. On his knees, a man comes face to face with his limitations and chooses to rely not on his own strength, wisdom, or strategy, but on the limitless power of God. In that quiet surrender, something supernatural happens - fear loosens its grip, clarity replaces confusion, and faith begins to rise. The posture of kneeling is not defeat; it is alignment. It is the moment a man exchanges self-reliance for divine reliance and discovers that heaven's resources far outweigh his own. What looks like weakness to the world becomes strength in the hands of the Lord. The world may see a man bowed low and assume he has given up, but in truth he is gearing up, being fortified from the inside out. Prayer builds boldness, steadies the heart, and anchors the soul in truth. When a man rises from his knees, he does not stand alone; he stands empowered, carrying a courage that cannot be shaken because it is rooted not in his ability, but in God's faithfulness.

Courage requires endurance. It is not proven in a single heroic moment but in the quiet, unseen choices made day after day. True courage is forged in consistency - in the decision to stand firm when emotions fluctuate, when opposition rises, and when results seem delayed. A godly man understands that faithfulness is not flashy; it is steady. He wakes up each morning resolved to obey, to lead with integrity, and to trust God regardless of how he feels. Godly men learn that perseverance is the pathway to promise. They trust that God is working beneath the surface, even when visible progress appears slow. Roots grow deep before fruit appears. In seasons of waiting, refining, and stretching, they hold their ground. They endure because they believe that obedience today produces strength tomorrow. Courage, then, becomes a daily decision to remain faithful, to keep building, to keep praying, and to keep walking forward confident that God's timing is perfect and His purposes are sure.

A courageous man speaks truth with both boldness and love. He does not tremble in the face of opposition, nor does he soften God's Word to win approval. He understands that truth is not his to edit, revise, or dilute - it is his to honor and proclaim. He speaks with clarity because he fears God more than man, and he stands firm because he knows that truth, when spoken rightly, sets captives free. His courage is rooted in obedience, not ego. At the same time, his boldness is wrapped in compassion. He does not wield truth like a weapon to wound, but like a light to guide. His words carry grace because his heart carries love. He understands that correction without care becomes cruelty, but truth spoken in love becomes transformation. A courageous man reflects the character of Christ. He is strong enough to confront, yet tender enough to restore. His courage is marked not by volume or aggression, but by a steady commitment to speak what is right with a spirit that heals rather than harms.

God does not call men to comfort - He calls them to courage. When the Lord speaks, He expects obedience, not negotiation. Hesitation is rarely neutral; it is often fear wearing the mask of wisdom. Delayed obedience is still disobedience, because partial surrender is not surrender at all. A godly man understands that obedience is not about having all the answers - it is about trusting the One who does. Courage is revealed not in bold words, but in decisive action when God has clearly spoken. Fear will always present itself as "waiting for the right time," "needing more clarity," or "being cautious." But faith moves when God moves. A courageous man steps forward even when the path is uncertain, because his confidence is anchored in God's character, not his circumstances. He obeys quickly, trusting that the outcome belongs to the Lord. When God speaks, the man of faith responds - not tomorrow, not when it feels safer, but now - believing that obedience opens the door for God's power to be revealed.

Courage is strengthened through community because God never designed men to fight life's battles in isolation. From the beginning, He declared that it was not good for man to be alone. When men gather in authentic fellowship - praying together and standing shoulder to shoulder - their faith is sharpened and fortified. Just as iron sharpens iron, godly relationships refine character, correct blind spots, and build spiritual resilience. In community, fear loses its grip, doubt is confronted with truth, and weary hearts are reminded of God's promises. Fellowship with other men fuels perseverance and reinforces the call to live boldly for Christ. When one man grows tired, another lifts him up. When one begins to waver, another speaks life and truth into his spirit. Brotherhood in Christ creates accountability, strength, and momentum. Courage grows stronger when shared, and together, men become steadfast, unmovable, and confident in their calling to stand firm and live boldly for Christ.

The world desperately needs courageous men who reflect the character of God in both strength and humility. In a culture often marked by confusion, compromise, and fear, true courage stands out as a steady light. When men choose integrity over convenience, truth over popularity, and service over selfish ambition, they become living reflections of God's heart. Darkness retreats when men of faith rise with conviction and humility. Courage fueled by pride may draw attention, but courage grounded in surrender draws people toward God. When a man stands firm in righteousness while remaining gentle in spirit, his life becomes a testimony that points others toward hope. His faith speaks through his actions - through forgiveness, perseverance, compassion, and bold obedience. In this way, courage becomes more than bravery; it becomes a witness, shining light into dark places and inviting others to discover the transforming power of God.

Godly courage is never confined to a single moment - it stretches far beyond the present and reaches into generations yet unborn. When a man chooses to stand firm in truth and to trust God when fear presses in, he builds more than character - he builds legacy. His children may not remember every word he speaks, but they will remember the strength of his convictions and the steadiness of his faith. Courage rooted in God becomes a foundation stone, something future generations can stand on when their own storms arise. The choices a man makes today echo into tomorrow. When he chooses faith over fear, integrity over convenience, and obedience over popularity, he plants seeds that will outlive him. Those seeds grow into confidence in his children, resilience in his family, and boldness in those who follow his example. One day, others will harvest the fruit of his unseen prayers, his steadfast decisions, and his refusal to bow to fear. Godly courage does not just change a moment - it shapes a lineage.

The call to courage is ultimately a call to trust God completely. Courage is not the absence of fear; it is the decision to move forward because God is faithful. When a man answers the call to courage, he is declaring that his confidence is not in his own strength, wisdom, or resources, but in the unchanging character of God. It is the deep assurance that God goes before him, preparing the way; stands beside him, strengthening his resolve; and remains faithful behind him, redeeming every step. A courageous man understands that he never walks alone. Even in seasons of isolation, opposition, or doubt, he is upheld by the steady presence of the Lord. When storms rise, he stands firm because he knows Who anchors his soul. When decisions weigh heavy, he steps forward because he trusts the One who guides his path. The call to courage is not a call to reckless bravery, but to steadfast faith - a life lived with the confident assurance that God is near, God is able, and God is always faithful.

Every godly man must answer this call. Courage is not optional; it is essential to faithful living. A man who walks with God will inevitably face moments that test his resolve, challenge his convictions, and demand that he choose obedience over comfort. In those defining moments, courage becomes the bridge between belief and action. It is the strength to trust God when the path is uncertain, to uphold righteousness when compromise is easier, and to remain steadfast when pressure mounts. When men rise in God-given courage, they fulfill their purpose and bring glory to the One who called them. Courage shapes families, influences communities, and honors heaven. A courageous man does not rely on his own power but stands firm in the confidence that God goes before him. His boldness reflects trust, his perseverance reflects devotion, and his obedience reflects love. Through courageous living, a man becomes a living testimony that faith is not merely spoken - it is demonstrated.

| 7 |

"THE SPIRIT OF COURAGE"

Courage empowers you to live a purposeful life because it pushes you beyond fear and into destiny. Purpose is rarely discovered in comfort; it is revealed when you choose to step forward despite uncertainty, opposition, or doubt. Courage gives you the strength to pursue what matters most, even when the path is unclear or the cost feels high. It fuels conviction, sharpens vision, and builds resilience. Without courage, purpose remains a dream. With courage, purpose becomes action. Every bold decision, every faithful step, and every refusal to quit shapes the life you were created to live. This is why you must live and walk in courage every day of your life. Courage is not a one-time act - it is a daily commitment to stand firm in your values, to speak truth, to rise after failure, and to move forward in faith. When you consistently choose courage, you strengthen your character and expand your influence. Walk boldly, live intentionally, and let courage guide you toward the fullness of your calling.

A purposeful life is built one courageous step at a time. The root word for "courage" is "cour" which is the Latin word for 'heart.' It refers to speaking one's mind by telling all that is in one's heart. It speaks of honesty and openness. Courage begins with honesty. It begins with admitting you cannot do the impossible on your own and that you desperately need God's help. True courage is not pretending to be strong; it is humbly acknowledging your weakness and inviting His strength into your struggle. When you confess your limits, you make room for His power. When you surrender your pride, you receive His grace. The bravest step you will ever take is not charging ahead in self-confidence, but bowing your heart in faith and saying, "Lord, I cannot do this but You can." Courage is trusting God to do the impossible in your life and leaning on Him at all times with confidence that He is faithful, powerful, and always working for your good. Doing that is where real courage is born.

Uncommon courage is mastery over fear. It is bravery that stands up for people and for a cause. 2 Tim. 1:7, "For God has not given us a spirit of fear, but of power and of love and of a sound mind." God wants you to be "bold and loving and sensible" (MSG). When Paul wrote these words to Timothy, he was encouraging a young leader facing pressure, persecution, and uncertainty. The challenges were real but so was the Spirit of God within him. God has placed within every born-again man a different spirit. The spirit of courage is a spirit of power that enables him to stand firm, a Spirit of love that keeps his motives pure and his heart compassionate, and a sound mind that gives him clarity, discipline, and self-control even in chaotic moments. Power means we are equipped. Love means we are anchored. A sound mind means we are steady. We are not called to shrink back, but to step forward in faith, trusting that the same Spirit who raised Christ from the dead lives within us.

Faith is not the absence of opposition; it is the courage to step forward despite it, trusting that the Lord goes before you. When you choose faith over fear, you shift from being a target to becoming a force, pressing ahead with divine confidence, knowing that no weapon formed against you will ultimately prevail. Your courage is an attitude that determines your altitude. It is not merely a feeling that rises when conditions are perfect; it is a decision you make when the road is uncertain and the outcome is unclear. Courage lifts your perspective, stretches your faith, and propels you beyond the limits of fear and doubt. The only impossible journey is the one you never begin. Every dream, every calling, every God-given assignment starts with a single bold step forward. When you choose courage, you choose growth. When you choose to begin, you choose possibility. Take the step, trust the process, and watch how your attitude elevates your life to heights you once thought were out of reach.

Live courageously and refuse to be a coward in a culture that often rewards compromise and punishes conviction. Courage is not loud arrogance or reckless behavior; it is steady obedience to God when fear whispers for you to back down. Revelation 21:8 gives a sobering warning that the cowardly are listed first among those cast into the lake of fire. This is not about momentary fear, but about a lifestyle of shrinking back from truth, denying Christ through silence, and choosing safety over faithfulness. God has called you to stand, to endure, and to overcome. Every day presents a choice: bow to fear or walk by faith. When righteousness costs you something, and when obedience requires sacrifice, choose courage. Speak up. Stand firm. The Spirit of God within you is greater than any opposition around you. Refuse to live small. Refuse to hide your faith. Live boldly, love fiercely, and follow Christ without apology because eternal rewards belong to those who overcome, not those who cower in fear.

Courage is taking a stand against what is wrong. It is choosing truth over comfort and conviction over compromise, no matter the cost. It means having the courage to speak up whenever you see others doing what is wrong or inappropriate, even when it's uncomfortable or unpopular. True integrity refuses to stay silent in the face of wrongdoing and chooses boldness over fear. Courage is speaking your mind with conviction, even when your voice trembles and others stand in disagreement. It is the strength to stand firm in truth, choosing integrity over approval and purpose over popularity. It's doing what is right regardless of the risks and potential consequences. It's when you follow your conscience, refusing to compromise your principles despite pressures and temptation. Have the courage, if need be, and the willingness to suffer for the greater good. With that willingness comes a special bond between you and the Lord, a bond that is not there if you're not suffering for His name's sake.

Paul said in Phil. 3:10 (NLT), "I want to suffer with Him, sharing in His death." King James said Paul wanted "the fellowship of His sufferings." There is just something deeply sacred about suffering for God and for the sake of the gospel that defies natural explanation. In the moment, it is not pleasant. It stretches you, humbles you, exposes your weaknesses, and often costs you comfort, reputation, relationships, or even opportunities. You may not enjoy the misunderstanding, the rejection, the sacrifice, or the loneliness that sometimes accompanies standing firm in your faith. Yet beneath the discomfort on the outside, there is a quiet, steady peace that settles in the soul - a peace that does not come from circumstances but from alignment. When you know that your hardship is not wasted, that your obedience matters, and that your stand honors Christ, there is a deep assurance that anchors you. It is the peace of knowing you are walking in truth.

It is the calm confidence that you are participating in something eternal, something far greater than your temporary discomfort. Suffering for selfish reasons leaves regret but suffering for righteousness leaves reward. Even while tears fall and prayers feel heavy, there is an inner strength that whispers, "This is worth it." The heart may ache, but the spirit rests. There is comfort in knowing that God sees that He is near to the brokenhearted, and that every sacrifice made for His name carries eternal significance. In that paradox - pain on the outside, peace on the inside - you discover a deeper fellowship with Christ, a sharing in His sufferings that produces endurance, character, and hope. And though you would not choose the hardship itself, you would not trade the peace that comes from faithfully enduring it for anything. The truth is that comfort is overrated. People tend to be closer to God when they're suffering than when they're not.

What is courage? It's the God-given ability to take a stand. Life has a way of responding to the size of your courage. When you choose safety over obedience, comfort over calling, and silence over conviction, your world slowly contracts; opportunities feel smaller, relationships become guarded, dreams are postponed, and purpose seems distant. But when you dare to step forward despite fear, despite uncertainty, despite the risk of failure, something remarkable happens: your life begins to expand. Courage stretches your faith, deepens your character, strengthens your resilience, and opens doors you once thought were locked. It is courage that moves you from the shoreline of hesitation into the deeper waters of destiny. It is courage that transforms adversity into advancement and setbacks into steppingstones. Every bold decision enlarges your capacity to lead, to love, to forgive, to build, and to believe again. Fear will always whisper limitations, but courage declares possibility.

The measure of your life is not determined by the absence of fear, but by your willingness to act in spite of it. When you confront challenges head-on, speak truth with grace, pursue your calling with tenacity, and trust God beyond what you can see, your influence widens and your impact multiplies. Life does not expand because circumstances change; it expands because you do. And as your courage grows, so does your vision, your authority, your joy, and your legacy proving that life will always shrink to the size of your fears or expand to the size of your faith-fueled courage. It takes courage to be extraordinary for God. Courage is taking the road least traveled. It's turning your crisis into an opportunity. Don't be afraid to put yourself on the line if you want the rewards that life has to offer, because every meaningful victory requires the courage to risk comfort, reputation, and security. That means it's better to go down swinging than to be called out on strikes.

Have the courage to think differently when the world pressures you to conform, because breakthrough begins where comfort ends. Have the courage to invent new things, to create what has never been seen, and to believe that your ideas carry purpose. Have the courage to travel the unexplored path, trusting that bold faith and fearless vision will lead you exactly where you are meant to go. Steve Jobs once said, "Your time is limited so don't waste it living someone else's life. Don't be trapped by dogma that is living with the results of other people's thinking. Don't let the noise of others' opinions drown out your own inner voice. And most important, have the courage to follow your heart and intuition." Courage is already inside you and everything you need to win has been placed within your hands. Step forward boldly, trust what God has deposited in you, and go after your purpose with relentless faith. No guts, no glory. Rise up and claim the victory that's waiting for you!

Courage is more valuable than confidence because courage comes first. Confidence is often the result of success, preparation, or familiarity—but courage shows up when none of those things are present. Courage steps forward when you feel unqualified, uncertain, or even afraid. It chooses action over comfort and obedience over doubt. While confidence waits for proof, courage moves without it. And it is in those courageous moments - when you speak up, step out, try again, or refuse to quit - that real growth begins. The truth is, confidence starts with courage. Every time you do what scares you, you build evidence that you can handle more than you thought. Each bold step strengthens your belief in yourself. The more courageous you are, the more confident you become - not because life gets easier, but because you grow stronger. And as your courage expands, so does your capacity for impact, fulfillment, and reward.

A courageous life is a meaningful life, and from that courage flows the confidence that transforms your future. So don't put the cart before the horse. Courage comes first, then comes confidence. Courage is like a muscle. The more you flex it, the stronger and more confident you become. At first, stepping out in faith or facing a difficult situation may feel uncomfortable, even intimidating. But every time you choose bravery over fear, you build resilience and inner strength. Small acts of boldness like speaking up when it matters, trying again after failure, standing firm in your convictions gradually develop a deeper confidence within you. Just as physical muscles grow through resistance and repetition, courage grows through challenges and persistence. Over time, what once seemed overwhelming becomes manageable, and what once felt impossible becomes achievable. If you don't feel confident to try something new, summon your courage and give it a try.

It takes courage to act outwardly on what you see inwardly, because faith is proven not in what you imagine, but in what you dare to pursue. Will you step out in bold obedience and live the vision God placed within you, or will you let fear silence it and die a dreamer? It takes courage to rise above comfort, push through fear, and pursue success with relentless determination. It takes courage to be successful. It takes courage to win. It takes no courage to fail. Just do nothing and failure is yours. Courage is the bold decision to challenge the status quo and choose what is better, even when it would be easier to stay the same. It takes strength to be different, to swim upstream against the current and pursue a higher standard. It takes courage to be exceptional. It takes courage to be wise. It takes courage to be educated and to prosper. It takes courage to break out of normalcy and go after your dream. With courage you discover the impossible.

It takes courage to be an overcomer, to rise above the hurdles in your path and refuse to be defined by them. Courage is standing firm when the storms of life rage against you, choosing faith over fear and strength over surrender. And sometimes, simply getting up each day and pressing forward is the bravest act of all. To the courageous, a failure, a refusal, a disappointment, a disability, or a fear is never the end of the story - it is the spark that ignites a deeper resolve within. What tries to limit them only strengthens their spirit, compelling them to rise higher, press harder, and overcome with unwavering determination. Never forget that the devil is a liar and a deceiver. Most fears look menacing but in reality, it's only an illusion. It's like a goldfish swimming near the surface of the water with a shark fin strapped to its back. On the surface your fears may look like a great white shark but below the surface it's nothing but a harmless goldfish.

To the army of Israel, Goliath looked like a hungry shark. To David, who had a different spirit in him, he was a goldfish. 1 Sam. 17:11 says, "When Saul and all Israel heard these words of the Philistine, they were dismayed and greatly afraid." But David said in vs. 32, "Let no man's heart fail because of him; your servant will go and fight with this Philistine." Plato said, "Courage is knowing what not to fear." Courage says, "No weapon formed against you will prosper"(Is. 54:17). Is the giant in your life real, or is it only an illusion magnified by fear? Trials and unexpected battles are part of every journey, but the illusion is the lie that whispers you are incapable of overcoming them. Fear exaggerates the size of the obstacle and minimizes the strength within you. The giant may stand tall, but it is not greater than your faith, resilience, and determination. What appears overwhelming today can become tomorrow's testimony when you refuse to believe the illusion and choose instead to stand firm and move forward.

When the army of Israel saw Goliath, they weren't facing an invincible giant - they were facing an illusion magnified by fear, yet they fled in dread because they believed what they saw more than what God had spoken (1 Sam. 17:24). Fear will always make giants look larger than life, but faith exposes the illusion and reminds us that no enemy stands taller than the promises of God. They thought their chances of defeating him were insurmountable. They asked, "Have you seen this giant? Look how big he is!" They didn't realize that the bigger the giant is, the harder they'll fall. What looks intimidating today only guarantees a greater testimony tomorrow. David said, "Who is this uncircumcised Philistine, that he should defy the armies of the living God?" (vs. 26). While the people saw the size of Goliath, David saw the size of the promise beyond him. He refused to focus on the giant in front of him and instead fixed his eyes on the reward, the purpose, and the God who guaranteed the victory.

Courage doesn't look to what you're going through, it looks to where you're going to. David said, "The Lord, who delivered me from the paw of the lion and the paw of the bear, He will deliver me from the hand of this Philistine" (vs. 37). David did not stand before Goliath trembling at the size of the giant; he stood there seeing the victory God had already promised. His eyes were fixed not on the obstacle, but on the outcome, and that vision filled his heart with unshakable courage. When you look ahead to the triumph God has prepared for you, fear loses its voice and faith finds its strength. David knew that God was not distant, but a mighty Deliverer who steps into the battles of His people. He trusted that no giant, no army, and no obstacle was greater than the power of the Lord who rescues and redeems. Because of that confidence, David faced every challenge knowing that behind every giant is a victory. You claim that victory with courage. Let the battle begin.

| 8 |

"THE NECESSITY OF COURAGE"

The necessity of courage is seen in Josh. 1:6 where God told Joshua and the people to "be strong and of good courage." The Israelites were about to cross the Jordan River to possess the Promised Land and God was saying it would take courage to get the job done. They would be going into battle against the fierce, brutal, heathen tribes who inhabited the land. Likewise, every man has battles to fight, and courage is necessary for dealing with life's challenges. It's wonderful to be a man of God but there are also battles to fight. Sometimes these battles can be very intense. There are battles against the tyranny of our moods, battles against resentment, bitterness, covetousness, jealousy, and depression. Sometimes we battle against addictions whether it's alcohol, drugs, overeating, immoral behavior, or laziness. Every day we have to battle the temptation to think, say, and do the wrong thing. It's going to take courage to step forward and fight these hard battles.

Without courage, there is no way you can know the fullness of life God wants you to have and enjoy. To experience life's highest and best, courage is absolutely, unquestionably necessary. Every man is born into a battlefield. Not a playground. Not a vacation. A battlefield. The battles may not always be visible, but they are real - battles for character, for integrity, for faith, for family, for purpose. Whether he acknowledges it or not, every man will face moments that demand courage. Courage is not the absence of fear. It is the decision to move forward in spite of it. Fear whispers, "Retreat." Courage declares, "Stand." Fear magnifies the obstacle until it looks bigger than the promise, louder than the calling, and stronger than the man himself. Courage, however, fixes its eyes on God magnifying His power, His faithfulness, and His authority over every challenge. In the life of a man, what he chooses to magnify will ultimately determine his direction, his decisions, and his destiny.

A man without courage slowly drifts into passivity. He avoids confrontation when truth demands a voice, postpones obedience when conviction stirs his heart, and shrinks back from responsibility when leadership calls his name. Fear convinces him that delay is wisdom and silence is safety, but in reality, it quietly erodes his strength, dulls his purpose, and robs him of the destiny God placed within him. Passivity is not peace. It is potential buried beneath hesitation. But a man who embraces courage rises differently. He steps into the unknown not because he has all the answers, but because he trusts that God has already gone before him. He confronts what others avoid, obeys when it is inconvenient, and carries responsibility as a calling rather than a burden. Courage does not eliminate fear; it anchors faith in the middle of it. And when a man chooses courage, he steps into alignment with heaven's design for his life, becoming the leader, protector, and example he was created to be.

Life will test you. Every season carries its own battlefield, and no one is exempt from the refining fire of adversity. There will be moments when the weight feels heavy, when resources seem scarce, when voices of doubt grow louder than the voice of faith. There will be days when you stumble and nights when you question your strength. But tests are not sent to destroy you, they are sent to expose what you truly believe, what you are anchored to, and how deeply your roots go when the winds begin to blow. The question is never if the battle will come - it is whether you will rise when it does. Rising is choosing courage over comfort, discipline over distraction, and faith over fear. It is standing firm when you could walk away, pressing forward when quitting feels easier. Every test carries within it the seed of promotion, growth, and transformation. When the battle arrives - and it will - rise anyway. Rise stronger. Rise wiser. Rise with the confidence that what tried to break you will ultimately build you.

Courage is necessary to lead a family. A family needs more than provision; it needs direction, protection, and an example to follow. It takes courage to pray when others are passive, to set standards when others lower them, and to speak life when circumstances try to silence hope. True leadership in the home means choosing patience over anger, integrity over convenience, and love over ego. It means standing firm in your values even when no one is applauding, knowing that the seeds you plant in private will shape generations to come. It takes courage to stand for righteousness in a culture drifting from truth. It takes courage to discipline your flesh, guard your mind, and remain faithful when compromise would be easier. Courage says no to the temporary so you can say yes to the eternal. In a world that rewards compromise, courage is the decision to remain faithful to God, to your calling, and to those who are watching your life as a blueprint for their own.

Many men pray for victory, asking God for breakthrough, favor, and triumph yet when the battle line is drawn, they hesitate. They want the crown without the contest, the testimony without the trial, the promotion without the proving. But heaven does not reward avoidance. Victory is not granted to spectators; it is given to those who step onto the field, who face opposition with faith instead of fear. The warrior who refuses the battlefield forfeits the crown, not because God is unwilling, but because courage is the doorway through which victory enters. God strengthens men who show up. He empowers those who engage the struggle, who confront their weaknesses, who stand firm when pressure rises. When a man takes his place in the fight - spiritually, mentally, and physically - grace meets him there.

Strength is released in motion. Courage grows in conflict. And the same God who calls him to the battlefield walks beside him in it, placing the crown on the head of the one who dared to contend.

There are silent battles that no one applauds. The fight to forgive when your heart still aches. The fight to remain pure in a world that celebrates compromise. The fight to keep believing when heaven feels quiet and prayers seem unanswered. These are not wars fought with noise or recognition, but with tears, discipline, and steadfast faith. No crowd cheers when you choose integrity over impulse. No headlines announce when you kneel again to pray after disappointment. Yet these unseen wars shape the soul more than any public victory ever could. This is why courage is so necessary. Courage is not only standing before giants - it is standing firm within yourself. It is choosing forgiveness when resentment feels justified. It is choosing holiness when temptation whispers. It is choosing faith when doubt grows loud. The deepest bravery is often invisible, but it is powerful. In those quiet, hidden battles, character is forged, trust is strengthened, and destiny is preserved.

Courage is spiritual before it is ever physical. Long before a man stands in the face of opposition, he has already fought and won a battle within his own heart. True courage is born in the quiet places where faith is formed, where identity is settled, and where a man decides who he will trust. When a man knows who he is in God, he carries an unshakable assurance that no circumstance can steal. Storms may rage around him, winds may howl against him, but his foundation is not built on emotion or public approval - it is anchored in truth. Physical bravery may impress people, but spiritual courage sustains a man when no one is watching. It begins in the heart and is strengthened through prayer, obedience, and unwavering belief in God's promises. A man rooted in his divine identity does not panic when pressure comes; he stands firm because he understands that his strength flows from a higher source. The world may measure courage by outward acts, but heaven measures it by inward faith.

Every generation stands at a crossroads where comfort tempts compromise and pressure tests conviction. What it needs most is not loud voices fueled by arrogance, nor impulsive strength driven by recklessness, but steady men anchored in truth. Courage is the quiet decision to stand when standing costs something. It is the strength to lead with humility, to protect without pride, and to remain grounded when culture shifts like sand. Faith-filled men do not bend to every storm; they plant their feet deeper in what is right. When pressure increases, true courage is revealed. It refuses to bow to fear and chooses integrity over approval and obedience over applause. Such men understand that legacy is built in seasons of resistance. Their courage becomes a covering for their families, a compass for their communities, and a foundation for the generations that follow. Courage sustains legacy because what a man refuses to surrender today becomes the inheritance of tomorrow.

The enemy rarely begins with a full assault - he begins with intimidation. His goal is to whisper doubt before he wages war, to magnify the threat before the battle ever starts. Intimidation is psychological; it attempts to paralyze your faith, distort your perspective, and convince you that defeat is inevitable. It paints giants as unbeatable and obstacles as immovable. Fear is his weapon of choice because a frozen warrior never advances. When intimidation succeeds, the fight is won before a single blow is struck. But when a man stands firm in faith, intimidation loses its power. A courageous man anchors himself in truth, refuses to surrender ground, and remembers who fights for him. Faith steadies his heart, strengthens his resolve, and silences the lies meant to shake him. When he plants his feet on God's promises, the enemy's threats become empty noise. The man who refuses to retreat is the one who ultimately prevails, because steadfast perseverance turns resistance into victory.

Courage says, "I will confront what I've avoided." It refuses to hide behind excuses, distractions, or delay. It walks straight toward the uncomfortable conversation, the neglected responsibility, the broken relationship, and declares, "I will fix what I broke." Courage understands that strength is not proven by dominance, but by ownership. It does not blame others for personal failure or wait for someone else to clean up the mess. Instead, it rises with resolve and says, "If my hands caused it, my hands will repair it." That is the heart of integrity. Courage also says, "I will apologize when I'm wrong." It recognizes that sometimes the greatest bravery is humility. To lower your pride, to admit fault, to seek forgiveness - these acts require more strength than winning an argument. Humility disarms conflict, restores trust, and builds character. Real courage is not loud; it is honest. It is not stubborn; it is teachable. And often, the strongest person in the room is the one willing to bow first.

There are seasons in life when courage feels expensive - when standing for what is right costs you comfort, convenience, and even companionship. Choosing righteousness may mean walking away from what is familiar. It may mean being misunderstood, overlooked, or even rejected. The easy road often promises applause and acceptance, but the higher road requires conviction and character. In those moments, courage is not loud or dramatic; it is quiet, steady obedience when compromise would be simpler. Yet though courage may cost you comfort, popularity, or ease, it never costs you honor. When you choose righteousness, you preserve your integrity, strengthen your character, and align your life with truth. Honor is not measured by how many stand with you, but by how faithfully you stand for what is right. Seasons change, opinions shift, and circumstances pass but the reward of a clear conscience and unwavering integrity endures far beyond the temporary price of courage.

A father who stands firm in adversity is quietly building more than his own character. He is shaping a legacy. His son watches how he responds to pressure, how he treats others, how he perseveres when quitting would be easier. His courage becomes a living example that says, "This is how we stand. This is how we believe. This is how we move forward." A father's courage becomes the foundation upon which the next generation learns to walk boldly. The same is true of leadership. When a leader chooses courage, it ignites confidence within the entire team. Courage multiplies. It spreads from one voice to many, from one decisive act to a culture of boldness. Fear loses its grip when someone dares to rise above it. And when courage becomes contagious, people discover strength they didn't know they had. They rise higher, reach farther, and step into challenges with faith instead of doubt. One courageous heart can transform a family, a team, and ultimately, a legacy.

God does not call perfect men - He calls willing men. Throughout scripture, the pattern is clear: ordinary men with flaws, fears, and fail-ures were chosen because their hearts were available. Moses doubted his speech, Gideon questioned his strength, Peter stumbled in denial yet each was used mightily because they surrendered their "yes" to God. The kingdom of God has never advanced on the shoulders of perfection, but on the backs of men who were willing to trust, obey, and step into what God asked of them. Courage is not the absence of fear; it is the willingness to move forward when your knees are shaking. It is saying "yes" when the assignment feels bigger than your strength, believing that God's power will meet you in your weak-ness. The call of God will always stretch you beyond your comfort, but it will never exceed His grace. When you step forward in obedi-ence, trembling though you may be, you position yourself for God to demonstrate His strength through your surrender.

When David stepped onto the battlefield to face Goliath, he did not measure the giant by his height, armor, or reputation. He measured him by covenant. While others saw an undefeated warrior, David saw "an uncircumcised Philistine" daring to defy the armies of the living

God. His confidence was not rooted in his own strength but in the faithfulness of the Lord who had delivered him from the lion and the bear. David's perspective was shaped by relationship, not intimidation. He understood that when God is involved, the battle is never about size - it is about sovereignty. Courage does the same for us today. It changes perspective. It shifts your focus from the size of the problem to the greatness of your God. When faith rises, fear loses its grip. Giants may still stand tall, but they no longer stand supreme. Courage reminds you that opposition is temporary, but God's power is eternal. When you see through the lens of faith, what once looked impossible becomes an opportunity for God to display His glory.

The battles you face today are not interruptions to your destiny - they are instruments shaping it. Every challenge that tests your patience or faith is forging something deeper within you. Without resistance, there is no strength. Muscles grow because they are stretched and strained. The pressure you feel is not meant to crush you but to condition you. What feels like opposition is often preparation in disguise, strengthening your resolve, sharpening your discernment, and building the endurance required for what lies ahead. Authority is not granted to the untested; it is entrusted to the prepared. Without pressure, there is no growth. Diamonds form under intense weight. Leaders are refined in hidden battles long before they stand in visible victory. Courage transforms struggle into preparation and pain into purpose. When you choose to stand firm, you convert adversity into advancement. The fight you are in today is equipping you for the influence, responsibility, and authority you will carry tomorrow.

There will be moments when no one stands beside you - no applause, no reassurance, no visible support. The room may feel quiet, the path uncertain, and the weight of the decision heavy on your shoulders. In those sacred hours, courage is no longer public; it becomes deeply personal. It is not about proving anything to others, but about standing firm in what you know God has spoken to your heart. It is in those unseen battles that character is refined, and faith is tested - not for performance, but for obedience. True courage is forged in the space between you and God. It is built in whispered prayers, in steady steps taken despite trembling hands, in choosing righteousness when compromise would be easier. When no one else understands the cost of your stand, heaven does. And in that private place, strength rises not from your own power, but from His presence. What you win in those solitary moments becomes the foundation for every public victory that follows.

So rise. Stand firm. Fight the good fight. The battles you face are not accidents; they are assignments. Fear will whisper retreat, but courage answers with obedience. Face what you fear with confidence in the One who goes before you. A man of conviction anchors himself in truth, stands on principle, and moves forward with unwavering resolve. When the winds rage and the ground shakes, he remains planted, knowing that what God has placed in his hands is worth defending. Lead with conviction. Live boldly for you are called to be a warrior. Every man has battles but the courageous man finishes strong. He does not quit when weary, nor surrender when wounded. He presses on, trusting that endurance produces strength and faithfulness produces legacy. Rise each day with purpose in your heart and fire in your spirit. Stand firm in the storm. Fight with honor. And when the dust settles, let it be said that you were faithful, you were fearless, and you finished strong.

| 9 |

"ACTS OF COURAGE"

One of the best ways to understand the meaning of courage is to see it in action. Courage is a force revealed in movement. It is faith stepping forward when fear whispers, "Stay where you are." When a believer chooses integrity over popularity, truth over silence, and obedience over convenience, courage becomes visible. Courage is shown when someone forgives though they've been wounded, gives though they are lacking, and stands though they are shaking. It is a holy momentum that moves the heart beyond hesitation and into purpose. Courage advances not because the path is clear, but because the promise is sure. Courage understands that growth lies on the other side of risk and that miracles often follow moments of trembling obedience. When you act in faith despite uncertainty, you reveal that your confidence is not in yourself but in the One who calls you forward. That is courage in motion - faith stepping forward boldly until conviction becomes visible through decisive, obedient action.

Courage is visible long before it is celebrated. It is forged in the quiet places where only God can see. It is the whispered "yes" in private prayer, the trembling but determined surrender that says, "Lord, I trust You," even when the outcome is unclear. True courage begins in hidden moments of obedience. It is the unseen decision to forgive, to step out, to let go, to believe again. Long before anyone applauds the victory, God honors the surrender. Courage is first an inward posture before it becomes an outward action. It is faith taking its first step in the dark, confident not in circumstances but in the One who leads. The world may celebrate the breakthrough, but heaven celebrates the trust that made the breakthrough possible. When you choose to move forward in obedience - when you say yes before you see results - you are already walking in courage. What is cultivated in quiet surrender before God will one day emerge in the open as undeniable strength, character, and radiant testimony in the light.

Scripture shows us courage in action through the life of David. Long before he ever stood before a giant, he stood before God. In the quiet pastures of Bethlehem, while tending sheep and worshiping with his harp, David developed a heart anchored in trust. His bravery was cultivated in seasons of obscurity. The private victories over the lion and the bear were not random events - they were divine training grounds where courage was shaped by communion with God. So when David faced Goliath, he was not stepping into unfamiliar territory; he was simply acting on a confidence he had already built in secret. The battlefield only revealed what the pasture had produced. His bold declaration before Israel and the Philistines flowed from a relationship with God, not a rush of emotion. True courage is born in the presence of God before it is displayed before people. Like David, we discover that the giants we confront publicly can only be defeated by the faith we have developed privately.

Courage does not wait for perfect conditions; it moves when obedience calls. Faith is not proven in calm seas but in storm-tossed waters. The wind may howl, critics may speak, and outcomes may remain uncertain, yet courage refuses to be paralyzed by what it sees or hears. It chooses to trust beyond logic and step forward despite discomfort. When everything appears unstable, courage anchors itself in the unchanging voice of the Lord and moves at His command. It is like stepping onto the water when Jesus says, "Come," even while the waves are still raging. The miracle did not begin when the storm stopped; it began when Peter stepped out of the boat. Courage believes that if Christ called you, He will sustain you. It understands that growth, breakthrough, and testimony are found beyond the safety of the shoreline. Courage does not wait for perfect conditions or peaceful circumstances. It moves forward with bold confidence because the Savior walks beside us. When He speaks, that is enough.

Consider Esther. She did not feel fearless when she approached the king uninvited. She felt the weight of risk pressing against her heart. The law was clear - approach uninvited, and death could be the consequence. She understood the danger. She counted the cost. Yet in the tension between fear and faith, she chose obedience over safety. Her words, "If I perish, I perish," were not a cry of despair but a declaration of surrender to purpose. Esther teaches us that courage is the decision that something greater than fear is worth stepping forward for. Courage is not the denial of danger; it is the embrace of destiny. It is the moment when you stand at the threshold of uncertainty and move anyway because you know you were called for such a time as this. Esther's bravery was rooted in purpose, and she understood that her position was not accidental but providential. Likewise, when you face overwhelming odds, or uncertain outcomes, courage whispers that your calling is bigger than your comfort.

Courage is seen in forgiveness. It takes uncommon strength to release someone who has wounded your heart and disrupted your peace. The natural instinct is to protect, to retaliate, to balance the scales - but forgiveness rises above instinct. To forgive is to refuse to let pain dictate your future. It is a declaration that the offense will not own you, define you, or chain you to bitterness. When you choose to release someone, you are not excusing their actions; you are freeing your spirit from captivity. It requires spiritual boldness to choose grace over revenge. The world may call retaliation power, but heaven calls forgiveness courage. Revenge keeps wounds open, but forgiveness closes them with healing. It takes a warrior's heart to lay down the sword of anger and lift up the shield of mercy. True strength is not found in how hard you can strike back, but in how boldly you can love when love is hardest. Forgiveness is an act of faith - trusting God to handle justice while you walk in freedom.

There is courage in obedience. When God speaks a difficult instruction, courage answers, "Here I am." It takes bold faith to say yes when the path ahead is uncertain, when the cost is high, or when the outcome is unclear. Obedience is not passive. It is an act of spiritual bravery that chooses trust over fear and surrender over self-will. When you obey God's voice, especially in the face of uncertainty, you step into courage that aligns your life with His divine purpose. It is choosing trust over fear, surrender over control, and faith over feelings. True courage is revealed in your submission to God's voice. Obedience often leads us beyond our comfort zones, but it always leads us closer to His purpose. The very place that stretches us is the place that shapes us. When we step where He directs, even trembling, we position ourselves for His power to be made perfect in our weakness. Every act of obedience aligns us with His will, refines our character, and advances His calling on our lives.

Think of Peter stepping out of the boat. The wind was strong, the waves were loud, and the other disciples chose the safety of what they could hold onto. But Peter chose something greater than comfort -he chose to trust the voice that called him. In that single step, he risked embarrassment, failure, and even sinking beneath the waves. Yet for a moment, in the middle of the storm, he did what no one else dared to do - he walked on water. Peter's faith faltered when he focused on the storm, but even then, he learned something the others never did: faith grows when it is exercised. Courage may stumble, but it is never defeated when it rises again. Every step forward - no matter how small - builds strength, resilience, and unwavering faith. Through decisive action, courage rises stronger within you, turning every fear you face into a steppingstone toward victory. The step may feel uncertain, but obedience in motion always leads to deeper trust and greater transformation.

Courage speaks truth when silence would be easier. It refuses to bow to comfort, convenience, or the fear of rejection. It understands that truth is not always popular, but it is always powerful. Real courage does not shout for attention; it stands steady, anchored in conviction. It chooses integrity over applause and obedience over approval, knowing that character is forged in the moments when speaking up costs something. Courage stands firm when compromise would be convenient. It declares righteousness in rooms where darkness has grown comfortable and complacency has settled in. It shines light not to condemn, but to restore; not to dominate, but to deliver. Courageous hearts refuse to normalize what is wrong simply because it is common. They rise with boldness wrapped in humility, grounded in faith, and committed to what is right. In a world that often rewards silence, courage dares to speak and, in doing so, it shifts atmospheres and awakens hope.

There is courage in starting over. When the plans you carefully built fall apart, it takes real strength to stand in the rubble and refuse to give up. Courage doesn't deny the pain, and it doesn't pretend the loss didn't happen. Instead, it gathers the broken pieces with trembling hands and lifts them toward heaven, believing that God is still a Master Builder. It whispers hope into places that feel empty and trusts that even shattered dreams can become the foundation for something stronger, wiser, and more beautiful than before. Starting over is an act of faith. It declares that failure is not final and that grace is greater than yesterday's mistakes. God's mercy is new every morning, and His purpose is not canceled by our missteps. When we choose to begin again, we are saying that our story is not defined by what went wrong, but by the God who makes all things new. In His hands, endings become beginnings, and what once looked like ruin becomes a testimony of redemption and renewed strength.

Joshua was told repeatedly, "Be strong and courageous," because he was standing at the threshold of destiny. Moses was gone. The wilderness season was ending. The promise of God was in front of him but so were fortified cities, trained armies, and unknown battles. God was reminding Joshua that fear cannot coexist with faith when it's time to move forward. The Promised Land was already given by covenant, but it still had to be possessed by courage. Every new season of leadership, growth, and promise requires strength of heart and steadiness of spirit. The land flowing with milk and honey would not fall into Israel's lap; they had to cross the Jordan, confront giants, and trust God with every step. In the same way, the promises over your life require movement, obedience, and unwavering trust. God gives the vision, but you must take the step. He declares the promise, but you must possess it. Strength and courage are not optional qualities; they are the bridge between prophecy and fulfillment.

Courage does not always roar with thunderous applause or stand boldly on mountaintops for all to see. Sometimes it is quiet. Sometimes it whispers in the stillness of a weary heart, "Try again tomorrow." It is the strength that rises after disappointment, the resolve that refuses to quit after failure, the steady breath taken before one more step forward. Courage is not always dramatic; often it is deeply personal. It is the decision to get back up when no one is watching, to trust God when answers are delayed, and to move forward even when feelings say retreat. True courage shows up in consistency. It wakes up early to pray when sleep would be easier. It keeps loving when love is not returned. It keeps believing when circumstances look unchanged. It keeps serving without recognition or applause. This kind of courage builds character, deepens faith, and shapes legacy. It is not loud, but it is powerful. And over time, that quiet perseverance becomes the very testimony of a life that refused to give up.

There is courage in generosity. It takes bold faith to open your hand when your resources feel small and your needs feel large. To give when it seems like there isn't enough is not irresponsibility - it is confidence in God's character. It is a quiet but powerful declaration that your security is not in what you can count, but in the One who cannot be depleted. Generosity, especially in lean seasons, is an act of spiritual bravery that defies fear and honors God. Faith-filled giving is a bold statement that God is the source, not circumstance. When you sow in trust, you proclaim that your provision does not come from a paycheck, an economy, or human approval, but from the faithful hand of the Lord. Every generous act says, "My God will supply." It shifts your focus from scarcity to sufficiency and from anxiety to assurance. Courageous generosity does more than bless others - it strengthens your own heart, anchors your trust deeper in God, and reminds you that the well of His provision never runs dry.

Courage is contagious. When one believer chooses to stand firm in faith, even in the face of pressure or uncertainty, it sends a ripple through the hearts of others. Strength has a way of multiplying when it is witnessed. One steady life becomes a testimony that God is faithful, that fear does not have the final word, and that obedience is always worth it. When one man walks in courage, he gives permission for others to rise up also and discover their own boldness. What seemed intimidating suddenly feels possible because someone proved it could be done. Acts of courage ignite communities and transform atmospheres. A single step of faith can shift an entire room from doubt to expectation, from hesitation to action. Faith becomes visible, hope becomes tangible, and unity becomes stronger. God often uses one willing heart to spark a movement, reminding us that bravery is not about perfection - it is about trust. And when trust in Him is displayed openly, it spreads like fire, lighting the way for many to follow.

The greatest act of courage the world has ever witnessed was displayed by Jesus Christ. Knowing full well what awaited Him, He did not retreat from betrayal, suffering, rejection, or the agony of the cross. In the garden of Gethsemane, He felt the weight of what was to come, yet He chose surrender over escape, obedience over fear. He stood firm when others fled, remained silent when falsely accused, and endured unimaginable pain with unwavering resolve. His courage was not reckless bravery - it was deliberate, sacrificial obedience to the will of the Father. Love compelled Him. Redemption required Him. With every step toward Calvary, He carried not only a cross, but the burden of humanity's sin. His courage tore the veil, defeated death, and opened the door to our salvation. Because He moved forward in faithfulness, we can move forward in freedom. The cross was not the end - it was the victory. And through His courageous obedience, we have hope, forgiveness, and eternal life.

Courage grows when it is exercised. It is not a gift reserved for the fearless; it is a discipline developed through resistance. Just as muscles strengthen when they are challenged, faith strengthens when it is tested. Trials are not signs of abandonment but opportunities for expansion. Every obstacle faced with trust, every fear confronted with conviction, and every step taken despite uncertainty builds spiritual endurance. Pressure does not weaken true faith - it refines it, shapes it, and prepares it for greater responsibility. Every act of obedience stretches the soul and deepens trust. When you choose to move forward in faith - especially when comfort invites you to stay still - you enlarge your capacity for courage. Obedience in the small moments prepares us for boldness in the larger battles. With each "yes" to what is right, even when it is hard, confidence in God's faithfulness grows. Courage is faith in motion. And the more we practice it, the stronger, steadier, and more unshakable we become.

We do not wait to feel courageous before we move. Courage is not something you wait to feel - it is a deliberate choice to stand firm, step forward, and act in faith even when fear is present. Faith does not consult fear; it confronts it. When God calls us forward, He is not asking for a surge of emotion but a step of obedience. The brave are not those who feel no fear - they are those who move despite it. Every time you choose obedience over hesitation, you openly declare that God's Word is greater than your worry. Feelings follow faithfulness. The moment you step forward in obedience, Heaven supplies strength you did not know you possessed. What seemed impossible begins to yield. What felt overwhelming becomes manageable. Strength rises as we walk, not as we wait. God meets motion with provision. When you act in faith, you discover that courage was never something you had to manufacture - it was something God was ready to release the instant you trusted Him enough to move.

To understand courage, watch it move when staying still would be easier. Watch it forgive when pride demands retaliation. Watch it obey when obedience costs comfort. Watch it endure when pressure mounts and the storm refuses to pass. Watch it love when wounds are still fresh. Courage is not loud bravado or reckless emotion; it is faith with feet. It is trust in motion. It steps forward when fear whispers, it kneels when ego resists, and it stands firm when circumstances shake. And when you choose to act even when trembling - you become living testimonies of the power of God at work within you. Courage is the evidence that faith is alive, breathing, and active. It transforms belief from something you say into something you demonstrate. Every obedient step, every patient response, every act of undeserved love becomes a declaration that God is greater than your fear. In those moments, heaven touches earth through your surrender, and your life preaches a sermon louder than words ever could.

| 10 |

"THE RISE OF COURAGE"

God wants you to be strong, bold, and very courageous. He wants you to face life head-on no matter what's happening. He wants you to be driven by courage, not ruled by fear. God never designed you to be intimidated, hesitant, or paralyzed by fear. Fear silences faith and magnifies obstacles until they look greater than the promises of God. But courage does the opposite - it lifts your eyes, strengthens your spirit, and reminds you that the One who called you is greater than whatever stands before you. When God speaks purpose over your life, He does not expect you to move forward trembling in doubt; He empowers you to advance with boldness. Throughout Scripture, we see that every person God used had to confront fear. Moses faced Pharaoh. David faced Goliath. Esther faced a king. In every case, the turning point was not the removal of danger, but the rise of courage. When you understand who stands with you, you gain the strength to stand firm against anything that comes against you.

Fear will try to rule you by whispering worst-case scenarios, reminding you of past failures, and exaggerating present challenges. It seeks to confine you to comfort zones and convince you that stepping out is too risky. But courage speaks a different language. Courage says, "If God is for me, who can be against me?" Courage moves forward even when the outcome is uncertain because it knows that obedience is more important than security. When you choose courage, you break fear's authority and align yourself with faith. Today, God is calling you to live driven not by anxiety, not by insecurity, not by the opinions of others but by holy boldness. The dreams He placed in your heart require bravery. The calling on your life demands faith-filled action. Fear may knock at the door, but it does not have to sit at your table. Let courage rise within you. Trust His promises. Step forward anyway. Because when you are driven by courage, you walk in the freedom and authority God intended for you all along.

Uncommon courage is always fueled by faith in the ultimate good of God and everything He has promised us. Good courage must be taken! You must take hold of the promises of God so that you can stand firm on the day the enemy attacks you (Eph. 6:13). Since "all the promises of God in Him are yes and in Him amen" (2 Cor. 1:20), you must not be a coward but let your heart take courage. Don't live a timid, weak, wimpy, fearful life. Be bold and live the life God wants you to live. Your own Promised Land is there waiting for you to come possess it. Don't let fear stop you from taking what's yours. Don't be afraid to try new things. Courage is not the absence of fear, it's going forward in the presence of fear. You're not a coward if you feel fear, you're a coward if you let fear control you. Courage means you step out according to what's in your heart and not letting your circumstances stop you. Get out of your boat of safety and start walking on the water. God is encouraging you to be bold and take a risk.

You will be amazed at all the amazing and wonderful things God has planned for your life if you will only be courageous and step out. So often, we stand at the edge of promise, aware that there is more, sensing that there is greater, yet hesitating because the unknown feels intimidating. But faith has never been about comfort - it has always been about trust. The same God who placed the dream in your heart has already prepared the path before your feet. What feels uncertain to you is already known by Him. When God calls you to step out, He is not asking you to rely on your own strength. He is inviting you to rely on His. The miracle is found in stepping into obedience. Every breakthrough begins with one act of faith that moves you beyond fear and into promise. Every testimony begins with a decision to trust God when the outcome is uncertain and the path is unclear. Every victory begins with courage, the bold resolve to stand firm, press forward, and believe that what God started, He will surely complete.

There are blessings attached to your obedience that you cannot access by remaining where you are. The provision, the connections, the growth, and the transformation are often waiting on the other side of your "yes." When you choose to trust God enough to move, you activate purpose. Doors you never could have opened on your own begin to swing wide. Opportunities you never imagined begin to unfold. Sometimes the greatest limitation is not the size of the challenge, but the size of your willingness. God does not call the qualified; He qualifies the called. If He is stirring something in your spirit, if He is nudging you toward a new season, do not shrink back. The courage to begin is often the very thing that releases heaven's help. Heaven responds to faith in motion. You may not see the whole staircase, but you do not need to. God rarely shows you the entire blueprint, but He does show you the next step. When you take that step, clarity increases. Strength rises. Confidence grows.

The journey itself begins to shape you into the person capable of carrying the promise. What once looked impossible begins to look inevitable. So be courageous. Step out. Trust Him. There is more ahead of you than behind you. The life God has planned for you is bigger, brighter, and more beautiful than your fears would ever allow you to believe. Take the step. Say yes. Move forward. You just might look back one day and realize that the moment you chose courage was the moment everything changed. Trust God and go forward. God will prove Himself to you if you'll be bold enough to follow Him and not the crowd. Step out with bold faith and God will increase the quality of life you're living. He'll expand the level of your contentment and sense of well-being. Be excited about the new things God wants to do in your life, because every new step of faith opens the door to greater purpose and blessing. Have the courage to follow Him wholeheartedly. For sure, this is the key to living a truly wonderful life.

Courage is the key that unlocks the door for God to move in your life. It is not the absence of fear, but the decision to trust God in the middle of it. Every person faces moments when stepping forward feels risky and retreat feels safe. Yet it is in those defining moments that faith becomes active. When you choose courage, you are declaring that God is greater than the obstacle before you. That declaration invites His power into your situation. Fear paralyzes, but faith mobilizes. Fear magnifies problems; faith magnifies God. When you operate from fear, you shrink back, hesitate, and second-guess the very promises God has spoken over your life. But when you walk in faith, something shifts. Faith strengthens your spirit and steadies your heart. It empowers you to move even when you don't see the full picture, trusting that God is already working behind the scenes. God cannot work through fear because fear closes your heart to His leading. Fear builds walls; faith opens doors.

Scripture consistently shows us that God responds to faith, to bold, unwavering trust in His character and His Word. Courage is faith in motion. It is stepping out of the boat, walking toward the unknown, and believing that the same God who called you will sustain you. When you act courageously, you position yourself for divine intervention. Courage doesn't mean you never feel anxiety or uncertainty. It means you refuse to let those feelings dictate your obedience. The more you trust Him, the more courageous you become. And the more courageous you become, the more room you give God to demonstrate His power in your life. Courage creates space for miracles. Every breakthrough begins with a step of faith. Doors of opportunity swing open when you choose to believe instead of doubt. Courage causes you to pray bigger prayers and dream bigger dreams. The rise of courage aligns your heart with God's promises so choose courage. Choose to trust God beyond what you can see.

Let faith rise higher than fear. When you do, you invite heaven into your circumstances. God works through faith-filled people who dare to believe, dare to step out, and dare to trust Him completely. Courage opens the door, and faith keeps it open for God to move mightily in your life. Courage comes from the heart. It's the spirit of aggression and boldness that says, "I'm going to step out. I will not let fear stop me." Courage knows that God has not given us a spirit of fear but of power, love, and a sound mind (2 Tim. 1:7). With courage you can face everything the enemy throws at you. Is. 12:2 says, "Behold, God is my salvation, I will trust and not be afraid." Ps. 118:6, "The Lord is on my side; I will not fear. What can man do to me?" Be fearless and bold no matter what is required of you. Step out and God will guide you every step of the way. Step out and God will prepare the way before you. He said in Is. 45:2, "I will go before you and make the crooked places straight."

God said in Josh. 1:9, "Be strong and of good courage; do not be afraid, nor be dismayed, for the Lord your God is with you wherever you go." God says that to you every single day of your life. When you let courage rise up inside you, you'll step out and try new things. You'll find God's destiny for your life. You'll find what's going to bring you fulfillment. You'll find who you're called to be and what you're called to do. You don't have to fear because the Lord Jesus Christ is living inside of you. No matter what season you are walking through - whether it feels like a mountaintop victory or a valley of uncertainty - God wants you to know that His presence is not dependent on your circumstances. He does not draw near only when life is easy, nor does He retreat when life becomes complicated. In moments of confusion, grief, transition, or unexpected change, He remains steady. His promise is not that you will avoid storms, but that you will never face them alone. Believing that brings about the rise of courage.

Know with certainty that His presence is constant, faithful, and unshakable. When you feel overwhelmed by responsibility, disappointment, or unanswered questions, God is not standing at a distance waiting for you to figure it out. He walks beside you in the middle of the tension. He sees the tears you do not show others, hears the prayers you whisper under your breath, and understands the burdens you struggle to explain. There is no detail too small and no crisis too large for His attention. His nearness is personal. He strengthens, comforts, guides, and sustains you in ways you may not always see immediately, but can trust completely. Even when the path ahead looks unclear, God's presence goes before you and surrounds you. He is with you in the waiting, in the rebuilding, in the healing, and in the breakthrough. He does not abandon His children when life becomes unpredictable. Instead, He uses every season to strengthen your faith and remind you that you are never outside His care.

Whatever you are facing right now, you can move forward with confidence, knowing that the One who called you is also walking with you. The first words spoken after the resurrection two thousand years ago was by an angel who said, "Do not be afraid" (Matt. 28:5). Then, a little while later, Jesus appears to some women and the first thing He says is, "Do not be afraid" (Matt. 28:10). The most common command in all the Bible is, "Do not be afraid." This command is given 365 times in the Bible. There's a "fear not" for every day of the year because fear is humanity's most common problem. It crosses every culture, generation, and background. It's also our oldest problem. From the Garden of Eden to the present day, fear has followed mankind like a shadow. It is everywhere. Yet into our oldest and most persistent struggle, God repeatedly speaks the same steadying command, "Do not be afraid." He gives us this command not because fear and trouble don't exist, but because His presence does.

After the fall of man the first recorded words of Adam were, "I was afraid because I was naked, and I hid myself" (Gen. 3:10). From that dreadful day until now, people have been hiding from God and fearing each other. They've been afraid and wearing masks ever since. The truth be told, fear is everywhere. It is universal, and it is ancient. Everyday people unconsciously make decisions based on hidden fears. People carefully choose what clothes they wear because they're afraid of what people might think about them. There is the fear of rejection, the fear of being unloved, and the fear of being alone. There is the fear of failure, the fear of losing your job, the fear of bankruptcy. There is the fear of losing your marriage, the fear of losing your mind, the fear of sickness, and the fear of death. The list goes on and on. Never give in to fear, because the moment you surrender to it, you allow it to divide your mind, shatter your emotions, and hinder the progress God has called you to make.

Stand firm in faith and courage and let confidence in His promises guard your heart and steady your steps forward. You're not to live in fear, you're to live in strength and courage, in faith and trust in the Lord. Courage is not just a matter of being strong. It's being calm in the midst of trial and fear. It's not a sin to experience fear. What matters is what you do when feelings of fear come. Fear is a powerful emotion, and when understood properly, it can serve a purpose in the life of a man. There are moments when fear acts as a warning system - alerting us to danger, sharpening our awareness, and helping us make wise decisions. It can keep us from reckless choices and guide us toward caution when necessary. In that sense, fear can protect you. It can wake you up, stir discernment, and push you to prepare, pray, and seek God more earnestly. Properly placed, fear can create urgency. It can ignite discipline. It can remind you that your calling matters and that your decisions carry weight.

At times, fear can also motivate you. The fear of failure can drive you to study harder. The fear of consequences can move you to live righteously. The fear of disappointing God can inspire deeper obedience. Properly placed, fear can create urgency. It can ignite discipline.

It can remind you that your calling matters and that your decisions carry weight. When fear points you toward wisdom and responsibility, it has served a temporary purpose. But fear was never designed to control you. It was never meant to dominate your thoughts, dictate your decisions, or paralyze your faith. When fear becomes the loudest voice in your life, it has stepped outside its assignment. A man of God cannot be led by fear and led by faith at the same time. Fear may knock on the door, but it must never be allowed to take a seat at the head of the table. Yes, fear may visit but it must never dwell. If you give it authority, it will try to control your thoughts, shape your decisions, and silence your purpose.

Let faith rise up and remind fear that it has no power where trust in God leads. Scripture reminds us that God "has not given us a spirit of fear, but of power, love, and a sound mind" (2 Tim. 1:7). That means fear does not have ownership over your identity. It does not define your calling. It does not determine your future. When fear tries to linger, you must confront it with truth. You must replace it with faith, courage, and confidence in the promises of God. A man of God will feel fear, but he will not dwell in it. He acknowledges it, learns from it, and then moves forward in obedience. Courage is not the absence of fear; it is the decision to trust God in the presence of it. Faith stands up when fear tries to sit down. Faith speaks when fear tries to silence. Faith advances when fear demands retreat. Let fear be a signal, but never a master. Let it sharpen you but never shackle you. Let it remind you to pray but never cause you to hide. You were called to walk by faith, not to live in fear.

What is courage? It's that attitude that enables you to face dangers and the challenges of life fearlessly, firmly, and calmly. Even in the midst of difficulty and hardship, there can be a sense of calmness and tranquility inside of you. Courage is the inner resolve that enables you to face dangers, obstacles, and the challenges of life fearlessly, firmly, and calmly. Courage does not deny that storms exist - it simply refuses to let the storm dictate your direction. Even in the midst of danger, difficulty, and hardship, courage produces a quiet strength that anchors the soul. There can be a deep sense of calmness and tranquility inside of you not because the battle has ended, but because your confidence is rooted in something greater than the battle itself. Courage steadies your heart in the storm, clears your mind of fear and doubt, and empowers your steps to move boldly toward the purpose God has placed before you. It allows you to remain unshaken on the outside because you are settled on the inside.

How do you obtain the courage you need for life's big challenges, for all the battles you have to fight every day? The Bible gives us the answer. First, you must make a firm decision to be courageous. God didn't suggest that Joshua be strong and courageous - He commanded it, because courage is not a feeling you wait for but a choice you step into. A command is not an appeal to your emotions; it is a call to your will. It does not ask how you feel; it demands that you choose to act, regardless of how you feel. God was saying, "Joshua, make up your mind to do what I've told you to do, and I'll empower you to do it." Phil. 2:13 (NLT), "For God is working in you, giving you the desire and the power to do what pleases Him." When you firmly decide to obey God's command to be strong and courageous, you step into alignment with His power and purpose. As you take that stand in faith, He will strengthen your heart, energize your spirit, and equip you to carry out everything He has called you to do.

| 11 |

"THE FOUNDATION OF COURAGE"

In order to be courageous, you must always remember that you are never alone. When God commissioned Joshua to lead Israel into the Promised Land, He did not begin with strategy, weapons, or military plans. He began with His presence. "As I was with Moses, so I will be with you. I will not leave you nor forsake you" (Josh. 1:5). The foundation of courage is not confidence in yourself - it is confidence in God's nearness. Joshua had every reason to feel overwhelmed. Moses was gone. The people were watching. The Jordan River stood in front of them, and fortified cities lay ahead. Yet God did not tell Joshua to look within; He told him to look upward. The same God who parted the Red Sea, who brought water from a rock, and who led by a pillar of fire was still present. Courage begins when you remember that the God who was faithful yesterday is faithful today. The same hands that carried you through past battles are still holding you steady now, and His promises have not changed.

We often feel alone when facing new seasons, new responsibilities, new battles, and new uncertainties. The enemy whispers that you must handle it by yourself. But God's Word declares the opposite. His presence does not fluctuate with your emotions. He does not abandon you in transition. Just as He stood beside Moses in the wilderness, He stood beside Joshua at the Jordan. Just as He stood beside

Joshua in courage and conquest, He stands with you now unwavering in every battle you face. The promise "I will not leave you nor forsake you" (Heb. 13:5) is more than comforting language; it is a covenant assurance. God binds Himself to His people. Even when you feel inadequate, remember that His presence does not diminish with your weakness. It surrounds you and stands strong on your behalf. Courage rises the moment you stop measuring your ability and start trusting His reliability. When you lean on His unshakable power and faithfulness, fear loses its voice and faith finds its footing.

True courage is born in relationship. Joshua had walked with Moses and witnessed God's faithfulness. Those memories became anchors for his future. In the same way, you must rehearse the victories God has already given you. Remember the doors He opened, the storms He carried you through, the prayers He answered. Each testimony becomes fuel for boldness in the next battle. God's presence also provides direction. When you know He is with you, you do not have to rush decisions or be paralyzed by fear. You can move forward step by step. Courage does not require knowing the entire map; it requires trusting the One who holds it. Joshua did not see the walls of Jericho fall before he marched. He trusted the voice of God and obeyed. When you internalize the truth that you are never alone, fear begins to lose its grip. You may still feel the tension of the moment, remember that the Creator of heaven and earth walks with you and His presence transforms intimidating places into holy ground.

God's presence is not a distant promise - it is a daily reality. From the rising of the sun to the quiet of the night, He walks beside you, surrounds you, and dwells within you. You are never navigating life alone. In moments of clarity and in seasons of confusion, in victory and in valley, His presence remains constant. It does not fluctuate with your feelings or circumstances; it is rooted in His forever faithfulness. Courage is not the absence of fear; it is the confidence that you are not facing fear by yourself. True courage is anchored in the awareness that God is near. When you know He stands with you, anxiety loses its authority. His nearness becomes your strength. His voice steadies your heart. His promises quiet the noise of doubt and remind you that you are upheld by something greater than the storm. This is why David could boldly declare in Psalm 23:4, "I will fear no evil, for You are with me." David did not deny the existence of the valley of the shadow of death; he walked through it.

David understood the Shepherd's presence outweighed the shadow. He also knew that the shadow of a dog never bit anybody. The valley may have been dark, but it was never empty. God was there. The same Shepherd walks with you today. Whatever valley you face, whatever uncertainty surrounds you, His rod and staff still comfort. His presence is your anchor. His nearness is your assurance. And because He is with you at all times you can move forward with unwavering courage, knowing that no shadow is stronger than the One who stands beside you. So stand firm. Be strong. Be courageous. Be this way not because you are fearless, but because you are never forsaken. The same God who promised Joshua His unwavering presence makes that same promise to you. Let that truth settle deeply in your spirit: you do not fight alone, you do not lead alone, you do not endure alone. And when you remember that, courage becomes not just possible but inevitable.

The assurance of God's abiding presence steadies your heart in uncertain moments. It reminds you that no valley is too dark, no mountain too high, and no storm too fierce for the One who walks beside you. True strength rises in your heart when you fully understand that nothing stands beyond His sovereign control. When you know the Lord is near, you stand taller in the face of opposition. You make decisions with boldness instead of hesitation. You move forward even when the path is unclear because your faith tells you that God sees what you cannot see. His nearness transforms insecurity into confidence and weakness into resilience. With His presence comes His power. God empowers you as an active defender and guide. The same power that formed the universe works within those who trust Him. When you rely on His strength instead of your own, you discover a supernatural endurance that carries you through trials you once thought would break you.

With His presence also comes His protection. This does not mean you will never face hardship, but it does mean that nothing can touch your life without passing through His sovereign hands. He guards your mind with peace, your heart with hope, and your steps with divine direction. In seasons of uncertainty, you can rest knowing that you are covered by His faithful care. And where God's presence abides, His provision follows. He supplies wisdom when you lack answers, peace when you feel overwhelmed, and resources when you feel insufficient. He opens doors no one can shut and makes a way where there seems to be none. You are never truly in lack when the Provider walks with you. So be strong and courageous. Anchor your confidence in the unchanging character of God. When you know He is forever by your side, boldness becomes your posture and faith becomes your foundation. His presence brings His power, His protection, and His provision. With Him beside you, you are never alone.

Courage comes when you have unwavering faith that God is with you in every single circumstance of life. King Hezekiah told the people not to fear the king of Assyria and the vast army with him. He said, "Be strong and courageous. Do not be afraid or dismayed for there are more with us than with him. With him is an arm of flesh; but with us is the Lord our God, to help us and to fight our battles" (2 Chron. 32:7). Have courage and boldly declare, "The Lord is my helper. I will not fear what man shall do to me" (Psalm 118:6). This is a warrior's confession of faith. When you anchor your heart in the truth that God Himself stands beside you, fear loses its authority. The opinions of people and the threats of adversity no longer control your steps. To proclaim that the Lord is your helper is to stand firm in the face of opposition, knowing that no human power can override God's purpose for your life. On the tombstone of Sir John Lawrence are these words: "He feared man so little because he feared God so much."

Giving proper attention to the Word of God is another essential for acquiring courage. Courage is born from truth rooted deep within the heart. When you consistently read, meditate on, and apply scripture, you anchor your life to promises that cannot fail. The Word reminds us that God is faithful, powerful, and present and who we are in Him - called, equipped, and never alone. As fear whispers uncertainty, the Word speaks assurance. It replaces doubt with conviction and instability with confidence. When you give God's Word your focused attention, you allow it to reshape your thinking. Courage is strengthened when our minds are renewed. The battles we face often begin in our thoughts, and Scripture provides the weapons we need to stand firm. Every testimony of deliverance, every declaration of God's faithfulness, and every command to "be strong and courageous" builds spiritual resilience within us. The more familiar you become with God's promises, the less intimidating life's challenges appear.

A courageous believer is not one who never feels fear, but one who knows where to turn when fear arises. By giving proper attention to the Word of God, you will develop a steady confidence that outlasts circumstances. You'll begin to speak what God says rather than what situations suggest. Your faith grows bold, your obedience becomes decisive, and your resolve strengthens. Josh. 1:8 says, "This Book of the Law shall not depart from your mouth, but you shall meditate in it day and night." Jesus said the same thing in Matt. 4:4, "Man shall not live by bread alone, but by every word that proceeds from the mouth of God." When you mediate on God's Word, you're taking the thoughts of God and placing them into your heart and soul. All of God's Word has the power to lift your spirit and fortify you for whatever it is you are facing. When the Word dwells richly within your inner man, courage becomes a natural response because you are standing not on shifting ground, but on the unchanging truth of God.

Not only must you read and meditate on the Word of God, but you must also do what it tells you to do. Meditation plants the seed, but obedience produces the fruit. The power of Scripture is released in your life when you align your actions with what God has spoken. Faith grows stronger when it is exercised, and courage is built when you choose to act on God's promises despite fear or opposition. When you forgive because the Word commands it, give because it instructs it, stand firm because it declares it, and love because it models it, you transform truth into testimony. The blessing is not in knowing the Word alone, but in doing it. Choosing to obey God in everything, regardless of personal cost, is the ultimate act of courage (Luke 9:23). When you are living in obedience to the Word of God, there is a strength that comes that will make you strong and courageous. Obedience to the Word of God brings stamina, energy, and confidence. There is boldness that overflows into your life.

The problem in the world today is too many men read the Bible but don't do what it says. The truth be told, obedience is an essential part of being a man of God. A real man does not follow his own impulses but humbly submits his will to the authority of the Lord, trusting that God's way is higher and better. In obedience, strength is refined, character is built, and true spiritual leadership is revealed. The act of taking up your cross and following Christ (Matt. 16:24) takes obedience. A man not obeying God's commands can rightfully be asked, "Why do you call Me 'Lord, Lord' and not do what I say?" (Luke 6:46). Obedience is defined as "dutiful or submissive compliance to the commands of one in authority." As a man of God, it is your duty and obligation to obey God, just as Jesus fulfilled His duty to the Father by dying on the cross for our sins. Obedience means complying with everything God commands you to do. It is your duty to do so. And, as you obey, courage grows strong in your inner man.

Another way to gain courage is to recall God's faithfulness in the past. He told Joshua, "As I was with Moses, so I will be with you" (Josh. 1:5). God is challenging Joshua to remember His faithfulness to Moses in the past. When we deliberately remember the prayers He answered, the doors He opened, and the strength He provided in seasons we once thought would break us, fear begins to lose its grip. The same God who sustained us then has not changed now. Reflecting on past victories - both great and small - builds confidence that He will guide us through present challenges as well. Testimonies of His provision, protection, and promises fulfilled become anchors for our faith, reminding us that we do not face today's battles alone. Courage grows when memory rehearses mercy, and trust rises when we remember that God has always been faithful. The Hebrew word for "faithfulness" means 'steadfastness; firmness; fidelity.' If God delivered you in the past, why should you be afraid now?

We learn to trust the character of a person by spending time with them - by listening to their words, observing their actions, and watching how they respond in moments of pressure. Trust is built through relationship, not assumption. In the same way, we learn to trust God's faithfulness by getting to know His character. As you study His Word, reflect on His promises, and recognize His hand at work in your life, you begin to see that He is consistent, unchanging, and true. God does not shift with circumstances or fail under pressure. When you study God's Word, you learn that He never changes and never lies. He is always true to His Word. Ps. 34:19, "Many are the afflictions of the righteous, but the Lord delivers him out of them all." When you recall God's faithfulness in the past, your courage will begin to soar. The more you know Him, the more confidently you can rest in His faithfulness. Trust grows where knowledge deepens, and faith becomes steady when it is rooted in who God truly is.

Courage comes when you remember the promises of God. It is not rooted in your own strength, talent, or certainty about the future, but in the unshakable faithfulness of the One who spoke the promise. When fear whispers that you are alone or unprepared, the Word of God reminds you that He goes before you, stands beside you, and remains within you. Every promise He has made has been proven true throughout generations. He has never failed, never forgotten, and never broken a single word. When you anchor your heart in that truth, boldness rises. You can step forward with confidence, face adversity with steadiness, and endure hardship with hope, knowing that the same God who fulfilled every promise in the past is faithful to fulfill every promise concerning you. Joshua told the people, "You know with all your heart and soul that not one of all the good promises the Lord your God gave you has failed" (Josh. 23:14). This is why you can be strong and courageous all the days of your life.

If you want courage, read your Bible daily and intentionally highlight every reminder of God's goodness and every promise He has spoken over your life. As you mark His faithfulness on the page, you'll begin to see it written across your own story. Courage grows when your heart is anchored in what God has already said. For example, He promised in Ps. 91:10-13, "No harm will overtake you, no disaster will come near your tent. For He shall give His angels charge over you, to keep you in all your ways. They shall bear you up in their hands, lest you dash your foot against a stone. You shall tread upon the lion and the cobra, the young lion and the serpent you shall trample underfoot." Never, ever, forget the promises and blessings of God. Ps. 137:6 says, "If I do not remember You, let my tongue cling to the roof of my mouth." Make a steadfast pledge today to remember and stand on God's promises, no matter what circumstances try to shake your faith. As you do, courage will come.

Sometimes God uses other people to build courage into our lives, placing examples before us so we can draw courage from their faith and step confidently into our own calling. When He spoke to Joshua, He reminded him of the strength and steadfastness of Moses, showing him what bold obedience looks like under pressure. Moses was afraid to stand before Pharaoh, feeling inadequate and unsure of himself, yet he chose to obey God's command despite his fear. Through that obedience, God transformed his weakness into courage and used him to deliver a nation. No doubt the memory of Moses' courageous obedience stood strong in Joshua's mind, reminding him of what fearless faith looks like in action. Watching Moses stand before kings, lead through wilderness, and trust God in impossible moments must have stirred Joshua's heart to rise with the same bold resolve. Inspired by that example, Joshua stepped forward determined to be a brave leader who trusted God completely.

On Paul's journey to Rome where prison and eventual death awaited him, several brethren came from a long distance to be with him. Acts 28:15 says, "When Paul saw them, he thanked God and took courage." Even mature spiritual believers need the inspiration and strength that come from genuine fellowship with other believers. No matter how deep one's faith or how seasoned one's walk with God may be, there are moments when encouragement, accountability, and shared worship breathe fresh courage into the soul. 1 Thess. 5:11, "Therefore encourage one another and build each other up." Vs. 14 says we are to "encourage the timid." Fellowship reminds us that we are not called to stand alone but to grow, serve, and persevere together, sharpening one another through prayer, testimony, and love. In the company of other faithful hearts, even the strongest believer finds renewed vision, strengthened resolve, and a deeper experience of God's presence.

| 12 |

"THE CLARITY OF COURAGE"

After being tempted in the wilderness for forty days, Jesus went into the temple and read a prophecy about Himself that was written in Is. 61:1,2, "The Spirit of the Lord is upon Me, because He has anointed Me to preach the gospel to the poor. He has sent Me to heal the brokenhearted, to preach deliverance to the captives and recovery of sight to the blind, to set at liberty those who are oppressed, to preach the acceptable year of the Lord." He had clarity when He said after the reading, "Today this scripture is fulfilled in your hearing" (Luke 4:21). Between clarity and purpose stands courage. It's the bridge that turns conviction into action. Jesus knew exactly what His life was about, and that clarity fueled His unwavering purpose. Because He understood His mission, He walked in the courage to teach, to serve, to suffer, and ultimately to fulfill the will of the Father. Jesus shows us that when we have clarity and gain a clear understanding of God's will for our lives, the courage to obey it rises up within us.

Clarity settles the heart. It silences confusion and anchors the soul in divine purpose. When we know what God has spoken, hesitation begins to lose its grip. Throughout His earthly ministry, Jesus moved with unwavering focus because He understood His assignment. He repeatedly declared that He came to do the will of the Father, not His own. That clarity shaped every decision, every conversation, and every confrontation. He was not driven by applause or intimidated by opposition - He was led by purpose. Clarity turns belief into bold conviction. When the vision is clear, hesitation dies. Once God makes His purpose known, the risk becomes obedience, and obedience carries its own strength. The clarity of courage is born when you become convinced that obedience to God carries greater value than any comfort, security, or approval you might surrender. When you truly believe that His calling matters more than what you could lose, fear loosens its grip and faith steps forward with bold resolve.

Jesus was courageous because He was committed to the purpose He stated at the beginning of His ministry. Clarity is knowing what your life is about, knowing the reason you were born. Jesus faced rejection, betrayal, and ultimately the cross, yet He did not retreat. Why? Because He knew the outcome was redemption. The pain was real, but the purpose was greater. Clarity about the Father's plan gave Him the courage to endure what others could not. In our own lives, confusion often paralyzes us more than danger does. We hesitate because we are unsure. But when we seek God in prayer, in His Word, and through the guidance of the Holy Spirit, He brings understanding. And with understanding comes boldness. If you are waiting for courage before you step forward, ask God first for clarity. Once you clearly see what He is asking of you, courage will rise from within like a steady flame. When purpose is settled, bravery follows. Clarity births courage, and courage carries you into destiny.

When people have clarity about who they are and why they're here, they can live a life that is focused on their purpose. Clarity gives rise to courage. You're more likely to take risks and do bold things when you have courage. If courage is lacking in your life, then perhaps you've lost clarity of what your life is about. When you lose sight of why you are here, what you are called to build, and who you are meant to become, hesitation naturally replaces boldness. Uncertainty clouds conviction, and fear grows in the absence of direction. But when clarity returns - when you recognize the assignment on your life, when you anchor yourself to a reason greater than comfort - courage rises almost effortlessly. Purpose fuels perseverance. Vision silences doubt. Knowing why you live gives you the strength to face what you fear. Clarity does not remove obstacles, but it gives you the resolve to confront them, because a life driven by purpose will always produce the courage to pursue it.

You are on a journey to become who you are called to be. Every step, every challenge, and every victory is shaping you into your God-given purpose. Just as Jesus walked with clarity and mission, your life carries divine intention, and heaven has placed greatness within you. On this journey of leaving your mark on the world, you must learn to see adversity through a new lens. No longer is hardship an obstacle, but as an opportunity for growth. The very challenges that test you are the tools that shape your character, refine your purpose, and prepare you to make a lasting impact. Have the attitude that nothing can hold you back and no obstacle can keep you from becoming who you were created to be. When you decide that your dreams and goals are worth the fight, every setback becomes a steppingstone, and every challenge becomes fuel for your forward progress. With courage in your heart, you can overcome fear and become the strongest, wisest, and best version of yourself.

Courage drives you to do the things you're supposed to do without fear and hesitation, even when the path ahead feels uncertain or uncomfortable. It empowers you to act with conviction, trusting that obedience and boldness will always produce growth, strength, and purpose. It takes intentional action to achieve your goals, fulfill your destiny, and accomplish what must be done. Dreams may inspire you, but only decisive steps forward will turn vision into reality. Don't be stagnant. Press on and go forward. That's what courage is prompting you to do. What is courage? It's the match that lights the fire inside of you. God is saying, "Burn, baby, burn!" Every day, fix your eyes on your dreams, your goals, and the aspirations God has placed in your heart. Let them shape your thoughts and guide your steps. Then rise with courage and boldly pursue them, trusting that faithful action today builds the future you were created to live. Chase your dreams and become the person you're supposed to be.

Yes, people are watching you and you have the opportunity and the ability to make a positive impact in their lives. People need your influence whether you realize it of not. Challenge yourself and change the world around you. All you have to do is use courage to become the person you are called to be. Each new day gives you a new opportunity to do something great, to make something special happen. Nobody can stop you but you. There are many great people in this world. Use courage and become one of them. Remember this, you will dwell in what you dwell on. "As a man thinks in his heart, so is he" (Prov. 23:7). Think well of yourself. Dwell on who God made you to be. Get excited about the wonderful future God had planned for your life. Those with courage think a certain way, operate a certain way, and have a certain mindset and mentality. You can do more and become more if you'll only believe more. Keep moving forward with courage and keep believing with unwavering faith.

It takes courage to live a great life. Courage is leaning into the things you're afraid of. Choose courage instead of fear. Mark Twain said, "Courage is the mastery of fear, not the absence of fear." When you master your fear, it turns into courage. The Lord stood by Paul's side when an angry mob of Jews conspired to kill him (Acts 23:10-12). The Lord appeared to him and said, "Be of good cheer, Paul" (vs. 11). Paul was alone, but in reality, he wasn't alone. The Lord met him in the barracks where he was being kept. We often demand that Jesus deliver us out of our circumstances when He wants to meet us in the midst of them. Everything changes when you know that Jesus is there with you. He stood by Paul in his hour of need and He'll stand by you also. Jesus said to Paul when he was down, "Be of good cheer" (vs. 11). In Greek, Jesus said, "Be of good courage." It takes courage to look adversity in the face and be of good cheer. This is, however, precisely what Jesus commands us to do.

Jesus does not waste words. Every command He gives reveals exactly what is happening beneath the surface. When He told Paul to "take courage," it was clear Paul was discouraged, and Christ spoke directly to the fear in his heart with timely strength and assurance. Paul never needed Jesus more than in that dark hour when everything around him seemed uncertain and overwhelming. It looked hopeless until Jesus appeared and spoke, and in a single moment, His presence turned Paul's darkness into divine purpose and direction. In the midst of hard times. Jesus said, "Be of good cheer, Paul. Take courage. Be unafraid." This wasn't a suggestion; it was a command. Jesus commands all men to have confidence and firmness of purpose in the face of danger and adverse circumstances. The command to "take courage" is in the present imperative which calls for this to be one's lifestyle. We're to be continually encouraged all the time and be consistently strengthened and uplifted.

You need to rely on the enabling power of the Holy Spirit to breathe fresh courage into your spirit and to energize you with supernatural encouragement. The same Spirit who raised Christ from the dead lives in you, empowering you to stand firm, move forward, and overcome. The Lord's greatest encouragement is not always a change in your circumstances, but the assurance of His presence in the midst of them. In every trial, His nearness strengthens your heart, steadies your faith, and reminds you that you are never walking alone. Courage empowers you to rise above negative circumstances, turning obstacles into opportunities for growth and strength. Instead of being defined by hardship, you become the master of it by shaping your response and refusing to let adversity shape you. The Lord did not condemn Paul for being discouraged but neither did He let him stay that way. The Lord would not have said "take courage" unless Paul needed to hear these words.

The presence of Jesus gives courage in every storm and every trial. Just as He reminded Paul that he was not alone, He stands with you in every challenge you face. Jesus was forsaken so that you would never be forsaken. Because of Him, you can walk boldly, knowing you are never alone. Jesus promised, "I will never leave you or forsake you," reminding us that His presence is our constant anchor in every season of life. Storms may rage and winds may howl, but when Christ is in the boat, we are never abandoned or alone. It is far better to walk through the fiercest trial with Jesus beside us than to stand in calm places without His presence. David wrote in Ps. 139:7,8 says, "Where can I go from Your Spirit? Or where can I flee from Your presence? If I ascend into heaven, You are there; If I make my bed in hell, behold, You are there." With Jesus by your side, when you go through rivers of difficulty, you will not drown. When you walk through the fires of oppression, the flames will not consume you.

Even in the middle of opposition, imprisonment, and uncertainty, God reminded Paul that his assignment was not finished, that there was still work to do. In Acts 23:11, the Lord assured him, "For as you have testified for Me in Jerusalem, so you must also bear witness at Rome," proving that no prison cell can cancel a divine calling. When God has a work for you to do, no obstacle can stop His plan, and no setback can silence your witness. In other words, it's not over until it's over. God said to Paul, "I have plans for you and I have a future for you." Likewise, your purpose in life is to be faithful in what God has called you to do, serving Him with obedience, courage, and unwavering trust. Jesus gave His life for you, demonstrating the depth of His love and the power of true sacrifice. Now you give your life to Him - fully surrendered, wholeheartedly committed, and determined to walk in His divine purpose every day. One day He'll say to you, "Well done, good and faithful servant" (Matt. 25:23).

Paul was called to be a witness for God, boldly proclaiming truth even in the face of hardship and opposition. In the same way, you are called to reflect Christ wherever you are, letting your life speak of His grace and power. It takes courage to shine as a light in a dark world, but your obedience can illuminate the path for others to follow. Speaking of the last days, Jesus said in Matt. 24:12, "Sin will be rampant everywhere, and the love of many will grow cold." Here in the last days, Christianity will be marked either by boldness or coldness. We will either rise with unwavering conviction or drift into a quiet compromise that numbs our faith and silences our witness. The hour calls for courageous believers who burn brightly and refuse to let their love for Christ grow cold. Dan. 11:32 says about the Antichrist, "Then with smooth words he will defile those who have rejected the covenant." That's the bad news. The good news is what he says next, "But the people who are loyal to their God will act valiantly."

The Bible says there are some believers who will grow cold. They'll be indifferent toward God because of the influence of sin. It then says there are others who will be bold and valiant, those who will do great exploits for the Lord their God. Pray for that type of boldness. Let your life be marked by strength and courage - the kind that stands firm in adversity and refuses to bow to fear. Walk in boldness, not coldness; let your confidence be fueled by faith and compassion, not pride or indifference. Be daring in purpose, steady in character, and warm in heart, so that your strength becomes a light that inspires others. This boldness that Daniel predicted comes from the outpouring of the Holy Spirit that God has reserved for these last days that we are in. Boldness stands up when everybody else sits down. It refuses to bow to fear, compromise, or silence. It is the courage to live out loud, shining unapologetically for the glory of God even when the crowd chooses comfort over conviction.

The power of God fills you with a boldness that fear cannot silence and doubt cannot shake. When His Spirit strengthens your heart, courage rises within you to stand firm, speak truth, and live faithfully before others. In these last days, His power makes you a living witness

- shining His light, declaring His hope, and reflecting His glory here on earth. Acts 1:8 says, "But you will receive power when the Holy Spirit comes on you; and you will be My witnesses." This God-given power awakens a prophetic voice within you, empowering you to speak truth with boldness and conviction. You declare without hesitation that Jesus is alive, reigning, and actively moving in the lives of His people. With courage and compassion, you proclaim that God has a divine purpose and a powerful plan for everyone who will believe. The truth is, if you are not boldly proclaiming your faith to others, you are not Spirit-filled. If you stand for nothing, you'll fall for everything. Don't fall for the nothingness this world is handing out.

Rom. 12:2, "Don't copy the behavior and customs of this world, but let God transform you into a new person by changing the way you think." Paul is urging believers not to conform to the patterns, values, and behaviors of the world around them, to resist blending into a culture that often opposes God's truth. Instead, he calls for transformation from the inside out, to have a renewed mind and heart shaped by God's Word and Spirit. In other words, stand out by living differently, thinking differently, and reflecting Christ in a way that clearly sets you apart. Coldness causes you to blend in with the crowd, settling for comfort and avoiding the risks that lead to growth. Boldness, however, sets you apart - igniting courage, inspiring others, and positioning you to live with purpose and impact. Don't blend in so you'll be accepted by everybody else, so they'll pat you on the back. People blend in so they won't make waves but that's precisely why you're here. Your purpose for living is to make waves.

It's a sad day when the light God placed inside you grows so dim that it blends into the darkness around you. You were never called to mirror the world's confusion, compromise, and chaos, but to shine with conviction, character, and courage. When there is no distinction, there is no influence because the power to change the world begins with refusing to look like it. The result of blending in is we'll be no different from the world around us. There will be no distinction at all, no difference. When we blend in, the enemy gets the upper hand because we've surrendered the very distinction God called us to carry. If there is no difference between us and the world, our witness loses its power and our light grows dim. The moment we compromise our identity, the enemy gains ground and influence. We were never called to fit in we were called to stand out, stand firm, and shine boldly. So what should you do? James 4:7, "Submit yourselves, then, to God. Resist the devil, and he will flee from you."

The message to all men here in the last days is to submit to God like never before, surrendering pride, fear, and self-reliance at His feet. True strength is not found in control, but in humble obedience to the One who reigns forever. As the world grows darker, the men of God must shine brighter. Every day they are to be living with courage, conviction, and unwavering faith. A bold faith is a daily reminder that this world is not our home, and we are called to reflect the light of Christ wherever we stand. God wants you to enjoy your life but don't get too comfortable here. You're in the world but not of the world. 1 Peter 1:17, "So you must live in reverent fear of Him during your time here as temporary residents." The end is near. There is not much time left. Pray for boldness so that you can share with others the saving grace of the Lord God. Acts 4:31, "After they prayed, the place where they were meeting was shaken and they were all filled with the Holy Spirit and spoke the Word of God with boldness."

| 13 |

"THE STAND OF COURAGE"

It takes courage to stand up for what you believe in. In a world that constantly shifts with trends, opinions, and pressures, conviction can feel costly. Voices grow louder, standards grow looser, and the temptation to blend in becomes stronger. Yet true courage is not loud or reckless. It is steady, the quiet resolve to remain rooted when the winds of culture try to uproot you. Courage means holding your ground with grace, speaking truth with love, and refusing to trade your values for acceptance. It recognizes that standing alone with integrity is far better than standing in a crowd without it. When your beliefs are anchored in something greater than public opinion, you gain the strength to endure discomfort and opposition. Every time you choose conviction over compromise, you build character. Once forged, character becomes a foundation no storm can shake. In the end, the stand of courage is the bridge between belief and action. It turns what you know in your heart into the life you live every day.

Every generation is summoned to sacred crossroads where the path of least resistance whispers for silence, and the road of purpose calls for resolve. In those pivotal seasons, comfort often disguises itself as wisdom, urging us to blend in rather than stand out. Yet history is not shaped by those who chose ease; it is marked by men who refused to bow to fear. The choice to stand may not always be loud, but it is always powerful. Courage becomes the dividing line between a life preserved, and a life poured out for something greater. It separates those who protect their comfort from those who pursue their calling. Speaking truth when it is unpopular, holding fast to faith when culture drifts, and choosing integrity when shortcuts beckon are the quiet battles that define a generation. In those moments, we discover that courage is the decision that obedience, purpose, and faith are worth more than safety. And when a generation chooses courage, it does more than survive its moment - it transforms it.

It takes real courage to hold to your values when others mock them. The crowd can be loud, persuasive, and intimidating, pressing you to compromise just to fit in or avoid criticism. But convictions rooted in truth are not weakened by volume or popularity. When you choose integrity over approval, you demonstrate strength that cannot be shaken by shifting opinions. True character is revealed not when everyone agrees with you, but when you remain steady despite opposition. Truth does not lose its power because it is unpopular. History repeatedly shows that what is right is not always what is embraced by the majority. Standing firm often means standing alone, but standing alone with truth is far stronger than standing with a crowd built on compromise. Courage is the decision that your values matter more than comfort or applause. When you refuse to bow to pressure, you become a quiet but powerful testimony that conviction, integrity, and faith still matter no matter how loud the crowd becomes.

Courage is born in the heart long before it is revealed in action. It does not begin with applause, recognition, or even visible strength it begins in the quiet chambers of conviction. It is formed in moments when no one is watching, when a person wrestles with fear, doubt, and uncertainty, yet chooses to believe that what is right is worth standing for. Before the public stand, there is a whisper in the soul that says, "This matters." Courage is a deep-rooted belief that justice, integrity, and faith are worth defending at any cost. It grows each time you refuse compromise, each time you align your life with what is honorable and just. When the moment of testing arrives, courage does not suddenly appear - it simply reveals what has already been planted within. The brave action others witness is only the outward expression of an inward resolve that has been strengthened over time. True courage is not impulsive; it is intentional. It is born in the heart, nurtured in conviction, and eventually displayed in action.

It takes courage to say "no" when everyone else is saying "yes." Peer pressure does not disappear with age; it simply changes form. As children, it may have looked like fitting in at school. As adults, it can look like compromising values for profit, approval, advancement, or comfort. The pressure to conform can be subtle - an unspoken expectation, a raised eyebrow, a promise of opportunity - but the cost of surrendering integrity is always greater than the reward of temporary acceptance. In business, relationships, ministry, and leadership, integrity often requires resisting the majority. True strength is revealed not in going along with the crowd but in standing firm when conviction demands it. Saying "no" may cost you applause, but it preserves your character. It may close certain doors, but it protects your calling. Leaders who shape history are not those who echo the culture, but those who anchor themselves in principle. Courage is not the absence of pressure; it is the decision to remain faithful in the midst of it.

Courage does not shout; sometimes it whispers. It is not always found in grand speeches or dramatic displays of strength, but in the quiet resolve of a heart that refuses to compromise its convictions. It is the steady voice that says, "I will not bend," even when bending would bring applause, comfort, or acceptance. Real courage stands firm when no one is watching and holds its ground when the pressure to conform grows heavy. It is revealed in integrity when shortcuts are offered, in honesty when deception would be easier, and in faith when doubt feels louder than hope. True courage is calm, confident, and anchored in conviction. It does not panic in the storm because it is rooted in something deeper than circumstances. It moves forward with assurance knowing that standing for what is right is more valuable than fitting in. Courage chooses obedience over popularity, character over convenience, and purpose over fear. It may not always be loud, but it is always powerful, forging a legacy that cannot be shaken.

It takes courage to defend the vulnerable. To step between harm and the helpless is to risk misunderstanding, criticism, and even rejection. Standing up for others can place you in uncomfortable positions where your motives are questioned and your comfort is sacrificed. Yet true character is revealed not in moments of ease, but in moments of conviction. Courage is the decision that someone else's safety, dignity, and worth matter more than your own convenience. History does not celebrate those who carefully guarded their image while injustice prevailed. It honors the men and women who chose integrity over applause and protection over popularity. Reputations fade, but righteous acts echo across generations. The ones remembered are those who shielded the weak, lifted the fallen, and stood firm when it would have been easier to stay silent. Defending the vulnerable may cost you comfort, but it builds a legacy of honor. In the end, it is far better to be known as a protector of people than a protector of pride.

Courage often costs something. It may cost popularity when you choose principle over applause. It may cost promotions when you refuse to compromise your values for advancement. It may cost partnerships when you will not bend truth to maintain convenience. Courage requires you to stand when it would be easier to sit, to speak when silence would protect you, and to act when hesitation would feel safer. There is always a price tag attached to conviction. Yet what courage gains is far greater than what it loses. It earns self-respect that no title can bestow and no critic can take away. It builds integrity that becomes the foundation of lasting influence. It secures honor - not the fleeting kind granted by crowds, but the enduring kind forged in character. When all is said and done, the person who chose courage remains steady, confident, and whole. In the end, what you keep within your character will always outweigh what you surrendered for the sake of doing what was right.

It takes courage to speak the truth with love. Anyone can blurt out facts without concern for how they land, and anyone can offer comfort without addressing what truly needs to be said. But the higher road requires strength of character. Truth without love can wound deeply, leaving scars that linger long after the words are spoken. Love without truth, however, can quietly mislead, allowing destructive patterns to continue unchecked. Courage steps into that tension and refuses to choose one at the expense of the other. The courageous person finds the balance - firm yet compassionate, bold yet gracious. They care enough to say what must be said, but they say it with a heart committed to restoration, not retaliation. Their words are not weapons; they are instruments of growth. Speaking truth with love demands patience, humility, and emotional discipline. Yet when handled rightly, it builds trust, strengthens relationships, and reflects a character anchored in both conviction and kindness.

Standing for what you believe requires preparation long before the moment of testing arrives. Convictions are not formed in the quiet places of understanding, prayer, reflection, and principle. When you take time to study truth, seek wisdom, and allow your faith to mature beneath the surface, you create a foundation that cannot easily be shaken. Preparation shapes perspective. It refines motives. It clarifies why you believe what you believe so that when opposition rises, you are not scrambling for answers but standing on solid ground. Courage is strengthened when your beliefs are deeply rooted truths. Shallow opinions shift with culture, pressure, and popularity, but rooted convictions remain steady because they are anchored in something greater than emotion or circumstance. When your heart has wrestled with truth, prayed through uncertainty, and reflected on principle, boldness becomes natural. You do not stand merely to be seen - you stand because you cannot be moved.

It takes courage to keep standing when the battle is long and the outcome is uncertain. Anyone can rise for a bold moment when emotion is high and the crowd is watching, but real strength is revealed in the quiet persistence that follows. Sustained courage is choosing to remain faithful when applause fades, when opposition intensifies, and when progress feels slow. It is the daily decision to hold your ground, to guard your convictions, and to refuse compromise even when weariness whispers otherwise. One bold stand may inspire for a moment, but endurance in conviction transforms a life. When courage is consistent, it shapes character, deepens integrity, strengthens resolve, and refines purpose. Others are influenced by steady faithfulness over time. Your perseverance becomes proof that your beliefs are not temporary passions but anchored truths. In standing firm through the long battle, you do more than survive - you become a living example of strength, resilience, and unwavering conviction.

Courage inspires courage. When one person chooses to stand despite fear, opposition, or uncertainty it sends a powerful message to everyone watching: it can be done. Boldness is contagious. A single act of faith, integrity, or conviction has the ability to break the silence in a room and shift the atmosphere of an entire community. When you rise, you become living proof that fear does not have the final word and that strength is not the absence of struggle but the decision to move forward anyway. Never underestimate the ripple effect of your stand. Someone is watching you fight through adversity. Someone is drawing strength from your perseverance. Your willingness to step forward may be the permission another person has been waiting for - the signal that they, too, can rise, speak, lead, and believe again. What feels personal to you may be profoundly prophetic for someone else. Stand firm, because your courage could be the spark that ignites a movement of boldness in others.

It takes courage to admit when you are wrong. In a world that often equates confidence with never backing down, it can feel risky to say, "I was mistaken." Yet true strength is not found in defending every misstep - it is revealed in the willingness to own it. Stubborn pride may protect the ego for a moment, but it quietly weakens character over time. Real conviction is not loud or defensive; it is steady and secure enough to withstand self-examination. When you have the courage to acknowledge error, you demonstrate a maturity that commands far greater respect than empty bravado ever could. Courage is having humility and the inner strength to correct course when necessary while still holding firmly to what is right. The brave heart listens, evaluates, and adjusts without surrendering its values. It models integrity and growth for others. Admitting you were wrong does not diminish your authority; it deepens it. Humble courage builds trust and paves the way for wiser decisions ahead.

There will be moments when fear whispers, "Stay quiet." Fear will try to convince you that silence is safer, that shrinking back is wiser, and that staying comfortable is the better choice. It will paint boldness as reckless and obedience as dangerous. In those moments, fear sounds reasonable. It speaks in logic and caution. But beneath its polished arguments is a single goal - to keep you from stepping into the purpose, calling, and conviction placed inside you. Yet faith and courage rise up and answer back, "This matters too much to remain silent." Faith sees beyond the immediate risk and into eternal impact. Courage is the decision that obedience is greater than comfort. When something is rooted in truth, conviction, and calling, silence becomes more costly than speaking. The world is changed not by those who avoid discomfort, but by those who choose conviction over convenience. When fear whispers, let faith speak louder. What matters most deserves a voice and that voice may be yours.

It takes courage to stand in your workplace, in your community, and in your home. Courage is not reserved for battlefields or bright spotlights; it is revealed in ordinary rooms, around conference tables, in neighborhood conversations, and at the dinner table. Everyday settings present daily opportunities to choose integrity over convenience, truth over popularity, and character over comfort. When you speak up with grace, refuse to compromise your values, or quietly do what is right when no one is watching, you are building a foundation that cannot be shaken. Small stands build the strength for greater ones. Each decision to act with honesty, patience, and conviction develops spiritual and emotional muscle. The quiet refusal to participate in gossip, the commitment to fairness when shortcuts are available, and the consistency of love and leadership at home all prepare you for larger moments of testing. As you remain faithful in the ordinary, you are being prepared to stand firm in the extraordinary.

Every time you choose to stand firm in the face of pressure, fear, or uncertainty, you are strengthening an internal muscle. The first step may feel uncomfortable, even intimidating, but with each decision to hold your ground, your confidence expands. What once seemed overwhelming becomes manageable, and what once felt impossible becomes attainable. Courage is cultivated when you decide to speak truth, protect your values, and refuse to retreat from what you know is right. When you consistently stand firm, you are not only overcoming external challenges; you are shaping your identity from within. Your character deepens because you are proving to yourself that you can endure, persevere, and remain steady. The more you practice courage, the more natural it becomes. Over time, your steady resolve builds a foundation of strength that cannot easily be shaken, and your life begins to reflect the bold, unwavering spirit you have chosen to cultivate.

In the end, courage defines legacy. Achievements may gather applause for a season, but convictions echo through generations. Titles fade, positions change, and accomplishments are eventually surpassed, yet the strength of a life anchored in principle leaves an imprint time cannot erase. Courage is revealed not merely in grand moments, but in daily decisions to stand firm when compromise would be easier. People may forget the details of what you accomplished, but they will remember the standard you carried. Your convictions become a compass for those who follow - your children, your community, and those influenced by your example. A courageous life gives others permission to rise, to hold their ground, and to pursue what is right even when it costs them. Legacy is not simply what you leave behind; it is what you plant within others. When your story is told, let it be said that you stood unwavering, lived boldly, and shaped generations through the power of steadfast courage.

Take your stand. Refuse to let your convictions live only in conversation while your actions remain silent. When your values guide your decisions, shape your responses, and determine your direction, they become visible. Integrity is proven not by what you say under easy circumstances, but by what you do when pressure mounts. Every choice to align your actions with your faith and principles strengthens your character and clarifies your identity. It takes courage to stand up for what you believe, especially in a world that often rewards compromise and convenience. But when you rise with conviction, you become more than a voice - you become a pillar. Your consistency provides stability for others who are searching for something solid. Your unwavering commitment to truth offers hope in uncertain times. And long after words fade, the example of your stand will continue to echo, reminding others that strength is found not in blending in, but in standing firm.

| 14 |

"THE BOLDNESS OF COURAGE"

Courage is not the absence of fear - it is the decision to move forward in spite of it. Fear may whisper of failure, rejection, or loss, but courage answers with action. It rises in the face of uncertainty and chooses progress over paralysis. True courage does not deny the presence of intimidation; it simply refuses to be ruled by it. It understands that growth lies beyond comfort and that purpose demands movement. Every step taken despite trembling knees is a declaration that fear will not have the final word. Boldness is courage that has found its voice, its stride, and its conviction. It is the fire in the heart of a man who refuses to bow to doubt, opposition, or the pressure to conform. Boldness separates the passive from the purposeful, transforming quiet belief into visible action. It speaks when silence would be safer. It stands when retreat would be easier. The bold do not wait for perfect conditions - they move with confidence rooted in conviction, knowing that destiny favors those who dare to advance.

Fear paints pictures of embarrassment, loss, and regret. It magnifies risk and minimizes potential. Fear keeps you calculating, overthinking, and standing still at the very moment movement is required. But courage speaks with a different tone. Courage understands that the greater tragedy is not failure - it is forfeiting destiny. Every great step of faith begins at the crossroads of fear and obedience. One voice urges retreat; the other calls you forward. The bold choose obedience.

They move when others hesitate. They act when others analyze them-selves into paralysis. They understand that faith is not the absence of fear - it is the decision to trust God in spite of it. Obedience un-locks doors fear told you were sealed. It builds strength, character, and confidence with every step taken. When you choose obedience, you silence fear's whispers and step into purpose. The question is not, "What if you fail?" The real question is, "What could happen if you trust God and move anyway?"

Courage is not loud arrogance that demands attention or seeks vali-dation. It is a quiet confidence born from deep conviction - an inner assurance that does not waver with the opinions of the crowd. True courage does not need to prove itself through noise or dominance; it stands steady, grounded in what is right even when no one is watch-ing. It is the calm strength that anchors the heart when pressure mounts, the unwavering belief that truth is worth holding onto re-gardless of the cost. Boldness is not about applause or recognition; it is about alignment. It flows from a life anchored in truth and shaped by integrity. When compromise would be easier, courage chooses conviction. When silence would be safer, boldness speaks with wis-dom and grace. It does not strive to be seen - it strives to be faithful. In the end, real courage is not measured by volume, but by consistency - the steady resolve to stand firm, rooted deeply in truth.

Throughout history, every breakthrough has been carried on the shoulders of courageous individuals. The builders who laid founda-tions where nothing stood before, the leaders who rose in uncertain times, the defenders who stood their ground, and the preachers who proclaimed truth all shared one defining trait - they all stepped be-yond comfort. They understood that progress requires pressure, and purpose demands risk. No wall was raised, no nation was strength-ened, no soul was restored by those who chose the easy path. Ad-vancement has always required someone willing to move when others hesitated, to believe when others doubted, and to act when others feared. Comfort has never built a legacy - courage always does. Comfort keeps us safe, but courage moves us forward. If you desire to leave a mark that outlives you, you must be willing to trade temporary ease for eternal influence. Step beyond the familiar. Embrace the challenge. Choose courage and watch your legacy unfold.

The boldness of courage begins internally. Before you ever stand before a crowd, confront an obstacle, or challenge injustice, you must first win the battle within. Courage is not first displayed in public; it is forged in private. It is developed in the quiet moments when no one is watching - when you choose faith over fear, conviction over compromise, and truth over comfort. Doubt will always try to whisper that you are not enough, not ready, or not capable. But boldness rises when you silence those lies and anchor yourself in who you are and what you are called to do. Identity must be settled before courage can be sustained. When you know who you are, you are no longer shaken by opinions, opposition, or uncertainty. Purpose must be embraced so deeply that retreat is no longer an option. The external victories you desire are rooted in internal alignment - heart, mind, and spirit united. When the war within is won, standing firm on the outside becomes natural.

Courage is not a single moment of bravery that defines a lifetime; it is a decision made over and over again in the quiet places of the heart. It is choosing obedience when compromise would be easier, choosing faith when fear whispers doubt, and choosing action when hesitation feels safer. True courage rarely looks like a spotlighted heroic act. More often, it looks like consistency - showing up, standing firm, and doing what is right even when no one applauds. It is boldness built through daily surrender and strengthened through daily resolve. Every day brings a crossroads: shrink back or step forward. Retreat into comfort or advance into purpose. The courageous understand that growth, calling, and impact live on the other side of forward motion. They do not wait to "feel" brave; they decide to be brave.

With each repeated choice to move ahead, courage becomes not just something they practice, but who they become. The courageous move forward until bold obedience becomes their way of life.

Boldness grows when you begin to understand that fear often shows up when you are standing at the edge of something meaningful, something that stretches you beyond comfort and into calling. Fear guards the doorway to growth because growth always requires movement into the unknown. The moments that make your heart race and your palms sweat are often the same moments that carry the greatest potential for transformation. Instead of retreating, lean in. Instead of shrinking back, step forward. What intimidates you today may be the very path that strengthens you tomorrow. Walk through the doorway fear is guarding. On the other side is new capacity, deeper wisdom, and resilience forged through experience. On the other side is strength you did not know you possessed, waiting to be awakened by action. Every courageous step reshapes you. Boldness is the decision to move forward trusting that beyond the discomfort lies growth, purpose, and power.

The courageous understand that opposition is often confirmation. When resistance rises, it is not always a warning to withdraw - it can be evidence that you are advancing into purpose. Growth disturbs comfort zones. Progress threatens complacency. When you begin to move with conviction, obstacles may appear not because you are wrong, but because you are right. Opposition has a way of revealing impact. If no one resists your movement, you may not be moving anything at all. Courage recognizes that friction is part of forward motion. When pressure increases, it is not a signal to retreat - it is a call to reinforce your resolve. Steel is strengthened by fire, and character is fortified by challenge. The moment resistance intensifies is often the moment breakthrough is closest. Instead of shrinking back, the courageous lean in. They pray harder. They stand firmer. Pressure does not define them; it refines them. And through that refinement, they emerge not weakened by opposition but strengthened by it.

Boldness of courage requires clarity of mission. When you truly know who you are and why you are here, fear begins to lose its authority over you. Intimidation may still whisper, but it no longer dictates your direction. A clear mission anchors your identity, reminding you that you are not wandering - you are walking with intention. When your purpose is defined, confusion fades, comparison loses its power, and distractions become easier to resist. You are not moved by every voice because you are guided by a greater vision. Purpose stabilizes your spirit and conviction fuels your steps. Clarity gives you confidence, and confidence strengthens your resolve. Even when opposition rises, you remain steady because you are rooted in something deeper than emotion - you are grounded in calling. Courage is not the absence of fear; it is the presence of purpose. When conviction burns within you, hesitation gives way to action. You move forward not because the path is easy, but because the mission is clear.

Courage speaks when silence would be safer. It rises up in moments when the cost of truth feels high and the pressure to blend in feels heavy. It stands when sitting would be easier, choosing conviction over comfort and integrity over approval. Courage defends what is right when others withdraw, not for applause, but because character demands it. It confronts what is wrong when others conform, understanding that compromise may be convenient, but it is never victorious. Courage is the quiet strength that refuses to bow to fear. Yet courage is not reckless - it is resolute. It does not act out of impulse, pride, or the need to prove something. It is steady, thoughtful, and anchored in principle. Courage weighs the consequences but chooses faith over fear and purpose over popularity. It understands that standing alone for a moment is better than standing ashamed for a lifetime. True courage is not loud bravado; it is unwavering commitment to what is right, no matter the cost.

There is a boldness that rises in a person who knows they are called. When you understand that your life carries divine intention, fear begins to lose its grip. Anxiety may whisper, but your assignment speaks louder. When purpose outweighs pressure, courage is no longer something you have to manufacture; it flows naturally. You move forward not because you feel no fear, but because what you are called to do matters more than what you are afraid of. Calling produces confidence because it is anchored in something greater than personal ability. It shifts your focus from "Do I have what it takes?" to "I was chosen for this." When your foundation is purpose, you stop measuring yourself against your limitations and start trusting the One who entrusted you with the mission. True boldness is born when you realize the assignment did not originate with you, so its success does not depend solely on you. That understanding transforms hesitation into faith and insecurity into steady resolve.

Courage often feels lonely because it requires you to step forward when others step back. The bold sometimes walk roads few are willing to travel, making decisions that are misunderstood, criticized, or even opposed. Yet throughout history, leadership has always required separation before celebration. There is often a season where you must stand apart choosing conviction over comfort, purpose over popularity, and obedience over approval. That lonely stretch is not a sign you are lost; it is evidence that you are leading. The path of courage may be narrow, but it leads to influence and impact. When you dare to walk it, you create space for others to follow. Your willingness to endure isolation becomes someone else's inspiration. True leaders are not formed in crowds but in moments of quiet resolve, where character is refined and vision is clarified. Stay the course. What feels like separation today is preparation for the influence and impact you were born to carry.

The boldness of courage transforms adversity into advancement. It refuses to bow to pressure or retreat in the face of resistance. Instead, courage steps forward when others step back. It sees what stands in the way not as a wall, but as a weight room - an opportunity to grow stronger. Every challenge becomes training. Every obstacle becomes strengthening. Every setback becomes preparation. The courageous heart understands that hardship is not punishment; it is the process through which character is forged, vision is clarified, and endurance is built. Courage reframes difficulty as development. It shifts the narrative from "Why is this happening to me?" to "How is this shaping me?" In that shift, adversity loses its power to intimidate and gains purpose instead. Trials refine perspective, deepen resilience, and awaken untapped potential. What once seemed like opposition becomes opportunity. When boldness leads the way, adversity becomes the very pathway to advancement.

Boldness is contagious. When one person stands firm in conviction, uncertainty begins to lose its grip on everyone around them. Strength has a way of stabilizing the atmosphere. When one voice rises with clarity and truth, it gives permission for other silenced voices to be heard. Courage is never confined to the individual - it multiplies. It travels across rooms, through teams, within families, and into communities. One decisive act of faith can awaken dormant bravery in the hearts of many. Courage ignites courage. Strength inspires strength. When someone chooses integrity over intimidation, faith over fear, and resolve over retreat, it creates a ripple effect that cannot be contained. Boldness becomes a catalyst. It reminds others that fear does not have the final word. It shows that standing firm is possible. And when enough people catch that fire, environments shift, cultures change, and ordinary individuals rise into extraordinary impact.

The courageous do not deny fear - they discipline it. They recognize the pounding heart, the trembling hands, and the whisper of doubt that tries to magnify the moment. They do not pretend those sensations are absent; instead, they master them. Courage is the decision to place faith, purpose, and conviction above it. The courageous understand that emotion is a signal, not a sovereign. They acknowledge it, steady their breath, and move forward anyway. While others wait for comfort, they step forward in commitment. While uncertainty looms, they anchor themselves in truth. Courage transforms fear from a paralyzing force into a refining one - turning trembling into tenacity and anxiety into advancement. Every bold step taken despite fear strengthens resolve and sharpens character. The courageous do not eliminate fear; they enlist it as proof that what lies ahead matters. And in that disciplined determination, they rise above emotion and walk boldly into their calling.

Boldness demands sacrifice. It often requires stepping away from comfort, risking reputation, and surrendering the illusion of security. Courage is rarely convenient. It calls you to speak when silence feels safer, to stand when retreat would be easier, and to move forward when certainty is absent. Every meaningful advancement carries a cost, and the bold understand that growth never comes without surrender. Comfort may feel safe, but it rarely produces transformation. Boldness is the decision to pay the price today, so you don't live with the consequences of hesitation tomorrow. The price of cowardice is always greater. Regret lingers longer than risk. Missed opportunities echo louder than failed attempts. While risk may bring temporary discomfort, regret brings lasting weight. The courageous choose risk over regret because they understand that failure refines, but avoidance imprisons. They would rather fall while pursuing purpose than sit safely while destiny passes by.

There comes a defining moment in every life when belief is no longer enough. Conviction can live quietly in the heart for years yet never reshape a single circumstance. Courage, however, was never meant to remain internal. It was designed to move. There is a line where what you believe must become what you do. That line separates intention from impact, potential from progress, and comfort from calling. Conviction without movement remains incomplete. The bold are those who cross that line. They allow their faith, values, and vision to step into risk, visibility, and responsibility. They understand that courage is the decision that something else matters more. When conviction becomes action, destiny begins to unfold. Doors open, mountains move, and influence expands not because belief existed, but because someone dared to move on it. The defining line is not drawn by talent or opportunity, but by action. And those who step boldly across it become the difference-makers they were meant to be.

You were not designed to live intimidated. You were created with capacity, authority, and divine potential woven into the very fabric of your being. Fear may whisper limitations, but it does not define your destiny. You were built to stand, to lead, to build, to love boldly, and to walk in confidence not because of pride, but because of purpose. There is strength inside you that intimidation tries to silence and influence inside you that doubt tries to bury. But what God placed within you cannot be canceled by what stands around you. Courage unlocks what fear tries to imprison. Boldness activates what hesitation suppresses. When you choose courage, you step into rooms you once avoided. When you choose boldness, you speak truths you once swallowed. Every act of faith pushes back the boundaries fear tried to set. The moment you move forward despite uncertainty, you reclaim authority over your life. You were not created to shrink back - you were created to rise up.

The boldness of courage is the mark of those who finish strong. It is not the absence of fear, but the decision to move forward in spite of it. Courage is the backbone of leaders who refuse to bow to pressure, the heartbeat of pioneers who step where no path exists, and the fuel of visionaries who see beyond the present moment. When obstacles rise and resistance pushes back, boldness anchors your spirit and steadies your resolve. It keeps you planted when others retreat. It keeps you focused when distractions multiply. It keeps you advancing when quitting seems easier. Stand firm in your convictions. Step forward into unfamiliar territory. Speak clearly with unwavering truth. Act decisively when opportunity appears. Be bold because courage was placed inside you for such a time as this. You were not created to shrink back but to rise up. The strength within you was designed for impact, for influence, and for endurance. Finish strong by choosing daily to let courage lead the way.

| 15 |

"THE PATH OF COURAGE"

The path of courage may be narrow, but it is the only road that leads to true influence and lasting impact. The broad way may promise comfort and applause, but it rarely produces character. The narrow path, however, refines the soul. It strengthens integrity, sharpens vision, and forges a spirit that cannot be swayed by pressure or popular opinion. Those who choose it understand that significance is the result of intentional, courageous steps taken when easier options are available. The narrow path requires resolve. It demands conviction rooted in unshakable truth. And it calls for a boldness that refuses to bow to fear, even when the cost is high. Every generation is shaped by individuals who were willing to stand when others sat, to speak when others were silent, and to act when others hesitated. If you desire influence that echoes beyond your lifetime, choose the path that stretches you the most. The narrow way may be difficult, but it leads to destiny, legacy, and impact that endures.

Courage is rarely convenient. It does not wait for perfect timing, ideal circumstances, or the comfort of unanimous approval. It moves when the path is unclear and the outcome uncertain. It steps forward when others hesitate because your purpose is stronger than theirs. Courage chooses obedience over popularity, conviction over comfort, and action over excuses. In moments where retreat seems reasonable, courage quietly whispers, "Advance anyway." Because of that, courage separates the ordinary from the extraordinary. The ordinary waits for guarantees; the extraordinary trusts God in the unknown. The ordinary blends into the background; the extraordinary rises with boldness and faith. Every breakthrough, every victory, every legacy worth leaving is marked by someone who chose courage when convenience was calling them back. Courage is steady resolve and when you answer its call, you step into a life that is not merely lived, but led with strength, purpose, and unwavering conviction.

The narrow path of courage is rarely crowded. It winds away from applause, away from comfort, and often away from the approval of others. Many admire bravery when they see it displayed in someone else's life, but far fewer are willing to pay the daily price required to walk it themselves. Courage demands quiet decisions no one notices, integrity when compromise would be easier, and perseverance when quitting would be applauded. It is not glamorous in the moment - it is steady, disciplined, and often lonely. Yet it is on that narrow road that true strength is formed. In the solitude of conviction, character is refined and purpose becomes unmistakably clear. The pressure, the resistance, and even the isolation shape a leader from the inside out. Those who choose the narrow path discover that loneliness is not a sign of failure, but evidence of focus. And in time, what once felt isolating becomes the very ground where vision is sharpened, resilience is built, and leaders are born.

Wide paths promise comfort, applause, and acceptance but comfort rarely produces calling. Applause may fill your ears, yet it cannot anoint your life with authority. Acceptance may make you feel included, but it does not guarantee assignment. The crowd often gathers on the broad road because it asks little and affirms much. It celebrates what is easy, familiar, and non-threatening. But purpose is rarely discovered in places that require no sacrifice. Growth is not born from convenience, and destiny is not forged in the echo of approval. The narrow path, though difficult, aligns you with destiny rather than popularity. It demands conviction when others choose compromise. It requires obedience when applause fades. It shapes character in silence and strengthens resolve through resistance. While the wide road offers visibility, the narrow road offers vision. When you choose the narrow way you gain clarity, calling, and the confidence that you are walking in divine alignment rather than public opinion.

Influence is not gained by blending in with the crowd; it is earned by standing firm when others waver. Anyone can echo popular opinions or shift with the cultural winds, but true leaders anchor themselves in conviction. When you choose courage over compromise, you demonstrate that your values are not for sale and your character is not negotiable. That kind of integrity commands attention. People may not always agree with you, but they cannot ignore someone who stands unshaken in the face of pressure. At first, your boldness may invite resistance. Some will question you, challenge you, or even misunderstand your motives. Yet over time, consistency builds credibility. When others see that you remain steady through criticism, adversity, and opposition, respect begins to replace resistance. Strength of conviction, lived out with humility and grace, becomes a quiet but powerful testimony. Influence grows not from fitting in, but from faithfully standing firm in what you know is right.

Courage shapes credibility. When people see you stand firm in the face of pressure they begin to trust the weight of your character. Any one can speak boldly when the stakes are low, but it is the tested voice that carries authority. When you endure criticism without retaliation, obstacles without surrender, and uncertainty without panic, your words gain substance. They are no longer just opinions; they are forged in experience. And people instinctively recognize the difference between noise and nerve. Influence does not rise from how loud you speak, but from how bravely you live. Valor gives gravity to your presence. It steadies your tone, sharpens your integrity, and commands attention without demanding it. Courage builds a reputation that cannot be manufactured - it must be demonstrated. When others witness consistency under fire, your leadership becomes undeniable. Your voice matters because your life backs it up. In the end, credibility is not granted by title or applause; it is earned by courage.

The narrow path also requires discipline. It is not a road for the impulsive or the easily distracted, but for those who are willing to train their hearts and minds to walk in truth. Courage is not reckless emotion or loud bravado; it is steady obedience to what is right. It is a daily decision to align your actions with your convictions, even when no applause follows and no recognition is given. True courage is revealed in the quiet places of life. It is choosing integrity when no one is watching and doing what must be done, even when it costs you something. It means standing firm when compromise would be easier, speaking truth when silence would be safer, and remaining faithful when the pressure to bend feels overwhelming. The narrow path may not be crowded, but it is the road where true character is formed and inner strength is refined. Those who walk it discover that lasting honor is not given by the crowd but earned through steadfast conviction and faithful perseverance.

Impact always demands sacrifice. The road that truly changes lives is rarely paved with comfort, convenience, or applause. It is carved through long nights, difficult decisions, unseen tears, and relentless obedience to a higher calling. The men who shape generations and leave lasting legacies understand that greatness is not accidental; it is purchased. It is built with perseverance when quitting would be easier, faith when outcomes are uncertain, and unwavering commitment when the crowd has disappeared. Those who choose this road recognize that temporary discomfort produces eternal significance, that sacrifice refines character, strengthens conviction, and deepens trust in God's purpose. While others chase ease, they pursue impact. While others avoid the cost, they embrace it. And in doing so, they discover that what feels heavy for a season becomes the very foundation of influence for a lifetime. Impact may demand sacrifice but sacrifice births legacy that outlives the one who made it.

Every great movement began with someone who chose the narrow road. While others searched for comfort, applause, or the ease of the crowd, they chose conviction. They understood that safety is too small a goal when eternity and purpose are at stake. When destiny calls and lives hang in the balance, comfort becomes insignificant compared to obedience, courage, and the lasting impact of faithfulness. Popularity fades but calling endures. The narrow road demands sacrifice, discipline, and unwavering faith but it also produces clarity, character, and courage. When one person dares to value purpose over popularity, it creates a path others can follow. Bold obedience becomes a beacon. Quiet faithfulness becomes a compass. And what begins as a solitary decision turns into a movement of transformed lives. The courageous path is rarely crowded at first, but it is always consequential. Walk it faithfully, and you won't just find direction for yourself; you'll become direction for someone else.

Fear will always try to widen the road. It whispers that compromise is harmless, that just a small step off course won't matter. It suggests that standing alone is too risky, that conviction costs too much, and that safety is found in blending in. Fear paints obedience as extreme and compromise as wisdom. It magnifies the crowd and minimizes the calling. But the widened road is rarely the better road - it is simply the easier one. And ease has never been the measuring stick of purpose. Fear has never built a legacy. It has never carved a path through impossible odds or raised a standard in the face of opposition. Fear's greatest achievement is the preservation of comfort, and comfort is the breeding ground of mediocrity. Legacies are built by those who narrow their focus, strengthen their resolve, and refuse to bow to the quiet voice of retreat. Courage does not mean the absence of fear - it means refusing to let fear make the decision. The road may be narrow, but it leads somewhere worth going.

Courage, on the other hand, expands your reach. When you confront adversity instead of avoiding it, you grow stronger in character, clearer in purpose, and deeper in conviction. Every challenge you face becomes a training ground for resilience. When you speak truth instead of shrinking back, you not only solidify your own foundation, but you also strengthen those around you who are watching and waiting for someone to lead. Courage is contagious. It gives others permission to stand, to believe, and to act with boldness. When you step forward in faith, doors begin to open that fear would have kept closed. Opportunities align with obedience. Strength meets surrender. What once seemed impossible becomes the very pathway God uses to elevate your life and influence. Courage doesn't mean the absence of fear - it means trusting God more than the fear. And as you choose bravery again and again, your world widens, your impact deepens, and your reach extends far beyond what comfort could ever provide.

The narrow path teaches endurance because it refuses to cater to comfort. It stretches your faith, disciplines your emotions, and strengthens your resolve when quitting feels easier than continuing. On the narrow road, you learn that storms are not sent to destroy you, but to develop you. Each trial becomes training. Each setback becomes instruction. When the winds rise and the rain falls, your spirit learns to stand firm not because the storm is small, but because your foundation has grown deep. That endurance builds a resilience that cannot be shaken by criticism, opposition, or unexpected challenge. You stop living for applause and start living from conviction. You stop reacting to pressure and begin responding with purpose. Over time, that quiet, steady strength becomes the bedrock of lasting influence. People are not moved by momentary passion; they are shaped by consistent character. And the resilience forged on the narrow path becomes the foundation upon which legacy is built.

True impact does not need a spotlight to validate its worth, nor does it depend on applause to prove its power. While trends rise and fall and public opinion shifts like the wind, true impact stands firm because it was rooted in conviction. It is the quiet decision to do what is right when compromise would be easier. It is the steady commitment to truth when silence would be safer. What is built on courage carries a weight that outlives noise and outshines momentary recognition. When the excitement fades and the crowds move on, what remains is the substance of what was sown. Lasting impact is forged in integrity, consistency, and sacrifice. It chooses faithfulness over fame and purpose over popularity. Courage lays foundations that convenience never could, and those foundations endure storms, criticism, and time itself. True impact is not measured by volume, but by legacy - by the lives changed, the character strengthened, and the example that continues to speak long after the applause has ended.

You cannot lead others into courage, growth, or faith unless you are first willing to walk that path yourself. Leadership is not a title you claim; it is a path you walk first. If you desire influence, you must first embrace bravery - stepping into uncertainty before asking others to follow. If you seek impact, you must first surrender comfort - choosing growth over ease, obedience over opinion, and conviction over convenience. True leaders model the standard. They absorb the cost. They carry the weight. They move forward when it would be easier to stand still. The narrow path is not accidental; it is intentional. It refines character, sharpens vision, and forges endurance. Wide roads attract crowds, but narrow roads cultivate calling. Every sacrifice shapes authority. Every act of courage builds credibility. If you want to guide others into promise, you must first walk through process. The path may be tight, but it leads to purpose and those who dare to travel it become the kind of leaders others trust to follow.

There will be moments when you question the journey - when the road feels steep beneath your feet and the progress you hoped for seems painfully slow. In those seasons, it's easy to mistake resistance for failure and delay for defeat. But growth rarely happens on wide, comfortable paths. The most meaningful transformation often unfolds in the tension of the climb, where endurance is strengthened, character is refined, and vision is sharpened. Just because the path is narrow doesn't mean you're lost; it may mean you're ascending. Narrow roads often climb higher, and higher ground always offers a broader view. What feels confining now may actually be positioning you for clarity later. The struggle is stretching you, the delay is developing you, and the climb is elevating you. When you reach that higher place, you'll see that every difficult step carried purpose. So keep moving forward. The view from the top will reveal that the narrow road was leading you somewhere greater all along.

Your courage today becomes someone else's confidence tomorrow. Every time you choose to stand firm - when it would be easier to shrink back - you are preaching a silent sermon of strength. People are watching more than you realize. They see how you handle pressure, how you respond to opposition, how you keep moving forward when circumstances try to hold you still. Your steady resolve becomes proof that endurance is possible. What feels like a private battle to you becomes public permission for someone else to believe they can overcome as well. When people see you stand firm, they discover strength within themselves. Influence multiplies when courage is visible. Boldness is contagious. Faith is transferable. Confidence spreads through example. One act of bravery can ripple through families, churches, workplaces, and generations. Never underestimate the power of your obedience, your resilience, and your unwavering stand. Someone is finding their footing because you refused to fall.

The world does not need more spectators sitting safely in the stands while history unfolds before them. It needs trailblazers - men who are willing to step onto uncharted paths and to move forward even when the way is uncertain. Progress has never been built by passive observers but by courageous individuals who dared to walk the road less traveled. Trailblazers understand that comfort rarely produces impact, and that significance is often found on the other side of risk, resistance, and responsibility. Now is not the time to blend in or bow out. It is the time to speak when it matters, to act when it counts, and to lead when others retreat. Leadership is not about titles; it is about initiative. It is about seeing a need and stepping into the gap. The world changes when ordinary people make extraordinary decisions to stand firm, to rise up, and to go first. Be the voice that brings clarity, the hands that bring help, and the example that inspires courage in others. The future belongs to those bold enough to blaze the trail.

Choose the narrow path. It is not the easiest road, nor the most popular, but it is the one that shapes strength, builds character, and forges conviction. The wide path promises comfort and applause, yet it rarely produces courage. The narrow way demands discipline, faith, and resolve. It calls you to rise when others retreat, to stand when others compromise, and to press forward when the journey feels steep. But every step taken on that road refines you, deepens your integrity, and aligns you with purpose. Embrace the challenge. Walk boldly, stand firmly, and live bravely. The path of courage may be narrow, but it transforms ordinary moments into eternal significance. Quiet obedience becomes a powerful testimony, revealing God's strength through surrendered hearts and steadfast trust. Though the way may test your endurance, it will also reveal your strength. And at the end of that faithful walk, you will discover that the narrow road was never a restriction, it was the gateway to a life that truly mattered.

| 16 |

"TYPES OF COURAGE"

Courage is something every man needs, for it is a defining attribute of good character and the foundation of true strength. It shapes integrity, commands respect and empowers a man to stand firm in conviction no matter the cost. Living with purpose and meaning begins when we lead from the heart, allowing love, compassion, and authenticity to guide our choices. A heart-centered approach toward life and ourselves empowers us to grow, serve, and walk each day with clarity, intention, and deeper fulfillment. Aristotle said, "You will never do anything in this world without courage. It is the greatest quality of the mind next to honor." Courage is not about being a hero in the spotlight; it's about choosing to stand firm when the moment demands strength. It's the grit and determination to make hard decisions, even when they are uncomfortable or unseen. True courage shows up daily facing challenges with a willful spirit that seeks to make the lives of other people better.

Courageous people are bold, choosing to step forward with strength when others shrink back. In Greek the word "courage" is described as 'boldness with confidence.' It is a fearless assurance rooted not in pride, but in unwavering conviction. Whenever you feel the urge to hesitate or retreat from a challenge, recognize it as the very moment growth is calling your name. Step forward anyway because when you continually step out of the boat in faith, you'll begin to see God meet you on the water again and again. Courageous obedience creates a pattern of breakthrough, and what once felt impossible will start becoming your new normal. You will accomplish things far above and beyond anything you can comprehend, imagine, or even dare to think. When you move forward in faith, God will do more through you than you ever believed possible. There are different types of courage that when activated will give you physical strength, endurance, mental stamina, and innovation.

Physical courage is the strength to move forward even when your heart is pounding and fear is whispering for you to retreat. This kind of courage requires a willingness to face danger, endure pain, and risk bodily harm or even death for the sake of something greater than personal safety. Whether on a battlefield, in a burning building, or standing between harm and the innocent, physical courage is revealed when a person values duty, conviction, or love above self-preservation. It is bravery in motion - the choice to step forward when every instinct says step back. A young lad asked a wise old man, "Can a man still be brave if he is afraid?" The old man replied, "That is the only time a man can be brave." Nelson Mandela said, "The brave man is not he who does not feel afraid, but he who conquers that fear." Fear and courage are brothers. It takes physical courage to run into a burning building to save a loved one. Physical courage is being terrified but going ahead and doing what must be done.

Strength, resilience, and awareness are all words that describe physical courage. Physical courage is the disciplined ability to act despite pain, pressure, or danger. Strength provides the capacity to endure and overcome physical challenges; resilience enables a person to rise again after being knocked down; and awareness sharpens the senses to recognize threats and respond wisely. Together, these qualities form a steady foundation that allows an individual to stand firm in adversity, protect others when necessary, and persevere through hardship. Physical courage is controlled power guided by alertness and determination. David had all these qualities when he faced Goliath. He had physical strength because he had tested strength. David killed a lion and a bear, so this uncircumcised Philistine was no problem for him. We develop physical courage when we step into a battle we've already won, strengthened by the memory that victory is possible because we've overcome before.

Social courage is the strength to stand firm in who you are, even when the crowd pressures you to be someone else. It means refusing to conform to expectations that compromise your values, character, or calling. True courage shines brightest when you boldly reveal your authentic self despite the risk of criticism, rejection, or misunderstanding. It's when you stand up for God in a respectful way when you're in a situation where others disagree with what the Bible says. Social courage is the strength to remain authentic and unwavering in adversity, choosing integrity over approval and conviction over comfort while still showing love and humility to those who disagree. It's choosing conviction without compromise, and grace without surrender. When you honor God with both your words and your attitude, you reflect Christ even in the middle of disagreement. Daniel had social courage when he prayed to God when it was against the law to do so. The greatest heroes stand up for what is right.

Righteous anger is the spark that awakens social courage within us. It stirs the soul when something sacred has been violated or truth has been ignored. When guided by wisdom and anchored in integrity, that anger becomes the prelude to bold action rather than reckless reaction. Speak your mind even if your voice shakes, for courage is not the absence of fear but the decision that truth matters more than trembling. Winston Churchill said, "Courage is what it takes to stand up and speak." Social courage is standing up tall and greeting the world with your head held high, regardless of who is watching. It is the strength to enter every conversation, every room, and every opportunity without shrinking back in insecurity. Social courage means feeling fully confident in the man God created you to be. When you embrace who you are, you no longer seek approval. You walk in assurance, authenticity, and quiet strength feeling fully comfortable being the man you are - authentic, secure, and unashamed.

Intellectual courage is the boldness to express godly wisdom with confidence and grace in any conversation you find yourself in. It means standing firmly on truth while speaking with humility, discernment, and love. When you choose to share God's perspective without fear or compromise, you become a light that elevates every discussion. This type of courage is cultivated through faithful study of the Bible and by immersing yourself in Spirit-led teachings written by anointed servants of God. As you consistently feed your mind and spirit with His truth, boldness rises within you to stand firm and speak with wisdom and conviction. It's the willingness to challenge old assumptions based on new revelations and insights gleamed from experience and research. When you know what you're saying is right and true, intellectual courage gives you the boldness to speak it out. Paul had intellectual courage when he boldly delivered a divine message that Gentiles had the same spiritual privileges as the Jews.

Intellectual courage is the willingness to stand firm in truth, even when it means disagreeing with popular opinion and challenging the status quo during times of social unrest. It requires bold conviction, thoughtful discernment, and the strength to speak with integrity when silence would be easier. It is a courageous willingness to take risks in the pursuit of truth, refusing to compromise what is right for what is easy. It is the strength to stand firm in your convictions - even if you must stand alone - trusting that truth is worth the cost. Galileo had intellectual courage to argue that the earth revolved around the sun and not the other way around. Many old assumptions have been disproved by research. You must have the courage to accept these new findings and how they apply to your life. Intellectual courage believes that old limitations, outdated thinking, and worn-out assumptions have passed away, making room for clarity and growth, wisdom and progress, and renewed understanding.

Emotional courage is the willingness to feel deeply. It is the strength to face fear, rejection, failure, and vulnerability without retreating, knowing that growth lives on the other side of discomfort. Every meaningful accomplishment is fueled by emotional courage, because nothing great is achieved without first daring to feel. Be aware of what your passions are, those things that continually occupy your thoughts and surface in your words as deep feelings and convictions. What you consistently think about and speak about reveals the direction of your heart and the calling shaping your life. Follow your heart for passion is what makes you do extraordinary things, to discover, to challenge yourself. Passion is the fire within that gives courage its heartbeat, empowering you to rise, stand firm, and pursue your purpose without fear. Steve Jobs said, "And most important, have the courage to follow your heart and intuition. They somehow already know what you truly want to become. Everything else is secondary."

Emotional courage is the daily practice of leaning into your feelings with honesty, allowing emotional awareness to guide your growth rather than suppress it. When you honor your experiences in life - both painful and joyful - you unlock deeper insight, stronger character, and a continual evolution of who you are becoming. Thornton Wilder said, "We can only be said to be alive in those moments when our hearts are conscious of our treasures." Emotional courage empowers you to make decisions rooted in your values rather than your fears. It gives you the strength to move forward with confidence, even when fear tries to hold you back. When you ignore your passions, when you deny or suppress your emotions, you risk the reduction of insight and the drive to go forward. If you choose to act boldly even while fear is whispering in your ear, you break the grip it has on your future. That's the power of emotional courage. It doesn't wait for fear to disappear; it moves forward anyway and becomes unstoppable.

Moral courage is the strength to stand for what is right even when it is unpopular, uncomfortable, or costly. It means choosing integrity over approval and conviction over convenience. True character is revealed when you remain faithful to your values despite opposition or discouragement. Doing the right thing often means standing alone when others choose the easy path. True integrity is revealed when you remain faithful to what is right, even if it brings shame, ridicule, or disapproval from those around you. It took unshakable moral courage for the three Hebrew children to stand tall when everyone else bowed before the golden image. In a moment where compromise was easy and consequences were deadly; they chose faithfulness to God over fear of man. It took unwavering moral courage for Daniel to kneel in prayer to God, even when the law forbade it and doing so could cost him his life. It took moral courage for Stephen to preach the gospel in front of those who were about to stone him to death.

It takes moral courage to honor your marriage vows, choosing faithfulness when feelings fluctuate and standing firm when storms arise. True love is proven not in ease but in the unwavering commitment to stay together through better or worse; trusting that perseverance strengthens the bond. It takes moral courage to remain sexually pure when you are not yet married, choosing conviction over culture and character over compromise. True strength is found in honoring God with your body, trusting that obedience today builds a foundation of blessing for tomorrow. Moral courage can be described as "daring integrity." It's when you refuse to compromise conscience for personal gain or convenience. It means holding on to one's biblical convictions, to be uncompromising under any influence that might tempt one to go against deeply held personal beliefs. It involves ethics and integrity. It's the daily commitment to align your words with your actions and your actions with your deepest values and ideals.

Moral courage is the strength to stand for what is right, even when it costs you comfort, approval, opportunity, or security. It is the unwavering resolve to choose integrity over popularity and conviction over convenience, no matter the consequence. Being a man of God requires you to have spiritual backbone - the inner strength to stand firm when pressure tries to bend your convictions. It means choosing obedience over popularity and truth over comfort, even when the cost is high. A man of God lives by faith, trusting the promises of God more than the opinions of people. He stands steady in storms, anchored in prayer, courage, and unwavering devotion to the Lord. Moral courage is standing up and acting when injustice occurs, when human rights are violated, or when people are treated unfairly. Take a stand to never become a coward morally. Always be willing to stand up for the virtues you believe in. Pontius Pilate lacked moral courage. He had the authority to release Jesus but refused to do so.

Moral cowardice recognizes truth but lacks the courage to stand for it. It knows what is right, yet bows to pressure, fear, or public opinion instead of conviction. Pilate declared that he found no fault in Jesus, yet he still handed Him over to be crucified, choosing comfort over courage. When we refuse to act on what we know is right, we allow evil to prevail through our silence. Leonardo da Vinci said, "He who does not punish evil commands it to be done." Moral courage requires us to make clear judgments about what actions and behaviors align with our highest values. It calls us to stand firm in truth even when it is unpopular, uncomfortable, or costly. When we choose integrity over convenience, we demonstrate the strength of character that shapes both our lives and the world around us. Moral courage calls us to stand firm in truth and righteousness, refusing to be swept away by the fear-driven narratives of this present world system. It compels us to rise higher - choosing conviction over comfort, faith over fear.

Spiritual courage is the quiet strength to stand firm when opposition rises and suffering presses in. It is choosing dignity over despair, trusting that God is present even in the storm. True spiritual courage does not pretend the struggle isn't real; it faces the storm head-on, rooted in the unshakable truth of God's promises. It walks forward with steady faith, trusting that every trial is already overshadowed by His faithfulness and victory. Aristotle said, "The ideal man bears the accidents of life with dignity and grace, making the best of circumstances." Spiritual courage empowers you to stand firm in the face of opposition, confident that you are never standing alone. When you trust that the power of God is at your disposal, fear loses its grip and bold faith takes its place. Spiritual courage causes you to be valiant in order to endure all things and overcome all obstacles. With spiritual courage you'll overcome all opposition as you unyieldingly engage in warfare and courageously persevere in your obedience to God.

Ps. 112:7 says the righteous man "will not be afraid of evil tidings; His heart is steadfast, trusting in the Lord." Spiritual courage makes you bold as a lion (Prov. 28:1), because when your heart is anchored in God, fear loses its grip and faith rises in its place. You can stand firm and unshaken, knowing that no weapon formed against you will prosper (Is. 54:17). Spiritual courage stands its ground with unwavering resolve, trusting God even when the cost is great. It presses forward with greater intensity and holy determination, knowing that eternal reward outweighs any temporary sacrifice. The courageous man confronts and conquers all fear and evil for there is no other way to obtain the desired promises of God. The effect of spiritual courage is a bold prevailing in every battle, not because of human strength, but because of unwavering trust in God's power and promises. It produces steadfast perseverance in obedience, standing firm in faith until victory is realized and God is glorified.

Spiritual courage is an extra dimension of courage that flows from intimacy with God and confidence in His promises. It is the boldness to stand firm in truth, love sacrificially, and obey faithfully even when fear, opposition, or uncertainty press in. This divine strength is a gift granted to the elect of God, empowering them to rise above natural limits and walk in unwavering faith. It is a quality of character that cannot be manufactured by human effort or perfected through discipline alone. It is awakened and strengthened by the power of the Holy Spirit. This divine work within us shapes our attitudes, refines our motives, and transforms our hearts from the inside out. It is, indeed, a sacred gift from God, bestowed by grace and revealed through a life surrendered to Him. Is. 40:29 says, "He gives power to the weak, and to those who have no might He increases strength." Spiritual courage gives you the strength and boldness to stand firm and do God's will, even when opposition rises and adversity presses in.

Spiritual courage believes the same promise God gave Joshua, "I will be with you. I will not leave you nor forsake you" (Josh. 1:5). Without spiritual courage, you will shrink back when God calls you to step forward, and fear will silence the purpose placed inside you. Spiritual courage is the strength that empowers a man to obey God in the face of pressure, resistance, and adversity. Without it, destiny is delayed, callings go unfulfilled, and the work of God remains undone. This is why three times God told Joshua to "be strong and of good courage" (Josh. 1:6,7,9). Three times God reinforced the command to Joshua to lead the Israelites with spiritual courage in the face of the dangers that awaited them. With spiritual courage you'll be able to "earnestly contend for the faith" (Jude 3). You'll be able to "fight the good fight of faith and lay hold of eternal life" (1 Tim. 6:12). Ps. 119:115 says, "Depart from me, you evildoers, for I will keep the commandments of my God!" Such is the nature of spiritual courage.

"THE DISCIPLINE OF COURAGE"

What is courage? It's being the only one who knows you're afraid. Ralph Waldo Emerson said, "A hero is no braver than an ordinary man, but he is braver five minutes longer." Mark Twain said, "It's not the size of the dog in the fight, It's the size of the fight in the dog." Most of your obstacles would melt away if, instead of shrinking back in fear, you made up your mind to walk boldly through them. Fear magnifies barriers, making them appear immovable and overwhelming, but courage has a way of shrinking what once seemed impossible. When you choose to confront challenges head-on with faith, confidence, and determination, you often discover that the mountain was more shadow than substance. The moment you decide to step forward rather than retreat, you shift from being controlled by your obstacles to commanding your path through them. Disciplined courage helps you to stay the course and persevere through the challenges of life and keep moving forward.

The discipline of courage means choosing to pause, reflect, and act with wisdom rather than reacting to every distraction or opposition that comes your way. It enables men to steadfastly address important issues and maintain a focus on the goal and desired outcome. It will anchor your heart with unshakable resolve, empowering you to remain steadfast and deliberate even when inevitable setbacks and failures arise. In every challenge, you will stand firm, knowing that perseverance in the struggle serves a purpose far greater than the momentary pain. Men with this type of courage walk with unwavering clarity, knowing exactly what they are called to build and who they are called to serve. Their vision is not self-centered but purpose-driven, focused on leaving a lasting impact that strengthens, inspires, and uplifts the lives of others. Disciplined courage is about clarity and mindfulness. Clarity about what you believe and mindfulness in the execution of those beliefs.

The discipline of courage is not loud, reckless bravery that demands attention or applause. It is steady. It is measured. It is rooted in deep conviction. True courage does not flare up in emotional bursts only to disappear when resistance comes. It is forged in prayer, refined in trials, and strengthened through obedience. Courage without discipline burns bright and fades fast, but disciplined courage endures. It is not driven by impulse but by purpose. It does not react in panic; it responds in faith. Disciplined courage is the quiet strength that keeps you standing when the winds of life press hard against you. It is the resolve to remain faithful when compromise seems easier, to speak truth when silence feels safer, and to move forward when fear whispers retreat. This kind of courage is anchored, not in feelings, but in conviction. It is sustained by character and guided by wisdom. While the world celebrates bold displays, Heaven honors steadfast endurance - the kind of courage that stays, stands, and finishes strong.

Disciplined courage is what keeps you steady when your emotions rise and fall like the tide. Anyone can start strong when excitement is high and motivation feels fresh, but the true test comes when feelings fluctuate and circumstances shift unexpectedly. In those moments, courage must be more than a burst of inspiration - it must be anchored. Discipline provides that anchor. It keeps you committed to your convictions, your calling, and your course, even when doubt clouds your vision, or distractions try to pull you away. Courage without discipline can be impulsive, but disciplined courage is focused, patient, and enduring. It chooses obedience over impulse and perseverance over convenience. When challenges arise, disciplined courage steadies your heart and reminds you why you began. It holds you in place when quitting seems easier than continuing. In a world of constant change, disciplined courage is the quiet strength that empowers you not only to start well, but to finish strong.

Life will test what you claim to believe. It is easy to declare faith, values, and convictions when the skies are clear and the path is smooth. But storms have a way of revealing whether your beliefs are merely convenient when comfortable or steady and immovable when pressure mounts. In the heat of adversity, what you truly trust rises to the surface. When circumstances shake you, what remains standing is what you have genuinely built your life upon. Disciplined courage is not loud bravado; it is steady resolve anchored in clarity. It comes from knowing what you believe, understanding why you believe it, and deciding in advance what you are willing to endure to remain faithful to it. Clarity fuels endurance. When your convictions are rooted deep, hardship does not redefine you - it refines you. Pressure does not destroy real men; it proves them. And when you stand firm in the face of testing, your life becomes living evidence that your faith is not fragile preference, but unshakable foundation.

Clarity gives direction. When you are clear about your values and your God-given purpose, you are no longer tossed around by every opinion, trend, or emotional wave that passes through your life. You understand who you are and what you stand for. Because of that, temporary pressures lose their power. You don't make permanent decisions based on temporary emotions. You pause, you pray, and you process before you act. Clarity anchors your heart so that fear and frustration do not drive choices that shape your future. Clarity sharpens your focus and strengthens your resolve. It removes distraction and aligns your energy with what truly matters. When your vision is clear, your steps become intentional. You move with confidence instead of confusion. You persevere because you know why you started. Clear values create firm boundaries, and a clear purpose fuels consistent action. In a world filled with noise, clarity becomes your compass guiding you steadily toward the life you were created to live.

Mindfulness is the companion of clarity because it slows the noise long enough for truth to be heard. It is the careful, intentional execution of what you believe as it aligns your thoughts, words, and actions with purpose rather than pressure. When you are mindful, you are not driven by emotion alone or pushed by the urgency of the moment. Instead, you create space to see clearly, to discern wisely, and to respond thoughtfully. Clarity is not accidental; it is cultivated in the quiet discipline of paying attention. Disciplined courage does not act impulsively; it acts intentionally. It pauses, evaluates, and then moves forward with steady determination. True strength is not found in rash reactions but in measured resolve. The courageous person considers the cost, commits to the conviction, and advances without wavering. In this way, mindfulness becomes the guardrail of courage ensuring that every step forward is guided by wisdom, anchored in belief, and executed with unwavering purpose.

Many abandon their path not because they lack courage, but because they lack discipline. Courage gets you started. It fuels the first step, the bold decision, the public declaration that you are going to change, build, lead, or overcome. But discipline is what keeps you moving when the excitement fades and the applause grows quiet. It is easy to feel brave at the beginning; it is harder to remain steady when progress is slow, opposition rises, and the outcome is uncertain. Without discipline, even the strongest start can dissolve into inconsistency. When pressure increases, it is often proof that you are pushing against something that matters. Growth invites friction. Purpose attracts opposition. The disciplined individual does not interpret resistance as a signal to retreat, but as confirmation to press forward with greater focus and resolve. They do not rely on feelings to sustain them; they rely on commitment. And while others turn back at the first sign of strain, disciplined courage presses forward to victory.

Perseverance is courage stretched over time. It is not proven in a single bold moment or a dramatic stand that everyone applauds. Rather, it is forged in the quiet resolve to keep going when the excitement fades and the spotlight disappears. Anyone can rise to a moment; few will rise every morning with the same commitment. True strength is revealed not in flashes of heroism, but in the steady rhythm of faithfulness - choosing again and again to press forward when quitting would be easier. Disciplined courage shows up in the small decisions no one celebrates, in the habits formed behind closed doors, and in the sacrifices that seem invisible to the world. These are the choices that compound over time, shaping character and building endurance that cannot be shaken. Long-term strength is not accidental; it is constructed daily. When you choose consistency over convenience and obedience over impulse, you are stretching your courage into perseverance and that is what ultimately defines a life well lived.

Challenges are inevitable. Sooner or later, failure will knock at your door. These moments are not signs that you are unqualified or forgotten - they are part of the refining process. Anyone can move forward when the path is smooth and the outcome is certain, but growth is forged in resistance. The weight of adversity reveals what is within you. It tests your resolve and invites you to rise stronger than before. Every obstacle carries a lesson, and every setback holds the potential to sharpen your character. Disciplined courage does not deny the pain of failure, but it refuses to let failure define the future. Instead, it pauses, learns, adjusts, and presses on without abandoning the mission. It understands that setbacks are not stop signs - they are training grounds. When others retreat, disciplined courage recalibrates. When others quit, it recommits. Victory is not reserved for those who never fall, but for those who rise with greater wisdom and unwavering determination each time they do.

Fear will speak. It will raise questions about your ability, your timing, and your worthiness. It will try to magnify uncertainty and shrink your confidence. But clarity reminds you of who you are, what you value, and why you began. Doubt may whisper in quiet moments, attempting to redirect your focus, but mindfulness steadies your thoughts and aligns your steps with truth. When you examine the facts instead of the feelings, you regain control of the narrative unfolding within you. Disciplined courage does not deny fear; it simply refuses to let fear lead. It acknowledges the pounding heart and the trembling voice yet chooses to move forward anyway. It understands that fear is a signal, not a commander. Through steady reflection and intentional action, disciplined courage transforms hesitation into wisdom and anxiety into awareness. You do not silence fear by pretending it isn't there - you overcome it by listening carefully, learning what you must, and then stepping forward with purpose.

Staying the course requires more than passion; it requires structure. Passion will ignite you, but structure will sustain you. Structure in your thinking keeps you anchored in truth when emotions fluctuate. It forces you to filter challenges through purpose rather than panic. Structure transforms good intentions into consistent action. When your days are ordered around what matters most, progress stops being accidental and starts becoming inevitable. Structure in your commitments strengthens your integrity because when you decide in advance who you are and what you stand for, distractions lose their power. Disciplined courage chooses consistency over convenience and faithfulness over feelings. Courage is not just standing firm in the storm; it is preparing before the storm ever comes. Daily disciplines like prayer, reflection, learning, and focused work create internal stability that external pressure cannot easily shake. When structure supports your passion, you don't merely start strong - you finish strong.

When your beliefs are clear, your path becomes straighter. You may still face resistance, criticism, and unexpected detours, but you are not confused about where you are headed. Conviction acts like a compass in your spirit pointing you in the direction you should go. Men who know what they believe are not easily swayed by popular opinion or temporary emotion. Their steps may slow, but they do not wander. Their progress may be tested but disciplined courage is what keeps their eyes fixed on the destination when the road grows rough and uncertain. It is the quiet resolve to keep moving forward when comfort calls you back. It is choosing faith over fear, commitment over convenience, and obedience over impulse. Obstacles will rise, but disciplined courage refuses to surrender focus. It strengthens your stride, sharpens your vision, and anchors your heart. When your beliefs are settled and your courage is trained, you don't just travel the path - you endure it, conquer it, and finish it strong.

Mindfulness guards against self-sabotage by bringing your thoughts, motives, and impulses into the light before they turn into actions. It creates a sacred pause between reaction and response - a space where you can examine whether your behavior reflects your deepest convictions or merely your fleeting emotions. When you live with that kind of awareness, you stop drifting and start directing. You become intentional instead of impulsive, principled instead of pressured. In that awareness, strength is cultivated. Not loud strength, but steady strength - the kind that anchors you when temptation whispers or fear pushes you toward compromise. Mindfulness aligns your daily decisions with your enduring values, reinforcing integrity one choice at a time. As alignment grows, so does confidence because you are no longer divided within yourself. You act from conviction, not confusion. And in that unity of belief and behavior, you build a life marked not by regret, but by purpose and resolve.

Disciplined courage is not rigid stubbornness; it is strength under control. Stubbornness refuses to bend even when wisdom calls for adjustment, but disciplined courage listens, learns, and responds without surrendering what is right. It is rooted deeply in conviction, anchored in truth, and unmoved by pressure to compromise. Yet it understands that methods may need to change as seasons shift. It knows the difference between standing firm and standing foolishly still. True disciplined courage is firm in foundation and flexible in strategy. It builds on unshakable values while remaining wise enough to adapt its approach. Like a tree with strong roots and moving branches, it can withstand the storm because it is both grounded and responsive. It adjusts tactics without abandoning truth, refines direction without forfeiting purpose, and embraces change without losing identity. This kind of courage is steady, thoughtful, and resilient - unyielding in character, yet agile in execution.

Through disciplined courage, perseverance becomes more than an occasional act - it becomes your lifestyle. You stop waiting for inspiration to strike or for circumstances to align perfectly. Instead, you train your mind and spirit to move forward regardless of how you feel. Discipline anchors you when emotions fluctuate, and courage steadies you when fear whispers doubt. Each consistent step builds resilience, shaping a character that does not retreat at resistance but rises to meet it. What once required great effort gradually becomes part of who you are. When perseverance becomes a lifestyle, you act because you have made a decision, not because the moment feels convenient. You push forward on hard days, trusting the process you have embraced. Feelings may come and go, but your resolve remains firm. Progress is no longer dependent on emotion; it is powered by purpose. And in that steady, unwavering commitment, you discover a strength that carries you farther than motivation ever could.

Every step forward under pressure builds endurance. When the weight is heavy and the path is steep, choosing to move anyway stretches your capacity and strengthens your resolve. Pressure is not your enemy - it is your training ground. Muscles grow by resistance, and so does the soul. Each time you refuse to retreat, complain, or compromise, you expand your endurance and prove to yourself that you are capable of more than comfort would ever reveal. Every refusal to quit strengthens character. Disciplined courage - showing up when it's hard, staying faithful when it's unseen, and standing firm when it would be easier to fold - shapes you into someone who can be trusted. Trusted with responsibility because you don't run from weight. Trusted with leadership because you don't collapse under pressure. Trusted with influence because your life backs up your words. Character is not formed in ease; it is forged in fire and those who endure become pillars others can lean on.

In the end, disciplined courage is the bridge between belief and breakthrough. It is not loud or reckless; it is steady, intentional, and rooted in conviction. It brings clarity to your thinking when confusion tries to cloud your vision, and it anchors your heart when fear attempts to pull you off course. Disciplined courage keeps your values in focus and your purpose in sight. It reminds you that what you believe is not meant to stay hidden in thought but to be expressed through consistent, faithful action. Clarity guides your mind, and mindfulness directs your steps. When storms arise and struggles press in, disciplined courage steadies you. It helps you respond instead of reacting, to stand firm instead of shrinking back. Stay clear in what you believe and let that clarity shape your decisions. Stay mindful in how you live, ensuring your actions align with your convictions. Then keep moving forward - one deliberate step at a time - knowing that breakthrough is built on the quiet strength of courage practiced daily.

| 18 |

"THE CAUSE FOR COURAGE"

There comes a defining moment in a man's life when God calls him beyond comfort, beyond fear, and into something far greater than he ever imagined for himself. It's the invitation to step into purpose, to trust the unseen, and to believe that the One who called him is faithful to lead him. In that moment, obedience unlocks a future bigger than his past and a destiny shaped by God's vision, not his limitations. God's plan for your life is so vast, so far-reaching, that from where you stand today it may seem impossible to imagine the journey ahead. Yet the distance between where you are and where He is calling you is crossed one faithful step at a time, not by sight but by trust. It takes uncommon courage to move forward when you can't see the whole path, but that courage is born in the confidence that the One who called you is already waiting at your destination. What should you do? Heb. 12:12 says, "So take a new grip with your tired hands and stand firm on your shaky legs."

Change happens to everybody. Because it often comes unexpectedly, disrupting our comfort and routine, we must be ready to face it with strength. More than anything else, courage is the anchor that steadies us and the fire that moves us forward when everything around us shifts. Courage is necessary because every season of growth begins with a decision to embrace change. Nothing truly transforms in our lives until we are willing to step beyond what is comfortable and familiar. When we choose courage first, we unlock the change that leads to greater strength, deeper faith, and lasting growth. Courage is the most important of all virtues, because without it we lack the strength to live out every other virtue when it matters most. The good news is courage is abundantly and readily available to you. It's on demand when you learn how to access it. What is courage? It's the strength to choose what is right and to stand firm in truth no matter the personal sacrifice required.

There are consequences for not having courage. When fear outweighs faith, progress is delayed and purpose is postponed. Because of a lack of courage, the children of Israel wandered in the wilderness for forty years because they refused to boldly step into the promise before them. Only Joshua and Caleb had the courage to go in, believing that with God's help they were well able to take the land (Num. 11:30). Courage is not optional in the life of faith; it is the bridge between God's promise and your possession of it. Having no courage is a silent curse that keeps you bound to fear, robbing you of the bold steps required to walk into God's promises. When you refuse to stand in faith, you forfeit the fullness of life, purpose, and victory that God has already prepared for you. On the other hand, there are benefits for having courage. With courage you'll move through the obstacles that stand in your way. With courage you'll break through those barriers that try to hold you back from fulfilling your destiny.

Like David did when he faced Goliath, courage compels you to run toward what others run from. Faith-filled boldness refuses to be intimidated by size, noise, or opposition because it knows that God is greater than any giant. When you choose courage, you don't retreat from your obstacle - you confront it with confidence, knowing victory belongs to the Lord. With faith and courage, you'll charge forward into your future with confidence, trusting that God has already gone before you. When you believe He is leading you, every step becomes bold, purposeful, and destined for success. Courage awakens your faith and reminds you that with the great God of the universe, nothing is impossible. When you stand boldly in Him, mountains move, doors open, and all things become possible through His power. When Moses died, God told Joshua it was time to lead the people across the Jordan River into the Promised Land (Josh. 1:1,2). He is giving Joshua a picture of what their future looks like.

When you need courage, you must connect with the cause for your courage. When fear rises, reconnect with the reason you started, the people you love, and the purpose God placed inside you. When you know why you need courage, the more fear begins to lose its grip, and the more courage will increase. Strength rises naturally and boldness follows. Purpose fuels bravery, and clarity strengthens your resolve. A greater cause awakens a deeper courage within you, pushing you beyond fear and into action. When the reason is bigger than your comfort, hesitation disappears and boldness takes its place. That's what drives a father to run into a burning building to rescue his trapped child. When your cause rises above comfort and self-preservation to something greater than yourself, your courage will rise with it, empowering you to face what once seemed impossible. Your perspective will change. You won't run into a burning building to save a set of golf clubs, but you'll do it to save your child.

When a hard decision must be made, don't focus on the discomfort - connect it to the cause that demands it. A clear cause fuels courageous choices, and courage grows wherever purpose is greater than pressure. God selected Joshua for the cause of bringing the children of Israel into the Promised Land. You also have been chosen and selected for the work of God. There is an assignment on your life, a divine cause placed in your hands, and when you embrace it, you step into the purpose God designed specifically for you. When you truly grab hold of a purpose greater than yourself and connect your heart to it, something powerful awakens within you. That connection fuels your courage, giving you the strength to take the first step even when the path ahead feels uncertain. It is God's will that you make a positive impact on someone else's life. You will fulfill your destiny because you are divinely connected to the cause that fuels your courage and empowers you to rise boldly into your purpose.

God is a personal God who desires an intimate, daily relationship with you. He wants to be involved in your life in a real and personal way, guiding your decisions, strengthening your heart, and walking with you through every season. To experience that closeness, you must remove sin and fear from your life because they block the fellowship and trust that allow you to fully embrace His presence. When you need courage, begin by cultivating the condition of your heart, because courage is born from within before it is ever seen outwardly. A heart strengthened by truth, discipline, and faith becomes unshaken in the face of fear or adversity. The stronger your heart, the greater your courage because bold actions always flow from a fortified inner life. When you cooperate with God as He cleans up what's inside of you, courage begins to grow. God will strengthen your heart from the inside out, building in you the courage, endurance, and faith you need to fulfill His will and purpose for your life.

Increased levels of courage are born as you cultivate your heart to do life with God, learning to trust His voice above your fears. As your relationship with Him deepens, boldness rises naturally, because you know you are never walking alone. It was God who said, "I will be with you." The question is, will you be with Him? The more you stay connected to God, the clearer His voice becomes, gently revealing the areas of your heart that need to grow. He doesn't expose what's broken to shame you, but to heal you - removing pride, fear, and doubt with patience and grace. In His love and kindness, He transforms you from the inside out, shaping you into the person He created you to be. When you allow God to shape your inner life, He strengthens your heart from the inside out. And as your heart grows stronger, your courage rises with it empowering you to stand firm, step forward, and live boldly. The way to do this is to stay connected to His presence at all times.

God told Joshua, "Study this book of instruction continually. Meditate on it day and night so you will be sure to obey everything written in it" (vs. 8). Those who follow in the way of God live a different kind of life, a life set apart, purposeful, and anchored in truth. In Him there is love that never fails, joy that overflows, and peace that steadies the soul through every season. As scripture declares, when we walk faithfully in His ways, we will "prosper and succeed in all we do" (vs. 8). Fill your mind with truth and your heart with the Word of God, and you will build your life on a foundation that cannot be shaken. Improved thinking leads to increased courage. When His promises shape your thoughts and guide your steps, fear begins to lose its voice. Stay rooted in His Word, and courage will rise within you to face every challenge with confidence and faith. Vs. 9 says, "This is My command - be strong and courageous! Do not be afraid or discouraged. For the Lord your God is with you where you go."

When you place your life fully in God's hands, you are stepping into divine guidance. He promises to order your steps, align your path, and lead you with wisdom when you trust Him completely. Surrender invites direction, and in His hands, your life is never without purpose. You can be directed by the Word of God; it is a lamp to your feet and a light to your path, guiding every step with divine wisdom and clarity. When you choose to follow what it says, courage is deposited into your spirit, empowering you to stand firm, move forward boldly, and trust God in every season. Remind yourself often that you are selected for the work of God. He has entrusted you with a unique assignment that only you can fulfill, and your obedience releases His purpose into the earth. Remember always that you are connected to the presence of God and with that connection comes divine direction. That direction comes through the Word of God. He wants to lead you and guide your steps. As He does this, courage will grow.

Courage helps us take the steps we're timid about taking, even when uncertainty whispers for us to stay still. It empowers us to move forward despite fear, doubt, or the comfort of what's familiar. True courage is the decision that purpose is greater than hesitation. When you choose courage, you unlock doors that timidity would have kept closed. The truth is that one brief moment of insane courage can unlock doors you never imagined and change the entire trajectory of your life forever. It can be the second you decide to speak when fear says stay silent, to step forward when comfort says stay put, or to trust God when circumstances look impossible. That single act of boldness can break chains that held you back and open doors you never imagined possible. Sometimes destiny doesn't require years of preparation - it requires one fearless act of courage. In a single moment of bold strength, you can step into doors God has already prepared and discover that courage, not comfort, was the key all along.

One step of courage can open a new beginning. One bold move can unlock a completely new chapter of your life. A moment of reckless faith can rewrite your story. One uncompromising act of courage can alter your legacy. In a matter of seconds, you can make the decisions that need to be made. You can repair the relationship that needs to be repaired. In one brief explosive moment of courage you can move forward and make a decision that entirely shifts the trajectory of your life. In one brief moment you can step into the fullness of the promises God has given you. When Joshua and the people arrived at the border of the Promised Land, they came face-to-face with a huge barrier. Before them was the massive Jordan River at flood stage. Tons of water separated them from the land of Canaan. There were no bridges to cross or boats to take them over to the other side. A massive obstacle stood between the people and where God called them to be. Thankfully, they were told what to do.

Josh. 3:3, "As soon as you see the ark of the covenant being carried by the Levitical priests, then you shall set out from your place and follow it." Notice that the leaders moved first. Every man is called to lead in some capacity, whether in his home, his church, his workplace, or his community. God is calling each of us to take the first step, trusting that when we move in obedience, He will guide, strengthen, and establish our path. In the Old Testament, the Ark of the Covenant represented the very dwelling place of God's presence among His people. It was not just a sacred object, but a reminder that victory, direction, and blessing flowed from staying near to Him. As you step out and move forward in life, make sure you remain in the presence of God because His presence is your true source of guidance and strength. Notice where it says, "As soon as you see the ark of the covenant..." They were being told to look to God and not the obstacle before them. Don't look at the Jordan River, look to God.

Your courage is either growing stronger or quietly shrinking based on what you allow your mind to dwell on. When you rehearse fear, doubt expands; but when you intentionally focus on truth, possibility, and faith, courage rises within you. Protect your mind diligently, for stronger thinking always gives birth to greater courage. The people were told, "When the ark moves, you move." Don't wait! Don't delay! Focus on obedience and not the obstacle before you. When God tells you to do something, don't hesitate or take time to think about it. Move now! Delayed obedience can mean missed opportunity, because divine instruction is often time-sensitive and purpose-driven. When He says move, trust His voice and step out boldly. When God tells you to do something, you don't have to pray about it. You have to do it. You have to obey. The longer the gap between hearing and doing, the less likely you are to do what God tells you what to do because delayed obedience slowly turns into quiet disobedience.

Don't obsess over the obstacle, obsess over the opportunity. When you fix your eyes on the problem, you magnify it; when you fix your eyes on the possibility, you activate faith, creativity, and courage. Obstacles are inevitable, but they are rarely the final word. The truth is, they are often the doorway to growth, innovation, and breakthrough. If you constantly replay the difficulty, you drain your energy and cloud your vision; but when you focus on the opportunity hidden within the challenge, you sharpen your perspective and position yourself to move forward. Obsessing over obstacles makes you miss life's greatest opportunities because your attention determines your direction. What you dwell on develops, and what you pursue produces. The more you focus on the obstacle, the bigger it becomes. Likewise, the more you focus on God, the bigger He becomes in your eyes. You need to obsess over the thing God has told you to do knowing there is no obstacle bigger than Him.

Obedience causes you to step into the fullness of the life God has called you to live. This is why you need to close the gap between the instruction and implementation. How you're doing spiritually is based on the size of that gap. The more you follow Jesus, that gap should decrease. The priests who carried the ark was given this command, "When you reach the banks of the Jordan River, take a few steps into the river and stop there" (Josh. 3:8). What is God saying? It's not the size of the step that matters; it's the direction of the step. Every morning when you wake up, before the noise of the day begins and the demands of life rush in, pause and ask God to point you in the direction He wants you to go. Invite Him into your thoughts, your plans, and your decisions. Direction comes through relationship, and purpose unfolds through action. When you surrender your day to Him, you align your heart with His purpose. Walk forward confidently, knowing that when God guides your path, every step has meaning.

God is still in the miracle business, and His power has not diminished with time. What He did before, He is more than able to do again in your life today. When He directs your path, trust His voice completely and step forward in faith. Do exactly what He tells you to do and watch Him turn your obedience into a testimony of His glory. Like the people who stepped into the Jordan River before it parted, obedience often comes before understanding. What God tells you to do may not make sense in the moment, but faith moves first and clarity follows. Trust Him enough to step in because the miracle is waiting on your obedience. Prov. 3:5,6 says, "Trust in the Lord with all your heart, and lean not on your own understanding. In all your ways acknowledge Him, and He shall direct your paths." As you faithfully take steps each day toward the destination God has prepared for you, know that your consistency and trust in Him will carry you to exactly where you are meant to be.

Don't sit still waiting on a miracle from God but start moving in the direction of your promise. Faith is not passive; it takes bold, obedient steps even before the breakthrough appears. Focus on movement over miracles, because when you move in faith, you position yourself for God to do what only He can do. The truth is, you shouldn't expect a miracle from God when He's expecting movement from you. Faith is not passive - it requires obedience, courage, and a willingness to step forward even when the path isn't fully clear. When you move in trust, God meets your obedience with His power. The people had to step into the Jordan River before the waters parted (Josh. 3:14-17). Because the people had the courage to obey, God made a way where there seemed to be none, and the entire nation crossed the Jordan River on dry ground. Their obedience unlocked the promise. Likewise, when we choose courageous obedience, we step into the life God designed for us to have and enjoy.

| 19 |

"COURAGE TO SLOW DOWN"

We live in a fast-paced world, in a culture that is constantly demanding more, pushing harder, and moving faster. Every notification, deadline, and expectation seems to whisper that if we slow down, we will fall behind. We are praised for busyness and applauded for exhaustion, as if a full schedule were the measure of a full life. Yet in the rush to keep up, we often lose sight of what truly matters, things such as our faith, our families, our purpose, and the quiet voice of God guiding our steps. Speed may produce activity, but it does not always produce depth. Motion does not guarantee meaning. Sometimes the greatest act of courage is not pressing the accelerator but gently applying the brakes. It takes courage to slow down in a world addicted to momentum. It takes wisdom to pause, reflect, and realign our hearts with what is eternal rather than what is urgent. When we slow down, we begin to see clearly again. We remember who we are, whose we are, and why we started the journey in the first place.

In the stillness, clarity is restored and our steps become purposeful instead of frantic. Slowing down is not weakness - it is disciplined strength guided by faith. Courage is the character trait that allows you to step into the life God has planned for you. Josh. 3:17 says, "Then the priests who bore the ark of the covenant of the Lord stood firm on dry ground in the midst of the Jordan. And all Israel crossed over on dry ground, until all the people had crossed over the Jordan." The people wanted to leave their old life behind and start afresh in the Promised Land. Josh. 4:10 says, "The people hastened and crossed over." They were in a hurry and two million people crossed over the Jordan River very quickly. Sometimes it is a good thing to hurry up and move quickly. At the same time, if we're not careful, if we move too fast, we may miss what God is doing at that particular moment. Sometimes we fail to see the significance of what is happening. We can be living in the midst of a miracle and completely miss it.

As soon as the people crossed over God told them to set up camp and slow down. He did not want His people to miss what He was doing in that moment, yet so often His presence moves quietly, beneath the noise of our routines and the weight of our distractions. When Jacob awoke from his dream and declared in Gen. 28:16, "Surely the Lord is in this place, and I didn't even know it," he revealed a powerful truth: God can be actively working, speaking, and revealing Himself even when we are unaware. The ladder reaching to heaven was not the beginning of God's presence - it was the unveiling of it. In the same way, there are sacred moments in our lives where heaven touches earth, where God is orchestrating purpose, positioning, and promise, and we must have spiritual awareness to recognize it. What we often call ordinary ground may, in fact, be holy ground, and what feels like a simple season may actually be a divine appointment. Beware of the danger of rushing through life too fast.

Sometimes God calls you to rise up, step out in faith, and move forward with courage and diligence. Other times, He lovingly whispers for you to slow down, be still, and trust Him in the waiting, knowing His timing is always perfect. Courage is not forged in chaos but built quietly in moments of stillness and reflection. When you get still before the Lord, something steady and strong begins to rise within you, bubbling up with confidence, peace, and holy boldness. If you don't slow down, you'll become more like a machine than a human being. If you rush through life, you may overlook the quiet, sacred moments where God's faithfulness is unfolding right before your eyes. Slow down long enough to notice His hand at work because often His greatest miracles are revealed in the stillness. Be intentional in developing the spiritual practice of slowing down, for it is in the quiet pauses of life that you hear God's voice most clearly, renew your strength, and realign your heart with His purpose.

In our fast-paced world, it's easy to get swept up in the constant motion of responsibilities, expectations, deadlines, and distractions. The noise of life can drown out our peace and leave us anxious, hurried, and spiritually drained. Yet in the middle of all the hustle and bustle, God gives us a simple but powerful command in Psalm 46:10: "Be still and know that I am God." Being still doesn't mean doing nothing; it means intentionally pausing. It means quieting your heart, turning down the noise, and shifting your focus from your problems to His power. When you slow down long enough to acknowledge Him, you begin to remember that He is sovereign, faithful, and fully in control. So what should you do? Make space daily to be still before the Lord. Carve out moments to pray, to reflect on His Word, and to listen rather than rush. Trust that while you rest in Him, He is working on your behalf. Surrender the pressures you cannot control and allow His presence to calm your spirit.

The Hebrew word for "still" is 'raphah" and it means 'to slacken, let down, cease, stop striving, to let go.' The word means 'to be still and stop frantic activity.' In some instances, the word carries the idea of 'to drop, be weak, or faint.' It's a picture of loosening your clenched grip on the circumstance and outcome and trusting God who is sovereign over both. When you choose to be still, you are declaring that God is stronger than your struggles and worthy of your trust. Being still allows us to let go of our anxieties, worries, and efforts to control our circumstances. God encourages us to embrace stillness in order to find peace and clarity in our relationship with Him. By resting in His presence, we can acknowledge His sovereignty and trust that He is in control of our lives and the world around us. Peace and security can be found when we fully surrender to God's will and recognize His ultimate authority over all things. This is why we need to intentionally set aside quiet moments to be still and focus on God's presence.

Being still is a healthy rest in the presence of the Lord, where your soul finds peace beyond the noise and pressure of life. It is the sacred moment when you stop striving and release the need to control what was never yours to carry. In that quiet surrender, God renews your strength and reminds you that He is faithfully at work on your behalf. It's when you reject all distractions and intentionally empty your mind of everything that is not spiritual that clarity begins to take root within you. In that quiet surrender, your values are refined, your discernment grows sharper, and a strong moral compass is formed to guide every decision you make. To be still means to refrain from needless fear and worry as you continue to learn and obey God's commands. When you get still before the Lord you acknowledge His sovereign control over all things. He is God and He is faithful, omnipotent, and unfailing. You seek spiritual strength from Him as you come to terms with your complete dependence on Him.

Stillness is a sacred mental posture of infinite peace, deep rest, and unshakable tranquility where a man quiets the noise of the world and silences the clamor of his own thoughts. In that holy calm, his senses are no longer ruled by distraction or impulse but are gently subdued as he abides in the presence of God. It is in this surrendered stillness that clarity is restored, strength is renewed, and the soul becomes anchored in divine truth. It is here in that quiet communion that a man's spirit is aligned with the heart of God. Focusing on God in our stillness enables us to listen to Him and hear His voice more clearly. He spoke to Elijah not in the mighty rushing wind, not in the earthquake, not in the fire, but in the still, small voice (1 Kings 19:11-13). It is God's desire to carry your burdens and fight your battles. Ex. 14:14

says, "The Lord will fight for you; you need only to be still." God is saying, "Get out of My way. Step back, open your eyes, and acknowledge who I am and what I can do."

Being still is a direct command from God, calling a man to cease his restless striving and surrender the battles that were never his to fight. It is the holy pause where human effort ends and divine sovereignty begins. In stillness, a man acknowledges that some matters belong solely to the Lord, and no amount of worry, manipulation, or force can improve upon God's perfect will. To be still is not weakness; it is disciplined faith and in that sacred surrender peace replaces pressure, clarity replaces confusion, and strength is renewed through quiet confidence in His power. The phrase "be still" can be rendered 'relax, let go, stop.' It means to become motionless and silent. Being still is an act of surrender, a release of striving with human effort to do what only God can do. It's a call to quiet our minds and hearts, making space for God to speak and work in our hearts. Embrace stillness. Practice the pause every day. Stop fighting a battle you cannot win. Be still and let God be God.

In the middle of a crazy, hectic world, give yourself permission to take a timeout and breathe. When everything inside you says go, go, go, choose instead to slow your pace and steady your heart. Clarity, strength, and peace are often found not in rushing ahead, but in pausing long enough to hear God's gentle direction. Select a time in your busy schedule to step away from the noise and be still before God. In that quiet place, listen for His voice reminding you who you are, why you are here, and how He desires you to live. When you make space for Him consistently, clarity replaces confusion and purpose rises above pressure. Develop the spiritual practice of having daily time alone with God. It's in these quiet moments where you'll hear God speak to you. Slow down and hear what God says about you instead of what the world says about you. God is saying, "Slow down and come away with Me. Spend some quiet time with Me and I'll speak courage into your life."

Psalm 37:7 (NLT) reminds us, "Be still in the presence of the Lord, and wait patiently for Him to act." This verse calls us to a posture of quiet trust rather than anxious striving. In a world that urges us to figure everything out, God invites us to slow our hearts and rest in His sovereignty. Being still is not passive resignation; it is active faith - choosing peace over panic and confidence over control. Waiting patiently means believing that God is already at work behind the scenes, aligning circumstances, shaping character, and preparing outcomes that serve His greater purpose. When we quiet our souls before Him, we discover that His timing is perfect, His plans are trustworthy, and His presence is enough. This is why God wants you to be still and rest in His presence, to hush the spirit, to be silent before Him, to wait in holy patience. Indeed, God is worth waiting for. Time is nothing to Him, let it be nothing to you. In other words, stop being in such a hurry all the time.

As you're being still before the Lord, you're maintaining an unwavering trust in God, even in the midst of challenging circumstances. Stop what you're doing. Be still and listen for God's still, small voice. God is speaking and this is why you need to tune out what's going on around you and get in His presence. Being still in the presence of God is not a sulky silence or hushed murmuring. It is simply resting in Him, trusting in His Word, and abiding in His love. In that quiet surrender we learn that His presence is more than enough. When you are quietly resting in His presence, the peace of God that passes all understanding begins to settle over your heart like a gentle embrace. In that sacred stillness, anxiety loses its grip and your soul is reminded that He is in control. As you trust Him completely, His peace floods every corner of your heart and mind with calm assurance. When you are quietly resting in His presence, the peace of God that passes all understanding will flood your heart and soul.

Being still before the Lord is a sacred invitation to cease striving, to loosen our grip on control, and to lay down the weapons of our own human effort. It is a deliberate surrender of pride, anxiety, and hostility - a quieting of the inner battle that insists we must win, fix, or defend ourselves. In that stillness, the noise of conflict fades, and the heart is freed from the exhausting need to prove its strength. Only after the fighting has stopped can true warriors lift their eyes from the dust of struggle and remember where their help truly comes from. It is in the calm after surrender that trust rises, faith deepens, and confidence in God becomes their greatest victory. God wants you to lay aside all your burdens and stand in awe of Him and His mighty power. Develop the habit of sitting in silence and reflect on all the good God has done in your life. As you intentionally practice stillness before God, your anxieties will begin to quiet, and your faith will grow stronger and deeper with every surrendered moment.

God wants you to experience His faithfulness for yourself personally in the quiet, sacred spaces of your own life. It is in those still moments that the foundation of your life is truly laid. That is where trust is strengthened, where doubt is answered, and where your heart learns that He is steady and sure. If you don't rush past those moments, if you linger long enough to listen and to trust, you will discover that courage begins to rise within you. Real courage is gathered in stillness. It is forged in the quiet moments when you choose faith over fear and conviction over comfort. In the silence where no one is watching, strength takes root and bravery is born. It is in those unseen moments of faithfulness, discipline, and trust that God shapes the courage that will one day stand unshaken in the light. It grows as you remember how He has carried you before. And when you pause long enough to see His hand at work, your faith deepens and your confidence climbs to a higher level.

When all the people finished crossing over the Jordan River, the first thing God told them to do was slow down. He wanted them to stop and build a memorial in remembrance to what just happened (Josh. 4:1-8). They had hurried across the Jordan in urgency and obedience, but now God was calling them to slow down, settle their hearts, and learn to walk with patience instead of pressure. God didn't want the people to ever forget what happened this day. He didn't want them to rush by this moment. He called them to pause, remember, and carry its significance forward so that the miracle would shape their faith for generations to come. In just a matter of days they would march into battle, but before they could face the war ahead, they had to quiet their hearts, steady their minds, and learn the strength that comes from slowing down. Sometimes you have to push back those things that are pressing you to always be on the go. Life lived at a fast pace will damage your soul and tear your heart apart.

Stop thinking if you slow down the world will pass you by. God never designed your pace to be driven by panic or pressure. When you walk in purpose and trust His timing, slowing down becomes strength, not setback. If you never slow down, the noise of life will eventually drown out the whisper of God, and what once felt clear will become distant and unclear. Make space to be still, because it is in the quiet moments that His voice becomes unmistakable and His direction sure. Your soul cannot discern His whisper when your life is filled with constant noise and motion. Slow down, be still, and create sacred space because God often speaks in a gentle whisper, not in the rush of a busy life. It's hard to hear God's small, still voice if you're on the go all the time. In time you'll be spiritually bankrupt. Your inner man is empty and thirsty, and this will cause you to make some very bad decisions. You'll trainwreck your life if you don't slow down. There is nothing inside of you from which to draw strength and wisdom.

Practice Sabbath living by intentionally setting aside time each week to rest your body, renew your mind, and refocus your heart on what truly matters. Slow your pace, step away from the noise, and create sacred space to breathe deeply and remember that God is your source, not your striving. Be still before Him, allowing His presence to restore your strength, realign your priorities, and refill your spirit with peace. Sabbath is not the day to mow the lawn, to catch up on other chores that need to be done. No, sabbath is a day of rest. Sleep in little bit longer, read a good book, go for a nice walk, meditate on all the good things God has done for you. You don't slow down just for the sake of slowing down. You slow down so your heart can connect with your Creator. This, in turn, will give you the courage to face whatever it is that stands in your way on your journey through life. As you spend time with God, personalize all His promises for your life. Believe that all God said was meant specifically for you.

As you rest, quietly rehearse in your mind every moment God has proven faithful to you, every door He opened, every prayer He answered, every burden He lifted. Remember the times He made a way when there seemed to be no way, turning impossibilities into testimonies. Let those memories settle your heart in peace, reminding you that the same faithful God who carried you then is carrying you now. Build a memorial of remembrance by reflecting on every personal moment God came through for you - each answered prayer, each open door, each unexpected provision. If He was faithful then, He will be faithful now; believe that truth, and courage will rise within you. If there's Jordan River in front of you, don't look for a bridge. With courage step into the water believing God will take you to the other side. His goodness and mercy are all around you every day, but you must slow your pace, quiet your heart, and open your eyes to truly see the evidence of His love surrounding you.

| 20 |

"COURAGE TO KEEP GOING"

So often, when we begin the pursuit of a dream, we get excited and start out strong. That's all well and good but, if the truth be told, a good beginning doesn't always guarantee a strong finish. It takes uncommon courage to keep going when the road grows long, the excitement fades, and the weight of responsibility presses heavily on your shoulders. Starting is easy - finishing is rare. Anyone can be inspired in the beginning, but only the steadfast remain when challenges arise, when progress feels slow, and when no applause is heard. To complete the assignment you've been given requires more than talent; it demands endurance, discipline, and an unwavering belief that what you are building matters. Courage is not the absence of fatigue or doubt—it is the decision to move forward in spite of them. Finishing well means refusing to abandon your post when the battle intensifies. It means honoring the commitment even when circumstances shift and comfort disappears.

The assignment on your life carries purpose beyond what you can always see, and quitting forfeits the fruit that perseverance produces. Those who finish well develop character, deepen resilience, and leave a legacy of faithfulness. Uncommon courage is choosing to stand firm, press on, and complete what you started knowing that completion brings fulfillment, growth, and impact far greater than the temporary relief of giving up. Oftentimes, the missing ingredient between where we are and where God wants us to be is courage. Courage is needed when your life is stuck in the mud or when you keep going around the same stupid mountain over and over again. It's courage that pulls you out of the rut you're in and sends you on your way to bigger and better things. We all need a fresh dose of courage to keep going, to continue when we want to stop. Courage will fill your tank up when you feel like you've run out of gas. We need fresh courage for fresh challenges. We need courage to finish what we start.

No matter what you've accomplished in your life, there's still more to do so don't get complacent thinking you can coast through life from this moment forward. No, get some fresh courage and keep going. The moment you decide to coast is the moment growth begins to stall. There are new mountains to climb, new lives to impact, and new depths of character to develop. Don't settle into comfort when there is still calling left in you. Get some fresh courage, renew your vision, and press forward with determination because the best chapters are waiting on your next bold step. When the children of Israel entered the Promised Land and won a few battles, the people wanted to take their shoes off and kick back for a little while. There was, however, more work to be done. The people wanted to settle in but there was still more land to conquer, more battles to fight. Josh. 13:1 says, "When Joshua was an old man, the Lord said to him, 'You are growing old, and much land remains to be conquered.'"

God had more in store for His people and now was not the time to kick back and relax and enjoy a do-nothing retirement. Caleb said to Joshua in Josh. 14:10-12, "Today I am eighty-five years old. I am as strong now as I was when Moses sent me on that journey. And I can still travel and fight as well as I could then. So give me this mountain that the Lord promised to me." Caleb was saying, "I am not finished. God has more in store for me." A great start may open the door, but it does not guarantee a great finish. The truth is that finishing well requires more than momentum - it demands perseverance, humility, and a fresh dose of courage from God. Every new season calls for renewed strength, and only His courage can carry you faithfully across the finish line. This is why you must make a commitment to move forward in courage when you're tempted to end the journey God has you on. Don't abandon the process in a moment of fear because the pressure you feel is often proof that purpose is being forged in you.

Make a commitment to work from God's eternal promises, not from temporary circumstances. Just as Caleb reminded Joshua that God had promised him his mountain forty years earlier, we must anchor our faith in what God has spoken no matter how much time has passed. When you build your life on His promises, delay does not weaken your confidence; it only strengthens your resolve to possess what He has already declared. Obtaining this promise fueled Caleb's courage because he was standing on something already spoken over his life. He worked from the promise given to him, not for the promise, and that confidence changed everything. Working "for" a promise means it hasn't yet been secured, but working "from" a promise means you move with boldness, knowing it has already been declared and guaranteed. You don't work hoping to receive a blessing, you work with excellence, gratitude, and purpose because you have already received the blessing God has bestowed on you.

When you work from a promise, obedience is always involved. Phil. 2:12 says, "As you have always obeyed, work out your own salvation with fear and trembling." God gives you the strength, but you must rise, move, and work out that strength through faith, discipline, and action. Caleb received his mountain as a promise fulfilled, but the promise still required possession. He didn't fight to earn what God had spoken - he fought from the confidence that it already belonged to him. Faith doesn't strive for approval; it advances from assurance, working the ground that grace has already granted. Don't let apathy rob you of the promises God has prepared for your life. Apathy is a quiet thief - it dulls your enthusiasm to step into new territory and slowly makes spiritual matters feel unimportant. Stir your faith, rekindle your passion, and pursue God wholeheartedly. Press forward with expectation because His promises are too great to miss by standing still. Surely, they are waiting on the other side of renewed commitment.

Don't let apathy and indifference rob you of the future God has already prepared for you. Refuse to stand still when His promises are calling you forward, and choose instead to move in faith, passion, and obedience. Make a bold commitment to partner with God's unlimited resources, trusting that with Him there is always more than enough to advance, overcome, and fulfill His purpose for your life. God has in abundance everything you need because there is no lack in Him. If you need wisdom, God has it freely and generously. If you need strength and courage, God has it in overflowing supply, ready to empower you for whatever you face. Live in such a way that you access what God has already given you. Don't focus on what you don't have, focus on what you do have. Don't be overcome with the enemy of entitlement, thinking you have the right to something without working for it. Caleb was given his mountain, but he had to work and go to war in order to drive the giants off his land.

Some people asked Joshua, "Why have you given us only one portion of land as our homeland?" (Josh. 17:14). These people had a mindset that they should be given more. They were saying they didn't have what they thought they deserved. That's entitlement. An entitled mindset says, "I deserve more," even when nothing has been earned or stewarded well. It focuses on what is lacking instead of taking responsibility for growth, gratitude, and effort. These are the people who think it's not fair when a neighbor gets a new car or a co-worker gets the promotion they think they deserve. True maturity shifts you from entitlement to empowerment, where you stop demanding increase and start developing the character to become worthy of the growth and favor you desire. Joshua replied, "If the hill country of

Ephraim is not large enough for you, clear out land for yourselves in the forest where the Perizzites and Rephaites live" (vs. 15). In other words, go to work. Take an axe and start cutting down some trees.

Prov. 12:27, "Lazy people don't even cook the game they catch, but the diligent make use of everything they find." What they need to do is go to work and develop what they already have in their hands. Growth doesn't begin with wishing for more - it begins with stewarding, sharpening, and maximizing what's already been given. You will be empowered the moment your mindset shifts from fear to faith, just like Caleb, who saw promise where others saw problems. When you think the way Caleb did - focused on God's power instead of the giants before you - you step into courage, confidence, and victory. Empowerment is the authority and power entrusted to you to act, to lead, and to fulfill a specific purpose. It is the process of growing stronger and more confident, taking control of your life instead of allowing circumstances to control you. When you embrace empowerment, you boldly claim your rights, step into your calling, and walk in the strength you were created to carry.

Take the time and make the effort to develop whatever God places in your hands, because what seems small today may carry eternal significance tomorrow. When you steward His gifts faithfully and cultivate them with diligence, He multiplies your obedience into impact beyond what you could imagine. If God gives you a spiritual gift, use it to bless others. If He gives you relationships, be faithful. If He gives you finances, be generous. Use everything God has placed in your hands to bring Him glory and advance His kingdom. When you surrender even the smallest act to Him, nothing remains insignificant. Every quiet step of obedience becomes a seed that God plants for eternal impact. Be faithful with the little, and in His perfect time, He will entrust you with more. Empowerment begins the moment you believe God can multiply what He's already placed in your hands.

When you trust Him with what you have, He turns your obedience into overflow and your faith into impact.

The resources God gives you are time, talent, and treasure. Time is the daily gift that cannot be stored or reclaimed, urging you to invest each moment wisely in what matters eternally. Talent is the unique ability and grace woven into your design, calling you to bless others with excellence and faithfulness. Treasure is the provision entrusted to you meant not merely for personal comfort but for kingdom impact. When you steward your time with intention, your talent with humility, and your treasure with generosity, you transform ordinary resources into extraordinary instruments in the hands of God. Sometimes you have more of one than you do the others. Young people usually have more time than money while older people may gain financial stability only to discover that time has become their most precious and scarce commodity. What you need to do is take what you have more of and use it to get the other two so that you can accomplish the purpose of God for your life.

2 Peter 1:3 (ICB), "Jesus has the power of God. His power has given us everything we need to live and to serve God. We have these things because we know Him. Jesus called us by His glory and goodness." You already possess everything you need for life and godliness. God has not called you to an assignment without first equipping you for it. The strength, wisdom, grace, favor, and spiritual authority required to fulfill your purpose have been placed within you through Christ. He has supplied every resource necessary for your calling. The gifts you carry, the experiences you've endured, the faith you've developed, and the Spirit who lives within you are more than enough. Walk boldly in confidence, knowing that what God has called you to do, He has already empowered you to accomplish. Live with gratitude and be faithful with what He has placed in your hands. Multiply the little He has given you and, when He finds you faithful, He will give you more.

Make a commitment to always work for God's greater purposes, even when the assignment stretches you beyond your comfort zone. Let your heart echo the bold surrender of Isaiah who declared, "Here am I! Send me" (Isa. 6:8), choosing obedience over hesitation. When you place yourself fully at His disposal, God will use your willingness to accomplish far more than you ever imagined. What matters most is not what we desire, but what God desires for our lives. Even Jesus surrendered His own will in prayer, saying, "Nevertheless, not My will, but Yours be done" (Luke 22:42), showing us that true faith is found in yielding to the Father's perfect plan. 2 Tim. 1:9 says God has "called us with a holy calling, not according to our works, but according to His own purpose and grace." God's will is planned in advance. Make no mistake about it, His purpose is absolute and certain to succeed. Acts 11:23 says Barnabas "encouraged them all that with purpose of heart they should continue with the Lord."

Rom. 8:28 talks about 'those who are the called according to His purpose." The purposes of God are the most important reality in one's spiritual life, because when we align with His divine calling, every circumstance becomes part of His greater plan for our growth and His glory. The greatest pursuit of your life should be the fulfilling of God's greater purposes, because nothing else carries eternal weight or lasting significance. When you align your heart with His divine plan, you step into a life that is not only meaningful on earth but impactful for eternity. The word "purpose" describes fixed intention in doing something or the reason for which something is done or for which something exists. It describes what one intends to accomplish and attain and suggests a settled determination that it is going to happen. Until you are willing to live for His purpose, life will have no meaning and will bring you no satisfaction. No achievement, possession, or applause can fill the emptiness of a misplaced calling.

Too many people become so consumed with the challenges in front of them that they lose sight of the greater calling God has placed on their lives. They are consumed with the little picture of their current situation, measuring everything by what they can see and feel right now. When our focus shrinks to our problems, we lose sight of the greater story God is writing across the earth through faith, obedience, and purpose. When we focus only on obstacles, fear grows larger and faith grows smaller. But when we lift our eyes back to God's purpose, we regain clarity, courage, and the strength to move forward in obedience. Lift your eyes beyond this moment, because what feels temporary to you is often eternal in God's hands. He is not just working in your circumstance - He is shaping your character, strengthening your faith, and positioning your life for greater purpose. Even now, in the quiet and in the chaos, trust that He is weaving every thread of your story into His divine plan to impact the earth for His glory.

When Joshua told the people to go to work and cut down some trees, here is how they responded. Josh. 17:16, "It's true that the hill country is not large enough for us. But all the Canaanites in the lowlands have iron chariots. They are too strong for us." The enemy that was coming against them fulfilling God's purpose for their life was fear. There is no obstacle in your life more dangerous than fear, because it whispers lies that shrink your faith, silence your courage, and attempt to keep you from stepping into the destiny God has already prepared for you. Fear restricts you from living in the will and purpose of God, keeping you from stepping into the destiny God has for you while limiting the impact your life was meant to make. There is so much fear in the world that it is sometimes hard to see what courage is. Instead of moving forward, the Israelites were stuck in fear. When you step into fear, you miss the purpose of God. It's courage that allows you to step forward and face your battles with confidence.

The length and breadth and depth and height of God's eternal plans and purposes stretch far beyond the boundaries of your present circumstances. What feels overwhelming today is only a small thread woven into a far greater tapestry He is designing with wisdom and love. Trust that His vision for your life is bigger than this moment, and His purposes are unfolding in ways you cannot yet see. The plans and purposes of God originate in His eternal wisdom, not our temporary circumstances. Yet in His unfathomable grace, He has lovingly woven us into His greater story, inviting us to participate in purposes far bigger than ourselves. Joshua responded to the people, "Since you are so large and strong, you will be given more than one portion. The forests of the hill country will be yours as well. Clear as much of the land as you wish and take possession of its farthest corner. And you will drive out the Canaanites from the valleys, too, even though they are strong and have iron chariots" (vs. 17,18).

Remember why you're here. Your life was not designed for comfort alone, but for calling. When the cause is greater than your fears, courage rises to meet the moment, and strength is born from conviction. The greater the purpose, the greater the courage it awakens within you. Israel had a mission from God who said in Is. 49:6, "I have called you to be a light to the Gentiles and bring My salvation to the ends of the earth." Jesus gave us all the same mission in Matt. 28:18-20. He said, "Go and make disciples of all nations; teaching them to obey all the commands I have given you." There must be a holy urgency about the mission you've been entrusted with, because time is too precious and the assignment is too important to delay. When you recognize that your calling carries eternal weight, you move with purpose, focus, and a fire that refuses to waste another moment. What's at stake here is your eternal destiny and the eternal destiny of those around you. With courage go out and take the world by storm.

| **21** |

"COURAGE TO CONFRONT GIANTS"

There comes a moment in every life when the path forward is blocked by something bigger than you. It stands tall, defiant, and intimidating daring you to retreat. In that moment, the battle is not merely against what stands before you, but against the fear rising within you. Giants magnify doubt and whisper defeat, hoping you will surrender before you ever lift a stone. Yet what appears overwhelming is often an invitation to rise up and remember who you are, whose you are, and what has been placed within you. The size of the giant is never the final word; courage is. What confronts you may be large, but every giant has a weakness, and every challenge carries within it the seed of your growth. When you refuse to bow, when you choose faith over fear and action over avoidance, you begin to shrink the very thing that once towered over you. When you stand your ground, you will discover that the giant was never greater than the strength God had already woven into your spirit.

Giants are not merely obstacles standing in your path; they are revelations standing in your mirror. They uncover what lies beneath the surface of your confession and expose the true condition of your courage. When a giant rises in your valley, it reveals what you truly believe about yourself - whether you see yourself as small and incapable, or as chosen, equipped, and anointed for the battle before you. Giants test your understanding of your calling. If you shrink back, they expose insecurity; if you step forward, they reveal conviction. They shine a light on whether your identity is rooted in past failures or anchored in divine purpose. More importantly, giants reveal what you believe about your God. When fear rules your heart, the giant appears massive and unstoppable. But when faith fuels your spirit, the giant becomes an opportunity for God to display His power through you. The valley becomes a proving ground where faith is strengthened, courage is refined, and trust is solidified.

Most giants grow because they are ignored. When fear goes unchallenged, it begins to narrate your future, shaping your decisions and shrinking your faith. The longer a giant shouts across the valley of your mind without resistance, the larger it appears until it seems immovable, invincible, inevitable. But giants do not grow stronger because they are powerful; they grow stronger because they are permitted to. Yet the moment courage speaks, intimidation begins to starve. Courage does not need to be loud; it only needs to be present. When you confront what you once avoided, the illusion of its size begins to collapse. Faith answers back. Action steps forward. Giants shrink when challenged because their strength was never in their size - it was in your surrender. When you refuse to stay silent, when you stand firm and speak boldly, you cut off the supply that feeds fear. And what once towered over you becomes nothing more than a stepping-stone to your next victory.

Courage does not mean you feel no fear. It means you decide that fear will not have the final word. Fear may knock on the door of your heart, whispering worst-case scenarios and rehearsing every possible failure. Your hands may tremble. Your voice may shake. Your mind may race. But courage rises when you choose conviction over comfort and obedience over escape. It is the quiet, powerful decision to move forward even when your emotions beg you to retreat. Courage says, "I will not let fear dictate my destiny." Courage is stepping onto the battlefield with trembling hands and knees that feel weak but also with a spirit that stands firm. It is doing what is right when it would be easier to hide. The brave are not fearless; they are faithful. They understand that fear may be present, but it does not get the final vote. Courage anchors itself in purpose, in calling, in truth. And when you act in obedience despite the shaking, you discover something powerful: fear may speak, but it does not rule.

Every giant has a voice. It whispers in your ear, "This is too much for you. You cannot win this battle." If you allow those words to echo unchecked in your mind, you begin to rehearse defeat before the battle ever begins. You imagine failure. You anticipate loss. The fight hasn't started, but in your thoughts you have already surrendered. Giants understand that if they can conquer your thinking, they won't have to conquer you on the battlefield. But the truth is, the voice of the giant is not the voice of your destiny. It is fear disguised as fact. It is intimidation masquerading as wisdom. You must decide which voice will shape your future - the whisper of doubt or the declaration of faith. Refuse to rehearse defeat. Instead, rehearse victory. Speak strength over your weakness. Speak courage over your fear. Speak faith over your circumstances. When you silence the giant's whisper and amplify the voice of truth, you step into the battle not as a victim of intimidation, but as a warrior prepared to win.

There is always another voice - the voice of truth. It does not shout like the giant; it speaks with steady authority and quiet confidence. This voice reminds you of who you are and whose you are. It calls you chosen when fear calls you incapable. It declares you equipped when doubt whispers that you are unqualified. Giants speak to your insecurity, but truth speaks to your identity. It anchors you in the unchanging reality that you are created with purpose, empowered by faith, and covered by grace. When the giant roars, it tries to define you by your limitations. The voice of truth reminds you that you are not fighting alone and that your worth is not determined by the size of the opposition but by the strength of the One who stands with you. If you will quiet the noise of fear long enough to listen, you will discover that truth has been speaking all along calling you to stand, to believe, and to confront the giant not from a place of weakness, but from a place of identity.

When you confront giants, you must first confront yourself. The battlefield is not only before you - it is within you. Doubt whispers that you are unqualified. Compromise tempts you to lower your standards just to survive the moment. These internal giants often loom larger than the visible threats, because they attack your identity, your calling, and your confidence. Before David ever faced Goliath, he had already settled in his heart who he was and who his God was. He refused to wear another man's armor, because he understood that victory requires authenticity and conviction, not imitation. Victory begins within long before it is seen without. When you silence doubt with truth, reject comparison by embracing your unique design, and refuse compromise by standing firm in your values, you shrink the giants on the outside. Strength grows in the hidden place. Courage is forged in quiet obedience. When your heart is steady, your faith anchored, and your identity secure, no external giant can intimidate you.

Preparation matters more than applause ever will. What the world calls a sudden act of bravery is rarely sudden at all - it is the visible eruption of a hidden life of faithfulness. The warrior who stands firm in the valley first learned obedience in solitude. The leader who speaks with boldness first listened in stillness. Long before the spotlight finds a person, discipline has shaped them, prayer has anchored them, and quiet growth has strengthened their resolve. Public courage is simply private commitment revealed. The quiet seasons are not wasted seasons; they are sacred training grounds. In moments when no one is watching, character is forged, convictions are clarified, and faith is deepened. The hours spent in study and the small daily decisions to choose integrity over ease become the foundation for future triumph. When the test finally comes, preparation speaks louder than fear. Victory in public is born from faithfulness in private, and those who honor the process will be ready when their moment arrives.

You do not need another person's armor to defeat your giant. Saul's armor would have crushed David under its weight. Borrowed confidence may look impressive, but it rarely fits the soul it's placed upon. When you try to fight life's battles dressed in someone else's calling, personality, or gifting, you lose mobility, clarity, and conviction. Giants are not defeated by imitation; they fall before identity. The strength that carries you through confrontation is not found in copying another warrior's strategy but in knowing who you are and whose you are. The courage that wins battles is forged in authenticity. It is refined through personal trials and strengthened by the quiet victories no one else sees. Authentic courage does not need applause or comparison; it trusts the preparation God has already woven into your life. Step into the field as yourself. The giant in front of you was not assigned to someone else's armor - it was assigned to your obedience, your voice, and your faith.

Giants are drawn to purpose. They do not gather around small dreams, weak commitments, or casual intentions. They rise up when a life begins to matter, when a calling starts to threaten the status quo, when destiny begins to take shape in the heart of a man who refuses to live average. The greater the assignment, the louder the opposition. Just as David's giant only appeared when he stepped into his anointing, your greatest resistance often shows up when you are closest to breakthrough. The size of the battle is not proof that you are failing; it is evidence that what you carry is significant. Hell does not mobilize against what is insignificant. Resistance is often confirmation that you are standing on ground worth defending. If there were nothing valuable in you, there would be nothing fighting against you. The very tension you feel is often heaven's reminder that you are advancing into territory that matters. Stand firm when giants roar. The battle is proof that you are defending something eternal.

There will always be spectators who criticize your courage. Some will question your strategy; others will mock your faith. Critics are comfortable in the crowd because the crowd requires no bravery. But courage was never meant to be understood by those unwilling to step into the arena. When you choose to confront the giant in front of you - whether it's fear, opposition, adversity, or doubt - you step into your calling. Giants are silenced by action. They do not retreat because someone debated well or criticized loudly. They fall when someone dares to move forward despite the noise. Courage is proven in motion, not in approval because true bravery steps forward in obedience to purpose, even when applause is absent and affirmation never comes. So let them talk while you prepare. Let them question while you advance. Let them mock while you believe. In the end, it will not be the spectators who write the story of victory - it will be the one who stepped forward when no one else would.

Courage requires movement. At some point, you must step forward. Faith, vision, and conviction all remain dormant until they are activated by action. You can pray about it, plan for it, and talk about it but eventually there comes a moment when standing still becomes disobedience to the dream placed inside you. Courage is not proven in contemplation; it is revealed in motion. The first step may be small, uncertain, even trembling but it is powerful. When you move, you signal to your fears that they no longer have authority over you. Waiting for perfect conditions is often disguised fear. We tell ourselves we're being wise, strategic, or patient, when in reality we are protecting ourselves from discomfort or risk. Perfect conditions rarely exist; growth is born in imperfect moments. The path does not clear before you move - it clears because you move. Step forward even if your confidence is still catching up with your calling. Courage is not the absence of fear; it is the decision to advance despite it.

Faith does not deny the size of the giant standing in front of you. It does not pretend the obstacle is small, nor does it close its eyes to the threat. Faith sees clearly. It acknowledges the weight of the diagnosis, the depth of the betrayal, the magnitude of the challenge. But then it does something powerful - it measures the giant against a greater reality. It compares the problem to the promises of God. It weighs the obstacle against the faithfulness of the One who has never failed. When David faced Goliath, he did not call him small; he simply declared that the battle belonged to the Lord. Faith does not shrink giants; it enlarges your understanding of God. Perspective is the turning point. When you only measure the giant against yourself, panic is inevitable. But when you measure the giant against God's power, possibility awakens. The same situation that once produced fear begins to stir courage. The same mountain that looked immovable becomes an opportunity for God to display His strength.

Sometimes the first stone you throw will miss. You step forward in faith, aim with conviction, and release what you believe is your best effort only to watch it fall short. But courage was never about perfect aim on the first attempt. It is about refusing to retreat when the outcome doesn't immediately match your expectation. Like David standing before Goliath, the power was not in a single swing of the sling but in the unwavering resolve behind it. Missed attempts do not define you; they refine you. They teach your hands to steady, your eyes to focus, and your heart to trust God more deeply than your fear. Courage is not a guarantee of instant success. It is a commitment to remain engaged until the battle is finished. It is choosing to pick up another stone when the first one fails. True courage understands that victory often belongs to those who refuse to quit. Stay in the fight. Adjust your aim. Strengthen your faith. The giant does not fall because you tried once - it falls because you refused to stop.

Giants rarely fall in a single moment; they fall in stages. First, their intimidation weakens. What once looked enormous and immovable begins to lose its grip on your mind. Fear shrinks when it is faced. The giant that taunted you with threats and doubt slowly loses its voice as you stand your ground. When you refuse to bow to intimidation, you reclaim authority over your thoughts. The battle always begins internally. The moment you stop exaggerating the giant's power is the moment its illusion begins to crumble. Then their influence diminishes. What once dictated your decisions, emotions, and direction no longer controls you. With every step of obedience, faith, and steady action, the giant's dominance erodes. Finally, its collapse becomes inevitable. Dominance gives way to defeat not because the giant was weak, but because you were persistent. Persistence is often the final blow. It is consistency that topples what once towered over you. Stay steady. Keep showing up. Giants fall when you refuse to retreat.

When one giant falls, others may appear. Victory is never the final chapter - it is often the doorway to the next battlefield. Just as David faced more than Goliath after that decisive day in the valley, so too will we encounter new giants that rise with different faces and voices. Courage, therefore, cannot be a one-time event; it must become a lifestyle. It is not a single moment of bravery but a daily decision to stand firm when new shadows stretch across your path. Courage wakes up early, prays when weary, speaks truth when it would be easier to stay silent, and trusts God when the outcome is uncertain. It understands that valleys are not permanent dwellings but training grounds for deeper strength. When courage becomes habitual, giants lose their power to intimidate. You learn that every challenge is another opportunity to demonstrate faith in action and that the same God who empowered yesterday's victory is faithful for today's fight.

Every victory, no matter how small, deposits confidence into your spirit for the next confrontation. The first time you stand your ground in faith, your knees may tremble and your voice may shake—but when you see God carry you through, something shifts inside. You begin to realize that the battle was never meant to destroy you; it was meant to develop you. Confidence in God grows with experience. The ground that once felt unstable beneath your feet becomes firm as you learn that faith is not fragile - it is forged. Each battle fought strengthens spiritual muscle. Just as resistance builds physical strength, opposition builds endurance, discernment, and authority in the spirit. What once intimidated you begins to lose its voice. Over time, territories that once felt forbidden become places you walk through with authority, not arrogance but assurance. You no longer enter battles hoping to survive; you enter knowing you are equipped. Growth transforms fear into familiarity, and familiarity into dominion.

The courage to confront giants is not about proving your strength. It is about trusting God's power working through your willingness. Too often we think bravery means showcasing our own ability, flexing our spiritual muscles, or demonstrating how prepared we are for the battle. But real courage is the decision to step forward even when your knees shake, because you believe God stands with you. Like David facing Goliath, it was never about the size of the stone but the size of his faith. When your confidence rests in the Lord, you stop fighting to impress people and start moving to obey God. When you step forward in faith, giants discover they are not as invincible as they once believed. The obstacle that once towered over your thoughts begins to shrink under the shadow of God's promises. Giants thrive on intimidation, but they crumble in the presence of obedience. And what once looked impossible becomes the stage upon which God reveals His strength through your surrendered heart.

| 22 |

"COURAGE IN THE FIRE"

Courage is not proven in comfort; it is revealed in the fire. Anyone can stand tall when life is predictable and peaceful, when prayers seem quickly answered and opposition is nowhere in sight. But spiritual courage is not measured by how steady you are in the sunshine - it is measured by how steadfast you remain when the storm clouds gather, and the heat begins to rise. The fire does not create weakness; it exposes it. It reveals whether your confidence was rooted in convenience or anchored in conviction. Yet for the person whose faith is genuine, the fire does not destroy - it refines. What enters the flames fragile can emerge fortified. Trials strip away pretense, burn off fear, and strengthen the very foundation of belief. When faith is authentic, adversity becomes a forge, not a funeral. The heat intensifies, but so does endurance. The pressure increases, but so does perseverance. And in the end, what stands after the fire is a purer, stronger, more courageous reflection of who you were always meant to be.

There are seasons in every believer's life when the flames feel overwhelming, times when trials rise without warning, prayers appear delayed, and doors close with no explanation. In those moments, faith is tested not in the spotlight but in the silence. Courage is not always a bold declaration or a dramatic stand; often it is the quiet resolve to remain steadfast when everything within you wants relief. It is choosing to believe that God is still working behind the scenes, even when the evidence seems absent. It is trusting His character when you cannot trace His hand. True courage in the fire is the heartbeat of endurance. It is the decision to stand firm when circumstances shout otherwise. Quiet endurance is the unwavering conviction that the same God who allowed the flames is present within them, refining rather than destroying, strengthening rather than abandoning. And when the season shifts, as it always does, you will discover that what felt like overwhelming fire was actually forging unshakable faith.

The fire has a purpose. It is not sent to destroy you but to develop you. Gold is purified in the heat where impurities rise to the surface and are removed. Steel is strengthened in the intense pressure of the forge. In the same way, God uses the heat of adversity to shape, purify, and strengthen His people. What feels unbearable in the moment is often the very process that is building endurance, character, and unshakable faith within you. The flames you fear may be what heaven is using to reveal the strength you did not know you possessed. Fire exposes weaknesses, but it also forges resilience. It burns away pride, fear, and self-reliance, replacing them with humility, courage, and trust in God. Do not curse the fire; let it complete its work. When the refining is finished, you will not look like what you have been through - you will look like someone who has been strengthened, purified, and prepared for purpose, greater responsibility, deeper wisdom, and stronger influence.

Courage in the fire means refusing to bow to fear when the heat rises and the pressure closes in. Fear whispers that the flames will consume you, that the trial will destroy your peace, your purpose, and your future. But courage stands firm and answers back with faith. Faith declares that the fire will not erase the promises spoken over your life. What feels like destruction is often divine development. The enemy wants you to focus on the intensity of the heat, but God wants you to lift your eyes and see His hand steadying you in the midst of it. The fire may surround you, but it cannot separate you from His presence. In the very place where fear tries to paralyze you, God draws closest reminding you that you are never alone. Courage is not the absence of fire; it is the decision to trust God while standing in it. When you refuse to bow to fear, you discover that the fire does not consume you - it reveals that you were built to withstand it, and that God has been with you every step of the way.

When you walk through spiritual fire, you discover who you truly are. The platforms, positions, and praise that once affirmed you can no longer sustain you. In the heat of testing, the only thing that remains steady is your relationship with God. In those intense moments, you learn that who you are in private with God matters far more than who you appeared to be in public before people. The fire strips away dependence on people and pushes you into deeper reliance on Him. It removes the comfort of constant affirmation and replaces it with the necessity of faith. When no one else understands, agrees, or applauds, you discover that His presence is enough. The very flames meant to weaken you become the refining process that purifies your motives, deepens your prayer life, and anchors your trust. What survives the fire is not performance - it is authenticity. And in that sacred place of surrender, you don't just endure the fire - you emerge refined, resilient, and more rooted in God than ever before.

The furnace reveals loyalty. It strips away the applause, the crowd, and the comfort of convenience, and it exposes what truly governs the heart. Fire has a way of forcing what we believe to confront what we fear. When the heat rises, neutrality disappears. The furnace demands a choice. Will you bow to pressure to preserve your position, or will you stand firm in truth even when standing alone? In the blaze of opposition, loyalty to God is no longer theoretical; it becomes visible, measurable, and undeniable. Courage in the fire means choosing obedience over comfort every single time. It means refusing to trade eternal reward for temporary relief. It is easy to declare faith when the air is cool, but true devotion is proven when the flames surround you. Those who stand firm discover that obedience invites the presence of God into the fire itself. And when you walk out unburned, without the smell of smoke, your testimony becomes a beacon to others revealing that loyalty to truth will always outlast the heat.

There is a breaking that happens in the fire. It is the breaking of pride that told you that you did not need God. It is the breaking of insecurity that whispered you were not enough. It is the breaking of self-reliance that convinced you your own strength could carry you through every storm. The fire exposes what was hidden and confronts what was fragile. It strips away false confidence and misplaced trust, not to destroy you, but to deliver you from the weight of what was never meant to sustain you. The fire burns away what cannot survive eternity. What remains is not weakness, but purified character. What remains is not fear, but unshakable faith. In the heat of refinement, motives are purified, convictions are strengthened, and dependence shifts from self to Savior. You emerge not charred but clarified. Not diminished but defined. The fire does not destroy you - it reveals you. And what stands after the flames is a faith that cannot be shaken and a life that reflects the glory of the One who refined it.

God never wastes a fire. What feels like destruction is often divine refinement. Every hardship carries hidden purpose, and every trial contains seeds of transformation planted deep within your spirit. The flames that feel unbearable today are not sent to consume you, but to cleanse you, strengthen you, and reveal what was placed inside you long before the fire ever came. Pressure exposes weakness, but it also reveals strength. Heat removes impurity, but it also forges resilience. What the enemy meant to scorch you, God is using to shape you. The fire you are walking through is expanding your capacity to carry greater responsibility and greater glory. The testimony you will share tomorrow is being written in the heat of today's struggle. Character is built in the furnace. Authority is forged in adversity. And the weight of future influence requires the strength that only fire can produce. Stand firm. Endure. Trust the process. When the smoke clears, you will shine with strength refined by the flames.

Courage does not mean you feel no pain. It does not deny the sting of betrayal, the weight of disappointment, or the heat of adversity. Courage acknowledges the fire but refuses to bow to it. The flames may draw tears from your eyes, but they cannot steal the trust rooted deep in your soul. You may feel the pressure, you may feel the stretching, but you make a decision that the fire will refine you, not define you. When you are anchored in God, even the fiercest flames become instruments of growth. What was meant to consume you becomes the very thing that strengthens you. Trials shape endurance. Pressure builds character. Heat produces purity. You are not fragile glass that shatters under intensity - you are forged steel, strengthened in the furnace of faith. The fire may bend you for a moment, but it will not break you. And when you emerge, you will shine with a deeper trust, a stronger spirit, and an unshakable confidence in the One who walks with you through the flames.

In the fire, distractions fade. The noise that once demanded your attention loses its power, and the clutter that crowded your heart begins to burn away. Trials have a way of stripping life down to its foundation. In the heat, priorities realign. You begin to see clearly again. You remember who you are, whose you are, and what truly matters. The fire does not come to destroy your purpose; it comes to refine it. The heat clarifies vision. It teaches you that faith is not optional, integrity is not negotiable, obedience is not conditional, and love is not weakness. These are the treasures that survive the flames. Everything else is temporary smoke - impressive for a moment but gone with the wind. When you emerge from the fire, you carry less, but you carry what counts. You walk with deeper conviction, stronger character, and a clearer focus. The fire may be uncomfortable, but it is also sacred because in it, God reshapes your heart and restores your sight.

The fire also exposes hidden strength. In seasons of pressure and uncertainty, you begin to see what God has placed inside you all along. What once felt overwhelming becomes the very tool that reveals your resilience. You discover courage rising when fear tries to speak, peace settling in when chaos surrounds you, and endurance carrying you further than you ever imagined. The heat pulls out of you a perseverance you did not know you possessed and shapes you into someone stronger, steadier, and more anchored than before. In the fire, prayer becomes deeper because you pray desperately and sincerely. Worship becomes purer because it is no longer based on comfort but on conviction. Trust becomes stronger because you have seen God sustain you in what you thought would break you. The very thing that tried to intimidate you becomes the soil where your faith takes root and grows deeper. What was meant to shake you will ultimately strengthen you and mature the faith God placed inside you.

Courage in the fire is contagious. When others see you stand firm in the heat of adversity they witness more than resilience; they witness faith in action. Strength under strain speaks louder than words ever could. It sends a powerful message that fear does not have the final say and that faith can hold steady even when circumstances shake. When you choose trust over panic and perseverance over retreat, you are silently preaching hope to those watching from the sidelines. Your endurance becomes someone else's encouragement. Your testimony becomes someone else's roadmap. The very fire that was meant to consume you becomes the light that guides others through their darkness. When people see that you made it through still standing, still believing, and still praising, it awakens courage in their own hearts. They begin to think, "If God did it for them, He can do it for me." And that is how courage multiplies. One life anchored in faith can ignite strength in an entire community.

The fire may isolate you, but it does not abandon you. There are seasons when obedience leads you into places that feel lonely, misunderstood, and painfully intense. In those moments, it can seem as though everything familiar has been stripped away. Yet the flames that separate you from comfort do not separate you from God. He does not watch from a distance - He steps into the furnace with you. What feels like isolation is often an opportunity to encounter His presence in a deeper, more personal way than ever before. Even when you feel alone, God is present in the midst of the flames. His nearness is often more tangible in the furnace than in seasons of ease, because hardship strips away distraction and reveals what is eternal. The fire becomes holy ground not because it is comfortable, but because He is there. What was meant to break you becomes the space where His glory is revealed. You are not abandoned in the fire - you are accompanied, strengthened, and transformed.

Do not rush the process. Refinement takes time. Gold is not purified in a single spark, and neither is a man shaped by God in a single moment. Impurities rise slowly to the surface, often through pressure, waiting seasons, and quiet battles no one else sees. Character is not built overnight; it is formed in the unseen choices, the disciplined responses, and the willingness to endure when shortcuts are available. Courage is forged layer by layer, decision by decision, prayer by prayer. What feels like delay is often divine development. What seems slow is often sacred. The longer you remain faithful, the purer your faith becomes. Faithfulness through testing deepens trust. Faithfulness through uncertainty anchors your soul. Each act of obedience refines your heart, burns away pride, and strengthens conviction. Over time, what once required effort becomes conviction; what once felt heavy becomes natural. Remain steadfast. Stay in the fire long enough for the impurities to surface and be removed.

There is promotion on the other side of the fire. God never wastes a trial, and He never allows a test without purpose. Every test precedes elevation. Every trial prepares you for new territory. The pressure you feel is not punishment - it is preparation. The fire refines, strengthens, and removes what cannot go where you are headed. Just as gold is purified by heat, your character, endurance, and faith are being developed in ways comfort could never accomplish. What feels like resistance today is actually resistance training for the level you are about to enter. What you survive in private becomes the strength you carry in public. The tears no one saw, the prayers whispered in the dark, the battles fought when no one applauded are building a foundation for visible victory. The fire is not your final chapter - it is preparation for your next assignment. When you step into your new season, you will arrive prepared. The very thing that tried to break you will become the evidence that God built you for more.

When the heat intensifies, remember who you are. You are not fragile - you are forged. Pressure does not expose weakness in you; it reveals the strength God has been building all along. You are not defeated - you are developing. Every challenge, every trial, every moment that feels too heavy is actually shaping endurance, deepening faith, and refining character. The fire is not proof of God's absence; it is evidence that He is near, working with intentional hands, crafting something stronger, wiser, and more resilient than before. Gold is purified by flame, and warriors are strengthened through battle. In the same way, your trials are not designed to destroy you but to define you. God is shaping you for greater purpose, stretching your capacity, expanding your vision, and preparing you for assignments that require strength you could not gain in comfort. Stand firm in the heat. Lift your head in the middle of the pressure. What feels like breaking is actually becoming. You are being forged for more.

Courage in the fire requires perspective. When the flames rise and the heat intensifies, it's easy to believe the moment will last forever. But flames are temporary while purpose is eternal. The trial you're walking through has a timeline, even if you cannot see the end from where you stand. Pain has an expiration date; it will not outlive the purpose of God in your life. What feels overwhelming today will one day be a testimony of endurance, refinement, and growth. Fire does not come to consume you - it comes to reveal what cannot be burned. Glory, however, does not fade with the smoke. When you keep eternity in view, the heat loses its power to intimidate. Perspective shifts panic into perseverance and fear into faith. You begin to understand that the fire is not your enemy but your furnace of formation. What is eternal in you cannot be destroyed by what is temporary around you. Lift your eyes higher than the flames. The moment will pass but the character, strength, and glory forged in the fire will remain.

One day you will look back at the very season that once frightened you and call it the turning point. What felt like uncertainty, pressure, and even loss will reveal itself as divine positioning. In the moment, the fire seemed threatening, but it was never sent to destroy you. It was sent to refine you. What you feared would consume you was actually shaping you, stripping away doubt, sharpening your faith, and strengthening your resolve. The same heat that tested you was also transforming you. The fire you feared will become the forge that formed you. You will thank God for the perseverance, wisdom, and strength it produced within you. You will see how every tear watered resilience, how every setback built endurance, and how every trial deepened your trust in Him. What once felt like a breaking point will stand as proof that you were being built for greater purpose. And when you stand on the other side, stronger and steadier, you will realize that the season that shook you was the very one that shaped you.

Stand firm in the fire. Trust while it burns. Worship while it refines. Pray while it purifies. The fire is not your enemy; it is your proving ground. It exposes what is weak, strengthens what is true, and burns away what cannot endure. When the pressure feels unbearable, refuse to retreat. Lift your voice in worship even when the flames crackle around you. Let prayer be your oxygen in the smoke. The same fire that threatens to consume you is the fire God uses to shape you. When the flames settle and the smoke clears, what will remain is not the fragile version of who you were, but a stronger, braver, purer version of you. You will carry the evidence of endurance, the quiet confidence of one who has walked through heat and did not bow. Courage is not the absence of fire; it is faith that stands unshaken within it. It is the steady heart in the storm, the lifted hands in the furnace, the unwavering trust that refuses to surrender. And when you emerge, your life will testify that the fire did not destroy you - it revealed you.

| 23 |

"COURAGE IN THE STORM"

Storms do not ask permission before they arrive. One moment the skies are clear; the next, winds are howling and waves are crashing against the structures of our confidence. Storms have a way of stripping away illusion. They reveal what is anchored and what is merely resting on the surface. What we believed was unmovable is tested, and what we assumed would last forever is examined under pressure. But disruption is not destruction - it is revelation. Storms are not sent to destroy the faithful - they are allowed to reveal them. Pressure uncovers perseverance. Adversity exposes authentic faith. When the winds rage, the roots of conviction go deeper, not weaker. What survives the storm stands stronger because it has been proven. Faith that endures hardship is no longer theoretical; it becomes testimony. The storm does not define the faithful - it refines them. And when the skies clear, what remains is not a broken believer, but a revealed one.

Courage in the storm is not the absence of fear; it is the decision to stand while fear screams. It is the steadying of your soul when the thunder rolls overhead and uncertainty flashes like lightning across the sky. Courage is not loud or dramatic. It does not need applause. It is the quiet resolve planted deep within a man of faith that says, "I will not move," even when the winds threaten to uproot everything around you. Courage is not found in perfect conditions; it is forged in imperfect ones. True courage is conviction anchored deeper than circumstance. It is a heart fastened to truth, not to comfort. When the ground trembles and the future feels unclear, courage chooses to trust what cannot be shaken. It stands because it knows who holds the storm. It endures because it believes that what is built on rock will remain when the winds pass. Courage is not the denial of fear - it is the mastery of it. It is faith with backbone, hope with grit, and obedience that refuses to bow to the noise of the storm.

Every believer will face moments when the sky darkens without warning. Prayers seem to echo back in silence, doors close without explanation, and the comforts that once felt secure slip quietly through our fingers. These seasons can feel unfair yet it is here that faith is tested and refined. Faith is no longer a declaration we make in bright sanctuaries; it becomes the lifeline we cling to in the valley. It is easy to speak of trust when the path is straight and the sun is shining. It is far more powerful to trust when the road bends sharply and the night grows long. In those moments, faith is the steady stance of a heart that refuses to bow to despair. It is the quiet lifting of the chin when tears blur the vision. It is choosing to stand, kneel, or even crawl toward God when emotions demand retreat. Faith fueled by courage is visible determination rooted in invisible conviction. It anchors the soul beyond circumstance. And though the sky may remain dark for a time, the man who believes knows that light is on the way.

Storms expose foundations. When the rain falls and the winds beat against the house, only what is built on truth will remain standing. In calm weather, every structure looks secure, every confession sounds convincing, and every dream feels durable. But when adversity strikes like thunder and uncertainty howls like wind - the true strength of your foundation is revealed. Character and faith are not proven in sunshine; they are proven in the storm. What is anchored in truth will not collapse under pressure, because truth does not shift with circumstances. The storm does not come to destroy you but to reveal you. It tests the depth of your roots, the integrity of your structure, and the authenticity of your belief. If cracks appear, the storm has done you a favor by exposing what needs reinforcement. Do not curse the wind - learn from it. Let the rain drive you deeper into faith, and deeper into alignment with what cannot be shaken. When the storm passes, what remains standing will be unmovable.

Many want the crown, but few embrace the storm that shapes the king. Everyone is drawn to the spotlight of authority, the honor of influence, and the weight of leadership yet far fewer are willing to endure the crushing seasons that prepare a man to carry it well. Crowns are not handed out to the comfortable; they are earned in the crucible. The storm exposes weaknesses, refines character, and strips away pride. It teaches humility when plans fail, courage when fear rises, and perseverance when quitting feels easier. The throne may represent power, but the storm produces the wisdom, restraint, and depth required to steward it. Just as steel is tempered by fire and shaped by repeated blows, so a leader is strengthened through trials that test resolve and refine integrity. If you desire lasting influence, do not resent the storm - embrace it. The very resistance you face today is shaping the capacity you will need tomorrow. The crown is sustained by the character the storm creates.

Courage in the storm begins with perspective. What feels like chaos on the surface may be divine construction beneath it. The winds that unsettle us are often the very forces God is using to strengthen our foundation. Storms expose cracks in our confidence, challenge our assumptions, and force us to anchor ourselves more deeply in truth. When we shift our perspective from panic to purpose, we begin to see that the storm is not sent to destroy us but to develop us. What appears to be falling apart may actually be falling into place under the careful hand of a faithful God. God often builds in ways we do not immediately understand. He shapes character through pressure, forms endurance through resistance, and establishes unshakable faith through uncertainty. Divine construction is rarely comfortable, but it is always intentional. In the middle of thunder and lightning, heaven is not absent - it is active. Courage grows when we trust that God sees the finished structure while we only see the scaffolding.

When waves rise high and visibility is low, courage chooses to trust what it cannot see. It stands firm when the horizon disappears and the winds howl against every promise once spoken. In the moments when certainty is stripped away and control slips from our hands, faith becomes our compass. We are reminded that we were never meant to navigate the storm alone. The unseen hand of God is steady, even when the sea is not. Trust grows strongest not in calm waters, but in tempests that demand we lean fully on Him. Faith requires full surrender. It asks us to release our grip on outcomes and anchor our hearts in the One who sees beyond the fog. Sometimes the greatest act of bravery is simply refusing to quit - refusing to abandon hope, refusing to surrender to despair. Endurance is holy ground. Perseverance is sacred strength. And in that steadfast refusal to give up, we discover that courage was never about seeing the way - it was about trusting the One who is the Way.

The storm will test your voice. When the winds rise and the thunder rolls, it will whisper lies into your spirit. It will try to convince you that you are finished, forgotten, and overwhelmed. In the chaos, it will tempt you to speak defeat, to declare despair, and to surrender the hope you once held with confidence. The storm wants your agreement. It knows that words carry power, and if it can get you to echo its fear, it can weaken your faith. But you must remember: the volume of the storm does not determine the truth of your future. Courage speaks life even when thunder roars. Courage declares promise when circumstances suggest loss. It lifts its voice above the wind and proclaims that God is still faithful, that purpose still stands, and that victory is still possible. You may feel the rain, you may see the lightning, but you do not have to speak the language of the storm. Speak life.

Speak hope. Speak faith. Let your voice align with truth and watch how even the fiercest storm begins to lose its power over you.

There is a refining fire hidden inside every storm. It does not come to destroy you, but to develop you. The winds may howl and the rain may fall hard, yet beneath the chaos God is doing a quiet, powerful work. The heat burns away doubt that once whispered defeat. It melts pride that convinced you that you did not need Him. It exposes the weakness of self-reliance and replaces it with holy dependence. What feels like pressure is actually purification. What feels like loss is often liberation from the very things that kept you small. When the storm passes and the flames settle, you will not emerge as who you were - you will rise as who you were meant to be. Stronger. Clearer. Anchored. The fire does not consume your calling; it confirms it. It does not erase your identity; it refines it. What remains after the fire is a purer faith, a steadier courage, and a deeper trust in the One who carried you through. The storm may have tested you, but the refining made you unshakable.

Courage does not always announce itself with thunder or spectacle. It is not always the bold speech, the public stand, or the dramatic victory. Sometimes courage is quiet. It looks like obedience when no one is watching. It is the steady whisper of "yes" to God in the middle of uncertainty. It is consistent prayer when answers seem delayed, faithful service when recognition never comes, and choosing integrity when compromise would be easier. Quiet courage is deeply rooted strength. It is a heart anchored in trust, moving forward one obedient step at a time. Sometimes courage is simply getting up again when you feel knocked down. It is wiping the tears and choosing to try once more. It is showing up when you would rather hide, believing when you feel weary, and enduring when the weight feels heavy. True courage is steady endurance that refuses to quit. And in those quiet, unseen moments, when you rise again, you are walking in a courage that heaven recognizes even if the world does not.

In the middle of the storm, it is easy to question whether God is present. The noise of adversity can drown out the whisper of His promises, and the darkness can make you wonder if heaven has gone quiet. But feelings are not facts. The same God who parted seas and calmed tempests has not stepped away from your situation. Often, when you cannot see His hand, He is steadying your heart. When you cannot hear His voice, He is strengthening your spirit. What feels like silence is often sacred work taking place beneath the surface. Divine silence is not divine absence. God is never more active than when you cannot trace Him. Roots grow deeper in hidden places, and faith matures when it must stand without visible signs. The storm may shake you, but it cannot remove the One who holds you. He is working in ways you cannot measure - aligning circumstances, building endurance, refining character, and preparing breakthrough. Trust does not grow in clear skies; it grows in the rain. So stand firm.

The storm reveals who you truly trust. When the winds rise and the waves crash against the fragile structures of your comfort, what you lean on becomes unmistakably clear. Do you trust your own strength or do you trust the One who commands the wind? Storms have a way of stripping away illusions, confronting pride, and revealing whether your security rests in self-reliance or surrendered faith. True courage is born when trust shifts from self to Savior. Courage is not the absence of fear; it is the presence of unwavering confidence in God's sovereignty. When you realize that the same voice that calms the sea governs your situation, panic gives way to peace. The storm may still rage, but your heart stands steady because it is anchored in Him. Strength built on self will eventually falter, but trust placed in the Savior produces endurance, boldness, and unshakable hope. When trust transfers from your hands to His, courage rises and the storm becomes a testimony, not a threat.

Every wave that crashes against you is not sent to destroy you - it is sent to develop you. Just as a muscle grows stronger under tension, your spirit grows stronger under resistance. The very pressures that seem determined to knock you down are actually building endurance within you. Faith is not formed in calm waters but in the pounding surf. Each setback, each challenge, each unexpected storm is adding weight to your spiritual training. And with every wave you withstand, your confidence in God deepens, your footing becomes steadier, and your inner strength expands. Resistance develops resilience. The pressure that tries to crush you is strengthening your core. What feels like strain is actually God fortifying your character, stabilizing your faith, and anchoring you deeper in truth. Diamonds are formed under pressure, and so are warriors of faith. When the waves keep coming, remember that the storm that tests you today is preparing you for the victory you will carry tomorrow.

The enemy hopes the storm will intimidate you into retreat. He counts on the wind, the waves, and the warfare to shake your confidence and silence your conviction. But storms do not come to destroy the called - they come to reveal them. The pressure you feel is evidence that something valuable is being formed within you. Every gust that pushes against you is also strengthening your spiritual footing. When you refuse to bow to intimidation, the very storm meant to drive you back becomes the force that launches you forward. Breakthrough is often born in resistance. When you stand firm, resistance becomes revelation. You begin to see what you're truly made of, and more importantly, you see who stands with you. The battle clarifies your calling. The struggle sharpens your faith. What tried to block you will instead build you. Hold your ground. The storm will pass, but the strength it produces will remain and, on the other side, you won't just survive, you will advance.

There is a kind of growth that only adversity can produce. Comfort may nurture us, but it is challenge that strengthens us. Roots do not stretch deeper when the soil is soft and the rain is steady - they press downward in seasons of drought, searching, stretching, refusing to die. In the same way, your faith and your character are developed when life demands more from you than you feel you can give. What feels like pressure is often preparation. What feels like resistance is often reinforcement. The very struggle you wish away may be the force that is making you unshakable. Anchors are proven in wind, not in still water. Sunshine can warm you, but it cannot refine you. Trials carve out spaces within you that peace never could, forming wisdom, endurance, and a quiet confidence that only survival can teach. Do not despise the season that stretches you for when the winds subside, you will not just have endured the storm - you will have become stronger because of it.

Courage in the storm is not born in the moment the winds begin to howl - it is strengthened by the memory of every storm God has already brought you through. When the thunder rolls and the waves rise, fear whispers that you will not survive this time. But memory answers back with testimony. You have faced giants before. You have walked through valleys before. You have stood in battles where the odds were against you and yet, you are still here. The same God who carried you through yesterday's fire has not changed, diminished, or abandoned His promises. If He sustained you then, He will sustain you now. Faith grows when memory fuels expectation. When you intentionally recall past victories, your heart begins to expect new ones. Yesterday's deliverance becomes today's confidence. Courage rises when you rehearse His faithfulness. The storm may be loud, but your testimony is louder. And the same God who carried you before will carry you again faithfully, powerfully, and right on time.

When the storm finally passes - and it will - you will not be the same person who first felt the wind begin to rise. The pressure that tried to bend you will have built your strength. The tears you shed in private will have watered roots you didn't even know were growing. You will stand taller not because life became easier, but because you endured what once seemed impossible. Your voice will carry a new authority, shaped by experience rather than theory. What once intimidated you will now testify to your growth. The very winds that shook you will become reminders of how far you've come. Challenges that once felt overwhelming will serve as evidence that you are stronger, steadier, and more resilient than you realized. You won't just survive the storm - you will emerge refined, with clarity where there was confusion and confidence where there was doubt. The storm was not sent to destroy you; it revealed you. And when the skies clear, you will recognize that the struggle didn't diminish you - it developed you.

The storm is not the end of your story - it is the chapter where courage is written into your character. Storms have a way of revealing what calm seasons cannot. They strip away illusions, expose foundations, and test what you truly believe. In the middle of the wind and rain, something stronger is being forged within you. Courage is not developed in comfort; it is carved in resistance. The very gusts that threaten to shake you are the forces shaping you into someone deeper, steadier, and more unshakable than before. You are not at the mercy of the storm; you are secured beneath it. Anchored hearts do not deny the storm's intensity - they simply refuse to surrender to it. This season will not define you by what tried to break you, but by how you stood when breaking was an option. Let the storm write strength into your spirit, resilience into your resolve, and faith into your foundation. When the skies clear you will not just have survived the storm; you will have become stronger because of it.

| 24 |

"COURAGE IN THE VALLEY"

Valleys are unavoidable in the journey of life. No one walks on mountain peaks forever. There will be seasons when the air feels heavy with uncertainty. It can feel as though progress has stalled and purpose has grown distant. But valleys are not detours from destiny - they are part of the design. The same God who meets us in triumph walks with us in trial. When the applause fades and the climb gives way to descent, faith becomes more than a confession; it becomes a lifeline. What we declared on the mountain must be demonstrated in the valley. It is in the valley that courage is formed. Courage is forged in the quiet places where trust is tested and perseverance is stretched. In the valley, we learn to listen more closely, pray more honestly, and depend more deeply. Roots grow deeper in low places. The mountain reveals God's power, but the valley reveals His presence and, when you rise again, you will carry not just a testimony of victory, but a testimony of endurance.

The valley is often misunderstood. We tend to associate it with those seasons when life is harder than we imagined. But scripture tells a different story. Valleys are not barren wastelands; they are channels of life. Rivers carve their way through valleys. Soil in the valley is rich and deep. Crops flourish there because water settles there. What feels like a low place may actually be a fertile place in disguise. The very pressure that pushed you down may be positioning you for growth. If you are walking through a valley season, don't mistake it for abandonment. It may be preparation. God often does His deepest work in the lowest places. Character is cultivated there. Faith takes root there. Dependence on Him becomes real there. The mountaintop may give you vision, but the valley gives you substance. There is water in the valley. There is growth in the valley. And in time, what once looked like a setback will reveal itself as sacred ground where strength, wisdom, and fruitfulness were quietly formed.

Courage in the valley is different from courage on the mountain. Mountain courage celebrates victory. It stands tall in the sunlight, arms raised, voice strong, declaring what God has done. It is the courage of conquest, the faith that shouts from the summit, "The battle is won!" Mountain courage is visible and inspiring. It carries the sound of triumph and the confidence of fulfillment. It is the kind of courage people applaud, the kind that builds monuments and marks milestones. But valley courage survives adversity. It does not shout; it endures. It walks through shadows with steady steps and refuses to quit when the path is unclear. Valley courage is quiet, steady, and unyielding. It is the strength to pray when answers delay, to stand when no one sees, to believe when feelings falter. And while mountain courage may draw attention, valley courage builds character. For it is in the valley that faith is refined, resolve is strengthened, and the foundation for the next mountain is formed.

In the valley, you do not always see clearly. The towering walls rise high on either side, blocking your distant view and narrowing your perspective. The path curves out of sight, shadows stretch long, and the future appears hidden behind rock and ridge. Valleys have a way of humbling us, reminding us how little control we truly have. But limited visibility does not mean limited purpose. Just because you cannot see the mountaintop does not mean it is not there. The valley is not a place of abandonment; it is a place of development. It is where faith is refined and where trust grows stronger than sight. Courage in the valley is choosing to take the next step when you cannot see the final destination. It is moving forward without a full map, believing that the One who leads you sees what you cannot. Courage does not require visible outcomes; it requires a steadfast heart. It is not the ability to predict the ending, but the decision to keep walking anyway.

It is easy to declare bold faith when the sun is shining, and the evidence of God's goodness is visible all around you. On the mountaintop, worship flows freely and confidence feels natural. But the valley strips away the applause, the excitement, and the emotional surge. It reveals whether your faith was built on a moment or on a foundation. In the quiet shadows of difficulty, when clarity fades and questions rise, you discover whether your trust in God was rooted in passing emotion or anchored deeply in unshakable conviction. When feelings fade and circumstances tighten, courage becomes a deliberate choice. It is no longer automatic; it is intentional. Courage in the valley means standing on what you know even when you cannot feel it. It means rehearsing God's promises when your heart is weary and walking forward when the path is uncertain. True faith matures in these hidden places. It is there that belief shifts from inspiration to discipline, from excitement to endurance.

The valley strips away distractions. In the valley, there are no stages, no spotlights, no cheering crowds. It's just you and God. The things that once affirmed you fall silent, and the titles that once defined you lose their echo. What remains is the raw condition of your heart. In that quiet struggle, when no one is watching and no one is praising, you begin to see what truly sustains you. The valley has a way of exposing whether you were living for recognition or resting in relationship. It is there, in the stillness and strain, that faith becomes real. When affirmation fades and visibility disappears, your dependence on God either weakens or deepens. The valley tests the source of your strength. If it came from applause, you will feel empty. But if it flows from intimacy with Him, you will discover a resilience that no crowd could ever give you. In the hidden place, character is refined, trust is strengthened, and your relationship with God becomes the only applause you need.

Courage in the valley means refusing to let fear narrate your story. Valleys are places of pressure, uncertainty, and vulnerability where the light feels dim and the path ahead unclear. Fear will whisper worst-case scenarios. It will magnify shadows and minimize promises. But courage recognizes fear's voice without surrendering to it. Courage understands that feelings are real, but they are not rulers. In the valley, you may hear fear but you don't have to agree with it. Courage speaks back with truth. It answers fear with faith, doubt with declaration, and uncertainty with unwavering trust. It reminds you that valleys are not permanent addresses - they are passageways. What feels like an ending may actually be preparation. When fear says, "You won't make it," courage declares, "God is with me." In the valley, courage is not the absence of trembling; it is the decision to move forward anyway, anchored in truth and confident that the same God who leads you through the valley will lead you out of it.

The valley is not evidence of God's absence; it is often proof of His guidance. We may feel surrounded by shadows, uncertainty, or silence, but the Shepherd has not abandoned the flock. In scripture, the valley is not a place of punishment - it is the path to a better life. Shepherds lead their sheep through valleys because that is where the water flows, where the ground is fertile, and where the journey continues forward. The path may feel narrow and unfamiliar, but it is intentional. What feels like detour is often divine direction. When God leads you through a valley, He is not losing you - He is positioning you. Valleys shape trust, strengthen endurance, and deepen dependence. They teach you to listen for His voice rather than rely on your own sight. The climb to greener pastures requires going through lower ground first. So do not mistake difficulty for distance from God.

If He is leading, even the valley is holy ground. The path may be tight, but it is purposeful for it always leads somewhere better.

Sometimes the valley is not a place of defeat, but a place of refinement. It is there, in the low places, that pressure exposes what comfort conceals. Just as fire draws impurities to the surface of precious metal, seasons of testing reveal hidden weaknesses we didn't know were there. The valley has a way of stripping away self-reliance and teaching us dependence on God. In the quiet shadows, God is purifying motives, reshaping character, and preparing us for greater responsibility. Hardship strengthens endurance in ways ease never could. Muscles grow under resistance, and faith grows under pressure. What feels like breaking may actually be God's hands molding you into something stronger, wiser, and more resilient than before. The valley is not your burial ground; it is your training ground. Stay faithful in the process. The same God who leads you through the valley is the One who refines, strengthens, and ultimately raises you to stand firm on higher ground.

Courage does not mean you feel strong. It does not mean your hands aren't shaking or your heart isn't heavy. Courage is choosing to take the next step when your strength feels small and your confidence feels thin. Real courage shows up in quiet obedience. It is praying when you are tired and worn out. It is trusting when you are confused and standing when everything in you wants to sit down and give up. The world often defines courage as boldness and power, but heaven defines it as faithfulness. Courage is getting up one more time. It is opening your Bible when your emotions say close it. It is lifting your voice in prayer when discouragement says stay silent. It is holding your ground when fear whispers retreat. Courage is not about how strong you feel - it is about how committed you are. And when you choose to move forward in weakness, God meets you there. His strength becomes perfect in your weakness, and what felt impossible becomes the very place where faith grows the strongest.

In the valley, comparison becomes dangerous. When you look up and see someone else standing on their mountaintop, it can make your own terrain feel darker, steeper, and more exhausting than it really is. You begin to measure your progress against their platform, your pace against their promotion, your prayers against their praise reports. But valleys are not punishments; they are preparation grounds. They are where roots grow deep, where character is refined, and where dependence on God becomes real. If you allow comparison to take root, it will distort your perspective and convince you that your process is proof of failure instead of evidence of formation. Your journey was never designed to mirror another's highlight reel. God writes unique stories, not carbon copies. The same God who appoints mountaintops also appoints valleys and both have purpose. True courage is staying planted where He has you, trusting that obedience in the valley will lead you exactly where you are meant to stand.

The valley also teaches compassion. When you've walked through dark places you begin to see others differently. You recognize the silent battles behind brave smiles. You hear the tremble in someone's voice that others overlook. The valley replaces quick judgment with patient understanding. God uses the shadows to deepen your heart, to stretch your empathy, and to shape you into someone who doesn't just speak about love but lives it. In the valley, you discover that brokenness is not a disqualification; it is often the birthplace of mercy. Those who have walked through dark places learn how to carry light for others. The comfort you cried for becomes the comfort you now give. The strength you fought to find becomes the strength you lend. Your pain may become someone else's hope. Nothing is wasted in God's hands. Every tear, every lesson, every scar can shine with purpose. When you emerge from the valley, you come out carrying light, ready to guide someone else through their night.

There is courage in staying. In a world that celebrates quick exits and easy escapes, remaining planted requires a deeper kind of bravery. It takes strength to stand your ground when the door out seems wide open. Staying means choosing commitment over convenience, faith over feelings, and purpose over pressure. That kind of courage is not loud or dramatic, but it is powerful. It is forged in the unseen moments where character is tested and loyalty is proven. Sometimes the bravest act is not escape, but endurance. Remaining faithful builds a deeper strength than quick exits ever could. Endurance develops spiritual muscle, emotional maturity, and unshakable conviction. When you stay - when you pray through the pressure, work through the weariness, and love through the disappointment - you grow roots that storms cannot easily uproot. Quick escapes may bring temporary relief, but steadfast faith produces lasting strength. There is courage in staying, because staying transforms you.

Valleys have echoes. What you declare there does not disappear into the silence - it comes back to you. In low places, when the light feels distant and the path feels uncertain, your words matter more than ever. If you speak defeat, your heart will rehearse defeat. If you speak fear, your spirit will magnify fear. But if you lift your voice and declare faith, even through trembling lips, that faith will echo back into your soul. The valley is not just a place of testing; it is a chamber of reinforcement. What you say there will settle into your spirit and shape how you rise. So speak life. Speak promises. Speak what God has said rather than what your circumstances suggest. Let your words reinforce courage instead of amplifying despair. Declare strength when you feel weak. Declare hope when you feel surrounded. Declare victory before you see it. Fill the low places with truth and let every echo remind you that you are not defeated, not abandoned, and not done.

The valley is temporary. No valley stretches endlessly; no shadow has the authority to outlast the sunrise. Yes, the air is heavier in the valley. Progress feels slower and prayers seem to go nowhere. But valleys are pathways, not permanent addresses. The terrain eventually rises. The same God who leads you down also leads you through - and He never forgets the way up. Courage holds onto that certainty even when the timeline is unclear. It does not deny the hardship before you - it acknowledges the struggle, stands firm in the storm, and refuses to surrender to anything less than victory. It says, "This is not the end of my story." It plants its feet in faith while the climb is still invisible. It trusts that elevation is coming even when the clock offers no reassurance. The valley may test you, but it cannot define you. Keep walking. Keep believing. The ground will rise again and, when it does, you will discover that the strength you gained in the valley was the very thing that prepared you for the mountain.

Mountains display glory. They rise high, visible to all, crowned with sunlight and wrapped in awe. From the mountaintop, victories are celebrated, prayers are answered, and faith feels unshakable. It is on the mountain that we see how far God has brought us. Triumph stands tall, confidence is strengthened, and others are inspired by the view. Mountains remind us of God's power and faithfulness. They are beautiful, breathtaking, and unforgettable but they are not where most growth happens. Valleys develop grit. In the low places, where shadows stretch long and the path narrows, transformation begins. Valleys cultivate maturity because they require trust when visibility is low and strength when applause is absent. While mountains inspire admiration from a distance, valleys produce depth within the soul. It is in the valley that character is refined, faith is proven, and resilience is forged. The valley cultivates transformation and those who endure it emerge stronger, wiser, and unshakably grounded.

When you walk through the valley with courage, you emerge different. Not untouched but strengthened. Not unchanged but refined. Valleys have a way of stripping away illusions and exposing what truly anchors your soul. In the low places your faith is tested, your character is shaped, and your dependence on God deepens. Courage in the valley is choosing trust over panic, prayer over despair, and obedience over retreat. And in that sacred tension, something powerful happens within you. The valley becomes part of your testimony rather than a tomb of your defeat. What once looked like a setback becomes the setting for transformation. God uses the pressure to purify, the struggle to strengthen, and the silence to speak deeply to your spirit. You come out with clearer vision, steadier faith, and a resilience that cannot be manufactured in comfort. You do not merely survive the valley; you rise from it carrying wisdom, humility, and a deeper revelation of who God is and who He has called you to be.

Do not despise the valley. The valley is not a punishment; it is preparation. It is the sacred classroom where God shapes character in quiet places, where roots grow deep before branches stretch high. In the valley, distractions fade and dependence deepens. It is there that faith is refined, motives are purified, and strength is built in ways the spotlight can never produce. Stand firm in its shadows. Let perseverance have its perfect work. Refuse to run from the pressure, because the very weight you feel is building the spiritual muscle you will need for what lies ahead. Walk boldly through its uncertainty. Courage forged in low places becomes authority carried in high places. The man who learns obedience in obscurity can be trusted with influence in visibility. The warrior who conquers fear in the shadows will stand unshaken on the mountain. For courage in the valley prepares you for authority on the mountain and when God lifts you higher, you will not only stand tall, you will stand ready.

| 25 |

"COURAGE ON DEMAND"

Courage is not a rare commodity reserved for heroes in history books or warriors on distant battlefields. It is not rationed out to a chosen few. Courage is abundantly available to you right here, right now. The difference between those who live boldly and those who shrink back is not supply, but access. Courage is on demand when you learn how to reach for it. It shows up the moment you decide to stand when it would be easier to sit, to speak when it would be safer to stay silent, and to act when fear whispers for you to retreat. Every day presents opportunities to draw from this limitless reserve whether in leadership, in fatherhood, in faith, or in the quiet battles no one else sees. The bold are not born with a greater portion of courage; they simply practice accessing it. They understand that courage is activated by conviction and strengthened by obedience. When you anchor yourself in purpose and trust God with the outcome, courage rises to meet the moment.

Many people believe courage is something that washes over them - a rush of bold emotion that suddenly makes them fearless. So they wait for the right mood, the right confidence, the right surge of inspiration. But courage is not a feeling you wait on; it is a choice you make. Feelings are unstable. They rise and fall with circumstances, opinions, and even the weather of your day. If you build your life on feelings, you will constantly retreat when fear whispers. But when you understand that courage is a decision, everything changes. Decisions are anchors. They steady you when emotions try to pull you backward. The moment you choose to step forward despite uncertainty, despite intimidation, despite the pounding of your heart - courage is activated. It does not require the absence of fear; it requires movement in the presence of it. Courage responds to commitment. Every time you choose forward motion over retreat, you strengthen the muscle of courage within you.

Fear is not the absence of courage; it is the invitation to it. Fear simply signals that something important is at stake. If nothing mattered, you would feel nothing. The very presence of fear is proof that you are standing at the edge of something significant. It shows up when you are about to step into new territory, make a difficult decision, speak an uncomfortable truth, or trust God beyond your comfort zone. Fear is a signal that tells you this moment carries weight, that destiny is pressing in, that purpose is within reach. Every time fear knocks on your door, courage is standing right beside it, waiting for you to choose which one you will entertain. Courage is not the absence of a pounding heart; it is the decision to move forward while it pounds. When you act despite fear, you silence its authority and strengthen your resolve. The question is not whether fear will show up because it will. The question is whether you will answer with retreat or with resolve. Choose courage and watch fear lose its voice.

Courage becomes accessible the moment you shift your focus. Fear feeds on whatever you magnify. When you stare at the size of the obstacle, rehearse the worst-case scenario, and measure your strength against the challenge, intimidation grows roots in your mind. But when you lift your eyes and focus on the size of your God-given purpose - on the calling, the assignment, and the reason heaven entrusted you with this moment - something changes. Your perspective begins to realign your power. What you choose to magnify will either paralyze you or propel you. When purpose becomes bigger than panic, courage steps forward on demand. You may still feel the wind of uncertainty, but you walk anyway because your focus has shifted from the threat to the mission. And when the mission fills your vision, panic loses its voice. The obstacle may remain the same size, but you rise above it because your perspective has enlarged your purpose. And where purpose leads, courage follows.

Inside you is a reservoir of strength placed there by God Himself. You were not designed to live intimidated, hesitant, or paralyzed by fear. Scripture declares that God has not given us a spirit of fear, but of power, love, and a sound mind. That truth reshapes how you see yourself. Power means you have divine ability backing you. Love means your courage is not harsh or reckless but rooted in confidence and compassion. A sound mind means you are not at the mercy of chaos or confusion. Courage is not something you beg God to create in you - it is something He has already deposited within you through His Spirit. That means you are learning to draw from what is already there. When pressure rises, you reach deeper. You remind yourself who placed that strength inside you. You stir up the gift. You stand firm because you know fear was never your inheritance. When you choose faith over fear, you tap into that reservoir and discover you were stronger all along than you ever realized.

Accessing courage requires intentional thought. What you rehearse internally shapes what you release externally. The battlefield is often not around you - it is within you. If your mind continually replays worst-case scenarios, imagined failures, and voices of doubt, your spirit begins to align with fear. Anxiety grows where negative expectation is nurtured. But when you deliberately turn your thoughts toward God's promises, you begin to strengthen your inner man. Scripture tells you to "take every thought captive" because they either build faith or feed fear. When you remember past victories and meditate on your calling, something shifts. Boldness begins to rise because courage responds to belief. If you believe God is with you, you step differently. If you believe He has equipped you, you act differently. You are summoning courage by aligning your thoughts with truth. What you repeatedly tell yourself becomes the lens through which you see every challenge. Choose to rehearse truth, and you will release strength.

Another key to accessing courage is action. Too often we wait to feel brave before we move, but courage is not a feeling we sit around and wait for; it is a response that rises when we step out in faith. The first step is usually the hardest because it demands trust in God beyond what we can see or control. It requires us to lean not on our own understanding, but on His promises. That initial act of obedience may feel small, but it breaks the grip of fear and positions us for God to meet us in motion. Once you step forward, momentum begins to build. Action feeds courage. Every small act of obedience unlocks a greater supply of boldness, strength, and clarity. As you move, God moves with you. What seemed intimidating begins to lose its power, and confidence grows with each faithful step. Courage multiplies through practice; it strengthens through use. When you choose action over hesitation, faith over fear, you discover that courage was never absent - it was waiting on your obedience to activate it.

Courage is strengthened by memory. When you pause and remember the battles you've already won, you remind your soul that victory is not foreign to you. Every trial that tried to break you instead built endurance, wisdom, and deeper faith. You are still standing. That alone is evidence of God's sustaining power in your life. The same strength that carried you through dark valleys and uncertain seasons is still available today. When you reflect on God's faithfulness in your past, you activate bravery in your present. Memory becomes fuel for momentum. What He brought you through before becomes proof of what He can bring you through again. Fear loses its grip when you remember that you've already faced giants and lived to tell the story. Your history with God is your evidence for today's battle. So rehearse the testimonies. Recall the breakthroughs. Let remembrance stir your confidence. The courage you need now is already anchored in the faithfulness you've experienced before.

You must also guard your environment. The voices you allow into your life shape the strength you walk in. If you continually surround yourself with negativity and people who rehearse doubt more than promise, your vision gets cloudy. Your confidence weakens. What enters your ears and eyes eventually settles in your heart. That is why protecting your environment is essential. You cannot expect bold faith to rise in a space where unbelief is constantly fed. But when you intentionally align yourself with voices that speak life, truth, and destiny, courage begins to flow freely. Faith-filled conversations ignite bold action. When you position yourself around people who call out your potential instead of your past, who speak promise instead of problems, and who remind you of who God says you are, your spirit rises. Courage becomes natural. Guard your atmosphere. Choose your influences wisely. Because the environment you cultivate will either suffocate your calling or empower you to walk in it boldly.

Prayer is another access point into the strength of heaven. It is not a ritual of weakness but a transaction of exchange. When you pray, you lay down your limitations and pick up divine enablement. Prayer is where anxiety is traded for assurance, where confusion gives way to clarity, and where trembling hearts become anchored in truth. In the presence of God, you are reminded that you are never fighting alone. His power flows where your strength runs out. In the secret place, courage is overflowing. You don't leave prayer smaller; you leave stronger. You rise from your knees with heaven's perspective and divine confidence filling your spirit. What once intimidated you now looks manageable because you have encountered the One who holds all things together. Courage is imparted, not manufactured. And when you step back into the world, you carry more than motivation - you carry impartation. Prayer transforms you from the inside out, equipping you to stand firm, move boldly, and live unshaken.

Courage is strengthened through obedience. It grows in the quiet, decisive acts of surrender when retreat would be easier. Every time you choose to obey God instead of bowing to fear, you lay another brick in the foundation of holy boldness. Obedience is not always loud or dramatic; often it is a simple "yes" when your flesh wants to say "no." Yet in those moments, heaven marks your faithfulness. With each step forward, you reinforce the truth that you are not controlled by fear - you are led by faith. Over time, those repeated acts of obedience reshape how you see yourself. You begin to recognize that you are not timid or defeated, but bold in Christ. Identity fuels behavior. When you believe you are courageous because your confidence is rooted in Him, you act accordingly. You pray when others stay silent. You stand when others shrink back. You speak truth when it would be easier to blend in. The more you obey, the stronger your identity as a faithful, fearless follower of Christ is established.

Sometimes courage is quiet. It doesn't always shout, charge forward, or demand attention. Sometimes courage is simply getting out of bed when grief presses against your chest and the weight of yesterday still lingers in your heart. It is choosing to show up when you would rather withdraw. It is taking one small step when you don't have the strength for ten. Quiet courage rises when you choose faith over fear, forgiveness over bitterness, and perseverance over surrender. It is found in the difficult conversation you've been avoiding, in the apology that humbles your pride, and in the steady decision to keep trusting God when the outcome is uncertain. Courage on demand meets you in both the spotlight and the shadows. It stands with you when you are called to lead boldly, and it sits beside you when you must forgive the one who wounded you deeply. It strengthens your voice when you must speak truth, and it softens your heart when you must extend grace.

You access courage through gratitude. When you begin to thank God for what He has already done, what He has already provided, and who He has already proven Himself to be, something shifts inside of you. Gratitude moves your focus from what is missing to what is present, from what is uncertain to what is secure. Instead of rehearsing fear, you rehearse faithfulness. Instead of magnifying lack, you magnify provision. Thanksgiving reminds you that the same God who carried you before will carry you again. In that remembrance, fear loses its grip and courage finds its footing. Gratitude stabilizes the soul. A grateful heart is not tossed back and forth by every challenge, because it is anchored in truth. When you thank God for what you have instead of fearing what you lack, your spirit steadies and your perspective clears. A stable soul steps forward in confidence. And when your heart is grounded in gratitude, courage is no longer something you chase; it becomes something you walk in.

Courage grows when you stop waiting for perfect conditions because perfect conditions rarely come. There will always be a reason to delay - a missing resource, an unanswered question, a lingering doubt, or the whisper of fear telling you that now is not the time. If you wait for fear to disappear before you act, you will wait forever. Fear does not leave before movement; it loses its grip because of movement. The truth is, clarity often follows obedience, and strength often follows the first step. When you decide to move in spite of imperfection, courage shows up immediately. It honors movement. Courage is not the absence of fear; it is the decision to advance while fear is still present. Each step forward builds momentum, and momentum builds confidence. The door does not open because you feel ready; it opens because you knock. Stop waiting for the perfect moment and create it by taking action. When you move, even imperfectly, you give courage permission to grow.

Courage is not the absence of risk. It is the willingness to trust God in the presence of risk. If there were no danger, no uncertainty, no possibility of failure, courage would not be required. Courage is born in the tension between what you see and what you believe. The world waits for perfect conditions, but men of faith move when conditions are imperfect. They step out not because the storm is gone, but because they know Who walks with them through it. Risk may surround you, but when trust anchors you, fear no longer controls you. Faith and courage are intertwined. When you truly trust that God is with you, you stand taller because your confidence is not in your own strength but in His presence. You move stronger because obedience has replaced hesitation. Faith changes your posture. Courage changes your action. Together, they transform the way you face challenges, opportunities, and battles. When you trust God in the presence of risk, you don't shrink back - you rise up.

There is also power in confession. What you consistently say, you eventually start to believe and what you believe shapes how you live. When fear whispers, courage must answer out loud. When weakness tries to define you, strength must be declared over you. Speak courage over yourself. Declare strength when you feel weak. Your words frame your reality. They set the atmosphere of your heart and the direction of your steps. Life and death are in the power of the tongue, and when you align your confession with God's truth, you align your life with His power. When you declare, "I can do all things through Christ who strengthens me," you are activating power. You are shifting your focus from limitation to divine enablement. Every time you speak God's promises over your life, you reinforce faith, silence doubt, and build spiritual momentum. Courage rises. Strength awakens. And what once felt impossible begins to bow to the authority of the Word you boldly proclaimed.

Courage is renewable. Every time you choose faith over fear, obedience over comfort, and conviction over convenience, you are building spiritual stamina. Courage works like a muscle; the more you engage it, the stronger and more responsive it becomes. The first step may feel heavy, the first stand may feel costly, but repetition rewires the soul. What once intimidated you begins to lose its grip. The timid become bold through practice. The hesitant become decisive through repetition. What felt unnatural at first becomes instinctive over time. Courage on demand becomes courage as a lifestyle. You begin to speak up without rehearsing fear, act without waiting for perfect conditions, and trust God without needing constant reassurance. Each act of bravery deposits confidence into your spirit, creating momentum for the next challenge. Courage multiplies with movement. The more you lean into it, the more you realize it was never a limited supply - it was a well that deepens every time you draw from it.

When you understand that courage is available at any moment, you stop seeing yourself as a victim of circumstance. You realize that courage does not wait for perfect conditions; it rises in imperfect ones. The moment pressure comes you are presented with a choice. Fear may knock first, but courage is always standing beside you, ready to be embraced. And when you choose courage, even in small ways, you reclaim authority over your attitude, your words, and your actions. You become a responder instead of a reactor. A reactor is driven by impulse, emotion, and external pressure. A responder is guided by conviction, clarity, and purpose. When you recognize that while you cannot control every situation, you can always choose your response. Circumstances may be unpredictable, but your character does not have to be. Courage empowers you to pause, to think, to pray, and then to act with intention. In that space between what happens to you and how you respond, your true power is revealed.

Today, courage is available to you. It is not locked away in some distant future moment, nor is it reserved for someone more gifted, more confident, or more qualified. It is present right now - on demand - waiting for your decision. Courage is not the absence of fear; it is the resolve to move forward in spite of it. When uncertainty whispers, you can answer with purpose. When pressure rises, you can respond with conviction. You do not have to wait to feel ready. You simply have to choose. Choose purpose over panic. Choose faith over fear. Choose obedience over hesitation. Every great step forward begins with a decision. The moment you align your heart with what is right instead of what is comfortable, courage rises to meet you. As you act in faith, strength follows. As you obey, clarity comes. As you take that first bold step, you will discover something powerful - courage has been within you all along. It has been waiting for your agreement, waiting for your yes. It is ready, abundant, and only one decision away.

| 26 |

"COURAGE TO OBEY"

ourage to obey is not loud or boastful. It does not seek applause, nor does it parade its sacrifices before others. True obedience is often unseen, forged in the quiet places where only you and God stand face to face. When Scripture calls us to "work out your own salvation with fear and trembling" (Phil. 2:12), it is an invitation to steward what He has placed within you. This kind of courage is steady and deeply personal. It is the daily decision to surrender your will, your pride, and your comfort so that the life of Christ can be fully formed in you. To work out your salvation is to cooperate with the transforming power of God, allowing your faith to move from confession to conduct. It is taking responsibility for the truth you claim to believe and letting it shape your thoughts, your relationships, your habits, and your ambitions. Courage to obey is not dramatic; it is disciplined. And in that quiet, consistent obedience, God brings to completion the good work He has already begun within you.

To work out your own salvation means you cannot live on borrowed conviction. You cannot survive spiritually on your pastor's fire, your spouse's discipline, or your parents' prayers. At some point, faith must become your own - personal, rooted, and tested. There comes a season when the spiritual training wheels come off. In that moment, what remains is not what others poured into you, but what you have chosen to embrace for yourself. True spiritual maturity begins when your obedience is no longer dependent on external pressure but flows from internal transformation. Courage is required because independence in faith removes excuses. When no one is watching, your decisions reveal the depth of your devotion. It takes boldness to obey God in private, to stand firm without recognition, and to choose righteousness when compromise would be easier. But this is where authentic faith is forged. The strength of your walk with God is measured not by public performance, but by private consistency.

"Fear and trembling" do not speak of cowering before an angry God, but of standing in awe before a holy One. It is the posture of a heart that understands it is dealing with sacred things - your soul, your calling, your eternity. When you handle something fragile and priceless, you do so carefully, intentionally, and with deep respect. In the same way, working out your salvation is not casual or careless; it is reverent. It is the awareness that your life carries eternal weight and divine purpose. Courage to obey grows in that soil of reverence. When you truly understand who God is - His holiness, His authority, His love, and His sovereignty - obedience no longer feels optional; it feels urgent. You don't obey out of fear of rejection, but out of honor and devotion. Reverence fuels resolve. The more clearly you see Him, the more boldly you follow Him. In that holy awareness of who God is and who we are in Him; obedience is transformed from a heavy obligation into a sacred privilege that draws us closer to His heart.

Obedience always demands movement. Faith that is never acted upon becomes stagnant and weak, like water that no longer flows. God never intended for His Word to simply inspire us in a moment of emotion; He calls us to step forward in response. When the apostle Paul wrote to the church in Philippi, he urged believers to grow up spiritually - to move beyond spiritual excitement into daily execution. Christianity was never meant to be admired from a distance; it must be walked out in real time. Courage to obey means you carry Sunday into Monday. It means the sermon does not end when the service does; it begins when you step back into your routine. Real maturity happens when inspiration becomes implementation, when forgiveness is extended, integrity is chosen, discipline is practiced, and love is demonstrated. Obedience is not passive agreement; it is decisive action. Every step taken in obedience strengthens faith, builds character, and positions you for greater responsibility in the Kingdom of God.

There is a trembling that comes when you realize the weight of your choices. It is not the trembling of fear alone, but the holy awareness that your life is being shaped one decision at a time. Every choice etches something into your character. Every act of obedience fortifies your spiritual backbone. Working out your salvation means you refuse to drift through life spiritually passive. Growth does not happen accidentally; it happens intentionally. It requires vigilance, humility, and courage to align your will with God's will. You examine your motives, guard your heart, and pursue obedience with purpose. Salvation is a gift, but maturity is cultivated. As you respond daily with reverence and resolve, you find that trembling gives way to transformation. What once felt fragile becomes firm. What once felt uncertain becomes anchored. Through deliberate obedience to God's Word, your faith is strengthened and rooted so deeply in Him that it stands unshaken when everything else around you begins to shake and fall.

Courage to obey will test your pride. Obedience often demands humility before it ever produces victory. It may mean apologizing first when you were misunderstood, forgiving fully when the wound still stings, or stepping back when your ego wants to step forward. Pride wants recognition, validation, and control but obedience surrenders all three. True spiritual courage is quiet, steady, and yielded. It chooses God's way over personal preference and bows the heart before it ever lifts the hands in action. Fear and trembling arise in that sacred tension when your flesh resists what your spirit already knows is right.

That internal struggle is the proving ground of spiritual maturity. In that moment, heaven watches to see whether you will protect your pride or crucify it. Every act of humble obedience chisels away at self-will and shapes Christlike character within you. The battle inside becomes the birthplace of strength, and what feels like loss to the flesh becomes lasting gain in the spirit.

Obedience is not about flawless performance; it is about faithful progression. Working out your salvation is a lifelong journey of growth, surrender, and transformation. There will be moments when you stumble, seasons when you question, and times when refinement feels like fire. Yet every step taken in sincerity shapes your character and deepens your dependence on God. Spiritual maturity is formed through daily decisions to align your heart with His will, trusting that He is shaping you through both trials and victories. The true courage of obedience is found in the determination to keep moving forward when you feel inadequate, unqualified, or uncertain. God does not honor perfection; He honors persistence. He blesses the man who rises after failure, who learns from correction, and who continues walking in faith despite weakness. When you choose to keep walking, even with trembling steps, you demonstrate a heart fully committed to becoming all that He has called you to be.

There is also courage in separation. Sometimes obedience will require you to distance yourself from influences that blur your spiritual focus. Not every voice speaking into your life carries God's wisdom, and not every relationship is assigned to your destiny. There are seasons when love remains, but proximity must change. When your convictions begin to cost you comfort, approval, or companionship, that is where real courage is revealed. Not everyone will understand your convictions, and some may even question your sincerity when you choose a different path. Fear and trembling appear when you stand alone, when you must trust God without human affirmation. Yet that trembling is often evidence that you are standing correctly. It is the natural response of a heart that reverences God more than people. When you choose holiness over popularity and obedience over acceptance, heaven takes notice. Standing alone with God is standing in alignment with His will, and that is where true strength is formed.

The refining fire of obedience burns away what comfort tries to preserve. When God calls us higher, He does not negotiate with our laziness or accommodate our selfish ambition - He confronts them. His refining fire reaches into the hidden corners of our hearts, illuminating motives we have disguised and sins we have tolerated. Courage to obey means you willingly step into that fire. You invite God to search you, examine you, and reshape you according to His will. Instead of resisting conviction, you welcome it as evidence of His love and commitment to your growth. You choose transformation over temporary comfort, holiness over convenience, and surrender over self-preservation. Obedience requires bravery because it asks you to lay down pride, repent quickly, and trust that God's correction produces righteousness. When you embrace conviction rather than run from it, you discover that the refining fire strengthens you, sharpens you, and prepares you for greater purpose.

Working out your salvation also means guarding your heart. The battles we face are not only outward but inward - thoughts, attitudes, desires, and distractions that try to quietly pull us away from God's best. To guard your heart means choosing what you allow to influence your spirit, what you meditate on, and what you dwell upon when no one else is watching. Spiritual growth requires discipline - intentional acts of surrender that keep your heart aligned with the will of God. Just as muscles grow through resistance, faith grows through consistent obedience. When you choose to pray instead of complaining, to trust instead of fear, and to obey instead of delay, you are strengthening your spiritual endurance. Guarding your heart is not passive - it is active, daily, and deliberate. It is the steady commitment to cultivate intimacy with God and in that consistency, your faith becomes resilient, your spirit becomes steadfast, and your salvation becomes something you live out boldly and faithfully.

Fear and trembling remind you that eternity is the backdrop of every decision you make. Time is a gift placed in your hands by God, and influence is a responsibility entrusted to you for His purposes. When you understand that your days are numbered and your opportunities are sacred, you stop living casually and start living intentionally. You begin to measure your steps, guard your heart, and align your priorities with what truly lasts. Courage to obey recognizes that one day you will give an account for how you lived, loved, and led. That awareness sharpens your focus when distractions call your name and strengthens your resolve when compromise whispers for attention. You choose integrity over convenience, faithfulness over applause, and obedience over comfort because you know eternity is watching. Fear and trembling will cause you to live with eternity in view, your courage to deepen, your leadership to mature, and your obedience to become a bold declaration that your life belongs fully to God.

Obedience will stretch your trust because it often calls you beyond what feels reasonable, predictable, or safe. God's instructions do not always align with human logic. Abraham had to leave everything familiar without a detailed map of the future. Moses had to speak when he felt inadequate and unqualified. David had to wait through seasons of obscurity and testing before stepping fully into his promise. In each case, obedience demanded courage because it disrupted comfort and challenged personal understanding. It required them to believe that God's wisdom was higher than their fears and greater than their limitations. Working out your salvation means trusting God beyond your understanding. It means choosing faith over feelings and surrender over certainty. When you obey despite confusion, delay, or discomfort, you declare that God's character is more reliable than your circumstances. That kind of courage refines your faith, strengthens your resolve, and aligns your life with eternal purpose.

There is also courage in consistency. It is easy to obey once in a moment of inspiration, when emotion is high and conviction feels strong. But it takes a deeper, quieter courage to obey God in the ordinary rhythms of life when no one is watching, when the feelings have faded, and when the task feels small. True spiritual strength is not proven in a single dramatic decision; it is revealed in daily faithfulness. Consistency is where character is formed. Fear and trembling create attentiveness. They keep you from drifting into spiritual autopilot, where familiarity dulls your sensitivity to the Spirit. A reverent awareness of God's presence guards your heart from complacency and sharpens your hearing. Courage to obey means you stay alert to God's voice in the routine as well as the remarkable. It means you treat every day as sacred ground and every instruction as significant. This kind of courage walks steadily proving that the bravest obedience is often the most consistent.

Spiritual maturity is revealed not in how deeply you feel in a moment of worship, but in how faithfully you obey God when no one is watching and emotions have faded. Tears may stream down your face in worship, and your heart may feel stirred in the moment, but heaven measures transformation by what happens after the music fades. Emotions can inspire you in the moment, stirring passion, compassion, and vision within your heart but feelings are often fleeting. Obedience, however, is what shapes your character over time, forging discipline, faithfulness, and spiritual maturity long after the emotion fades. Real maturity is courage in motion. It is salvation being worked out in real time - faith translated into action, conviction expressed through character. Spiritual depth is not about how high you can lift your hands, but how faithfully you can walk out His Word. Steady, daily obedience is the quiet but powerful proof that a heart is no longer fractured by compromise but is truly being made whole in Christ.

You are not working for salvation; you are working from salvation. Redemption is not a wage you earn - it is a gift you receive. God has already initiated the work in you. Before you ever lifted a hand in obedience, He moved first in grace. Before you ever chose righteousness, He planted the desire for it in your heart. Salvation is not the finish line you strain toward; it is the starting line from which you now run. You obey not to secure His love, but because you are already secured by it. The cross settled your position; obedience now reveals your transformation. The courage to obey is empowered by Him. When you choose holiness over compromise, forgiveness over bitterness, surrender over pride, you are cooperating with divine power already at work within you. Courage to obey is partnership with the Spirit. This means you are never alone when you choose to obey God. Every step of faith you take is supported, strengthened, and sustained by the power and presence of heaven itself.

There will be moments when obedience feels costly. Relationships may shift when you choose conviction over compromise. Opportunities may close when you refuse to bend your integrity. Comfort may decrease when God calls you out of what is familiar and into what is faithful. Obedience is rarely applauded in the moment; often it is misunderstood, sometimes even resisted. But the cost of obedience is never greater than the cost of disobedience. What feels like loss on the surface is often heaven rearranging your life for something deeper, stronger, and more eternal. When you work out your salvation with reverence and resolve, something powerful is formed within you. Obedience produces spiritual depth, inner stability, and a confidence that cannot be shaken by circumstances. It builds a foundation that storms cannot erode and criticism cannot dismantle. In the hidden places where you choose God again and again, He shapes you into a vessel of strength trusted with greater responsibility.

Fear and trembling anchor your heart in the awareness that you are not the source of your own strength. The courageous man does not swagger in spiritual confidence; he kneels in reverence. He understands that every victory over sin, every act of obedience, and every step of growth flows not from self-sufficiency but from divine empowerment. What appears to be boldness on the outside is actually deep reliance on the inside. Obedience without grace is impossible. No amount of discipline, knowledge, or willpower can substitute for the sustaining power of God's Spirit. True courage to obey is not rooted in personality strength but in humility before a holy God. It is the quiet confession that says, "Lord, without You I cannot do this." That humility becomes the doorway through which grace flows. When a man trembles before God, he becomes strong in God. When he bows low, he is lifted high. Courage to obey is born not in pride, but in reverent surrender.

In the end, the courage to obey is the truest evidence of authentic faith. It does not shout for attention, yet it moves mountains in the unseen places of the heart. Real faith is proven not in emotional moments, but in daily choices when you choose integrity over compromise, humility over pride, and surrender over self-will. Courage to obey means trusting God enough to follow His Word when it stretches you, corrects you, or calls you higher. It is reverence in action and conviction lived out. When you work out your own salvation with holy awe and steadfast resolve, you step into the person God designed you to be. You become refined through obedience, strengthened through discipline, and shaped by trust. Each act of faithfulness builds spiritual maturity and lasting character. Through steady obedience, your life becomes a living testimony. Others may not hear you preach, but they will see you walk. And in that faithful walk, courage transforms from a concept into a witness of faith in action.

| 27 |

"COURAGE TO FINISH STRONG"

Courage that refuses to quit is not loud, reckless, or impulsive. It does not need a spotlight or applause to validate it. It is steady. It is anchored. It is the quiet determination in a man's soul that says, "I will not stop until God finishes what He started in me." This kind of courage is born in prayer, strengthened in trials, and proven in consistency. It shows up when feelings fade, when progress is slow, and when no one is watching. It is the resolve to keep obeying, keep believing, and keep building even when the results are not yet visible. Anyone can begin with excitement. Inspiration is easy in the early stages. But few finish with endurance. Finishing strong requires a courage that outlasts emotion. It demands faith when the fire cools and discipline when motivation disappears. Real courage is not measured by how loudly a man starts, but by how faithfully he endures. The man who refuses to quit becomes the man God can complete because he stayed anchored long enough for the work to be finished.

Starting is easy when passion is high and the crowd is cheering. In the beginning, energy is fresh, vision is clear, and encouragement comes from every direction. There is something powerful about momentum and noise - about knowing others see your potential and celebrate your first steps. But the true measure of character is not revealed in the excitement of the launch; it is revealed in the discipline of the journey. Finishing strong often happens when the crowd has disappeared, when the applause has faded into silence, and when the road ahead feels longer than you imagined. Courage to finish strong is built in lonely places. It is formed in quiet mornings, in unseen sacrifices, and in moments when excuses seem easier than endurance. The decision to keep going and to refuse surrender when progress feels slow is what separates starters from finishers. Champions are not crowned because they began with passion; they are remembered because they endured with courage.

There will be moments when quitting feels logical. The resistance will seem justified. The obstacles will look immovable. But courage does not consult comfort - it obeys conviction. It does not bow to pressure or negotiate with fear. Courage stands anchored in what God said, not in what circumstances suggest. When doubt grows loud and progress seems invisible, courage remembers the assignment, the promise, and the purpose that were spoken long before the struggle appeared. Courage remembers the calling when circumstances try to erase it. It recalls the fire that once burned clearly in your heart and refuses to let temporary resistance rewrite a permanent destiny. Obstacles are not confirmations to quit; they are often confirmations that what you are pursuing matters. When quitting feels reasonable, courage chooses obedience. When the path looks blocked, courage looks beyond what is seen. And when everything around you says "stop," courage answers to something higher and says, "Press on."

Finishing strong is not about how fast you run but whether you refuse to leave the track. The Christian journey is a lifelong pursuit marked by steady obedience, daily surrender, and unwavering trust in God. There will be moments when your pace slows, when fatigue sets in, and when others seem to surge ahead. But faithfulness means you keep showing up. You keep praying. You keep believing. You keep walking when you cannot run. Many begin the race with intensity, but only those with resilient courage cross the line. Resilient courage is the quiet determination that refuses to quit when storms rise, when applause fades, and when progress feels invisible. It is the courage to endure hardship and to press forward when quitting would be easier. Finishing strong means you remain planted in your calling, anchored in truth, and committed to the course God set before you. In the end, victory belongs not to the fastest starter, but to the faithful finisher who stayed on the track until the very last step.

The enemy of finishing strong is not failure - it is fatigue. Failure can be confronted, corrected, and overcome. But fatigue is subtle. It seeps into your spirit after you've fought long battles, carried heavy responsibilities, and stood firm through storms. Weariness whispers, "You've done enough." Discouragement adds, "It's not worth it." It doesn't attack boldly; it erodes quietly. And if you are not careful, you will mistake exhaustion for completion and settle for stopping short of the promise. Many don't quit because they lost - they quit because they're tired. But courage rises in the weary heart knowing that the same grace that sustained you in the beginning is available for the end. The strength that carried you through the trial will carry you across the line. Finishing strong is not about having no weakness; it is about refusing to surrender to it. When your body is tired and your emotions are drained, lean into His strength. Lift your eyes beyond the moment and remember the promise. You are closer than you think.

There is a holy defiance in a man who refuses to quit. It is persistence anchored in the unchanging promises of God. This kind of defiance is born in the quiet place of prayer, forged in seasons of delay, and strengthened by the memory of what God has already done. Holy defiance does not shout to be seen; it stands because it knows. It understands that the same God who called, anointed, and appointed will also sustain and complete the work He began. This is the courage that whispers through clenched teeth, "Though I am tired, I will trust. Though I am tested, I will stand." It is not the absence of struggle; it is the decision to remain faithful in the middle of it. When storms rage and answers seem distant, holy defiance plants its feet and declares that feelings do not override faith. The believer may bend, but they will not break. They may weep, but they will not walk away. For their confidence is not in their own strength, but in the steadfast character of a faithful God who rewards those who endure.

Every great work of God faces resistance. Every calling encounters opposition. The moment heaven breathes purpose into a life, hell seems to take notice. Resistance is not a sign you missed God; often it is confirmation that you found Him. The enemy does not fight what is insignificant. He resists what carries weight, what threatens darkness, what advances the God's kingdom. When opposition rises, it is not time to retreat in fear but to root yourself deeper in faith. The measure of spiritual maturity is not how loudly you begin, but how steadfastly you endure when pressure increases. True maturity is proven in perseverance when prayers feel unanswered, when progress feels delayed, when the weight feels heavier than expected. Endurance is the quiet strength that refuses to let go of God's promise. It is the resolve that says, "I will remain faithful even when the fire burns." For in the endurance of pressure, character is refined, calling is clarified, and the work of God within you is made unshakable.

Courage to finish strong understands that pain is temporary, but purpose is eternal. Every assignment from God carries resistance yet the courageous heart sees beyond the moment. It recognizes that today's strain is not the final chapter - it's the refining fire shaping tomorrow's reward. Temporary discomfort cannot outweigh an eternal assignment. The ache in your body, the fatigue in your mind, and the opposition around you are all subject to time but the purpose placed inside you was born in eternity. When you remember that, endurance becomes possible. The cost of quitting is always greater than the cost of pressing on. Quitting may offer immediate relief, but it forfeits future impact. Pressing forward may demand sacrifice, but it preserves destiny. Finishing strong requires the bold decision to value purpose over pain and calling over comfort. The courageous man declares,

"This moment will pass, but my obedience will echo in eternity." So stand firm because what God started in you is worth finishing.

There are seasons when progress is invisible - when nothing seems to be moving, changing, or breaking through. Yet just because you cannot see growth does not mean it is not happening. Seeds do their most important work underground. Roots stretch deep before branches ever reach high. In the quiet, unseen places of your life, God is developing depth, resilience, and stability. What feels like delay is often divine preparation. What feels like silence is often sacred construction. Strength is forming beneath the surface, anchoring you for what is ahead. Courage holds steady in those hidden seasons. It understands that God is always working beyond what human eyes can perceive. When there are no visible results, faith becomes your sight and obedience becomes your movement. The underground season is not a wasted season - it is a rooting season. And when the time is right, what has been forming in silence will rise in strength, and what was hidden will become undeniable.

Finishing strong requires discipline when motivation fades. Anyone can start with excitement, but it takes maturity to continue when the thrill is gone and the feelings have shifted. Feelings fluctuate but commitment remains. Discipline is the bridge between where you are and the promise you're pursuing. It is the quiet decision to keep showing up, to keep praying, to keep building, to keep believing even when nothing around you seems to be moving. The finish line is not reached by bursts of emotion; it is reached by steady obedience. Courage is not sustained by emotion; it is sustained by devotion. Emotion may spark the fire, but devotion keeps it burning through the night. Devotion says, "I will remain faithful regardless of how I feel." It anchors you when enthusiasm wanes and strengthens you when doubt whispers. To finish strong, you must train your heart to follow your commitment rather than your feelings. When devotion leads, discipline follows. And when discipline is consistent, victory is inevitable.

The man who finishes strong does not wait until the battle intensifies to decide who he will be - he has already settled it in his spirit. Long before the pressure mounts, before fatigue sets in, before opposition rises, he has made a covenant with himself and with God that quitting is not an option. His resolve is not built in the storm; it is established before the storm ever forms. Because his decision is made in advance, he is not negotiating with adversity when it comes. He has already determined that the finish line is not a suggestion; it is his destination. For him, setbacks are not signals to retreat but stepping-stones to rise higher. Every delay develops endurance. Every hardship strengthens character. Every closed door refines his focus. His courage is predetermined. The man who finishes strong lives with a settled conviction that obstacles may slow him down, but they will never stop him. And because his courage is decided beforehand, his victory becomes inevitable.

There will be critics. There will be doubters. Some will question your calling because they cannot see what God showed you in private. Others will measure your progress by their comfort, not by your conviction. But you were never assigned to win their approval - you were called to walk in obedience. When God gives you an assignment, He does not consult the crowd for permission. Courage begins when you decide that faithfulness matters more than applause. Courage to finish strong is not fueled by approval; it is anchored in obedience. Approval fades. Applause quiets. Opinions shift with the wind. But obedience roots you in something eternal. When your steps are ordered by God, you can endure misunderstanding, opposition, and even isolation because you know Who sent you. Finishing strong is not about proving them wrong; it's about honoring Him right. Stay the course. Keep building. Keep believing. In the end, it is not the critic's voice that will matter - it is the Master saying, "Well done."

When the battle intensifies, courage recognizes that pressure is not a signal to quit but an invitation to lean in closer to God. When opposition rises and the weight feels heavier, courage prays deeper. It seeks wisdom instead of reacting in fear. It stands firmer, not because the storm has lessened, but because its foundation has strengthened. The heat of the fight refines focus, clarifies purpose, and strips away distractions. Finishing strong means adjusting strategy without abandoning mission. Warriors of faith understand that perseverance is not stubborn repetition; it is Spirit-led adaptation. You reassess, you realign, and you advance with renewed clarity. The mission remains sacred even if the tactics must evolve. When the battle intensifies, you do not shrink back - you grow wiser. You do not abandon the field - you fortify your position. And in doing so, you prove that true courage is not the absence of adversity, but the steadfast commitment to finish what God began in you.

Some victories are not celebrated publicly. There is no applause when you resist temptation in the quiet of your own thoughts. No spotlight shines when you choose forgiveness instead of bitterness, discipline instead of compromise, faith instead of fear. Yet those hidden moments are often the greatest battles you will ever fight. The world may not recognize them, but they shape your character, strengthen your spirit, and deepen your resolve. And though no crowd may cheer, those victories matter more than many that are displayed on public stages. Heaven records every act of endurance. Every unseen decision to continue and every step forward fueled by faith are testimonies of unwavering courage. God honors the steadfast heart that refuses to quit. The courage to keep going when no one is watching reveals a strength that is not dependent on recognition but rooted in conviction. What you endure faithfully today becomes the foundation of the breakthrough you will walk into tomorrow.

To finish strong is to guard your heart against bitterness. Along the journey, wounds will come, disappointments will sting, and prayers may seem delayed. The temptation is not merely to quit - it is to grow cold. Bitterness quietly convinces you that what hurt you has the right to define you. But finishing strong means you refuse to let pain write your story. You protect your spirit with forgiveness, humility, and trust in God's greater purpose. You understand that what tried to break you can instead build you, if you keep your heart tender and your faith steady. The fire does not choose the outcome - you do. Courage chooses refinement. It leans into the heat and refuses to allow hardship to corrupt character or distort vision. Instead of shrinking back, courage submits to the process, confident that God wastes nothing. To finish strong is to emerge from adversity with deeper compassion, stronger faith, and a purified heart - proof that endurance, when surrendered to God, becomes transformation.

Strength grows in resistance. Muscles do not develop in comfort; they are forged under tension, stretched beyond what feels easy, and rebuilt stronger because of the pressure placed upon them. In the same way, your spirit is strengthened when it pushes against opposition. Every challenge you face is an opportunity to grow beyond yesterday's limits. When you refuse to run from difficulty, you position yourself to become stronger, wiser, and more disciplined than you ever were before. Faith matures in adversity. It is easy to speak of belief when the skies are clear, but unshakable faith is born in the storm. Courage that refuses to quit becomes immovable because it has been tested and proven. When you stand firm and trust God despite uncertainty - you are building a foundation that cannot be easily shaken. What survives the trial becomes resilient, steady, and confident. Tested courage is lasting courage, and proven faith becomes the anchor that holds you secure no matter what rises against you.

One day, the race will end and the assignment will be complete. What will matter is not how loudly you started, but how faithfully you finished. Many begin with passion; few endure with perseverance. There will be hills that test your strength, valleys that challenge your faith, and stretches of road where no one is cheering your name. Yet courage is proven not in the excitement of the starting line, but in the quiet determination to keep moving when the path is long and the finish line is not yet in sight. Courage to finish strong is the legacy of a life fully surrendered to God's purpose. It is the steady "yes" whispered daily to His will, even when it costs comfort, recognition, or ease. A surrendered life understands that faithfulness in the unseen places carries eternal weight. When the final chapter is written, and the race is complete, may it be said that you did not merely begin with zeal, but you endured with integrity, trusted with unwavering hope, and crossed the finish line still holding firmly to the hand of God.

Stand firm. Refuse to quit. There will be moments when fatigue whispers that you have done enough, when pressure clouds your focus and the weight feels heavier than your strength. In those moments, lift your eyes higher. Fix your vision beyond the strain, beyond the noise, beyond the temporary battle in front of you. When discouragement knocks, remind yourself why you started, who you are, and what you are called to do. Let your courage be relentless, not dependent on circumstances but rooted in conviction. Let your faith be immovable, anchored deep where doubt cannot uproot it. The finish line is not reserved for the swift alone, but for the steadfast. It belongs to those who hold their ground when others retreat, who stay faithful when it would be easier to fold. Every step forward, even the small and trembling ones, is a declaration that quitting is not an option. And when you cross that finish line, do so with your head lifted high knowing you honored the call placed upon your life, and finished strong.

| 28 |

"COURAGE THAT COUNTS"

Not all courage is created equal. Some courage is loud, visible, and applauded by crowds. It stands on stages, charges into obvious battles, and receives recognition for its bold display. But there is another kind of courage that rarely gets celebrated and rarely draws applause. It is the courage to stand firm when no one is watching, to choose integrity when compromise would be easier, to forgive when pride demands retaliation, and to keep believing when doubt whispers defeat. This courage does not need an audience because its strength is not fueled by attention but by conviction. The courage that truly counts is often quiet, unseen, and tested in the private battles of the heart. It is not proven in the spotlight but in the secret place where character is shaped and destiny is determined. Public victories are simply the overflow of private obedience. The world may celebrate the visible triumph, but heaven honors the hidden resolve that made it possible.

Courage that counts is the strength to obey God when obedience costs you something. It is choosing righteousness when compromise would be easier, more profitable, or more popular. Real courage does not always look dramatic; often it is unseen and uncelebrated. It is forged in private decisions, in moments when no one is watching but God, and it is proven when the pressure to conform is greatest. Standing firm when bending would bring temporary relief requires deep conviction.

True courage is not about bravado, loud declarations, or outward displays of toughness; it is about an inward anchor that refuses to drift. It is the settled assurance that obedience to God is worth any sacrifice. Conviction steadies the heart, strengthens the spine, and fixes the eyes on eternal reward rather than temporary ease. Courage that counts chooses faithfulness over fear, integrity over impulse, and obedience over convenience trusting that God honors those who honor Him.

The world celebrates bold personalities and headline-making confidence. It applauds the visible and the victorious. But heaven honors faithful hearts. The courage that truly counts is not driven by applause or recognition; it is anchored in obedience. It does not ask, "How will this make me look?" but rather, "How will this honor God?" Real courage is often quiet. It shows up in unseen prayers, in integrity when no one is watching, and in steadfast commitment when compromise would be easier. Courage that counts does not seek attention; it seeks alignment. It asks one question above all others, "What does God require of me in this moment?" And then it acts accordingly. Whether the step is small or monumental, public or private, faithful courage moves in step with heaven's will. It chooses obedience over popularity, conviction over comfort, and surrender over self-promotion. In the end, the boldest life is not the one that draws the most eyes, but the one that remains aligned with the heart of God.

This kind of courage is not loud, reckless, or driven by ego - it is forged in surrender. Before it ever stands before people, it kneels before God. It understands that true strength does not begin with self-confidence but with God-confidence. Before it speaks publicly, it listens privately, allowing the whisper of the Holy Spirit to shape its words and steady its heart. This courage is not rushed into action; it is rooted in communion. The courage that truly counts is born in prayer, strengthened in scripture, and refined through obedience. It is developed when no one is watching and proven when everyone is. It grows each time we choose faith over feelings and obedience over comfort. As the Word of God renews the mind and aligns the heart, boldness becomes the natural byproduct of intimacy with Him. This surrendered courage does not strive for applause - it seeks God's approval. And when it finally rises to stand, it carries the authority, peace, and power that can only come from a life first bowed in reverence.

Many want courage for the spotlight of victory, but few desire courage for the silent grind of the process. It is easy to celebrate boldness when the battle is won and the outcome is visible. But true courage is not proven in applause - it is forged in obscurity. It is developed in the long nights of prayer, the unseen sacrifices, and the steady obedience when nothing seems to be changing. Real courage is revealed in endurance. It is the quiet decision to keep believing when prayers seem unanswered, to keep serving when recognition is absent, and to keep loving when appreciation is lacking. It is choosing faith over feelings, commitment over convenience, and character over comfort. This kind of courage does not shout - it stands. It does not quit - it continues. And in the end, the courage to endure becomes the very strength that carries you into the victory you once prayed for. The process you survived becomes the platform you stand on, and the perseverance you practiced becomes the power you walk in.

Courage that counts is not the absence of fear; it is the mastery of it. Fear may knock at the door of your mind, whispering doubts and painting worst-case scenarios across your imagination, but courage answers with faith. It does not deny the presence of uncertainty - it stands firm in spite of it. True courage looks fear in the face and declares that feelings are not final and circumstances are not sovereign. It chooses trust over panic, obedience over retreat, and conviction over comfort. Real courage declares that God is greater than uncertainty, stronger than opposition, and faithful beyond what eyes can see. It anchors the heart when the winds of adversity blow and steadies the soul when the path ahead is unclear. Courage rooted in faith says, "I will move forward because God goes before me." It rises not from human strength alone, but from confidence in a faithful Father who never fails. When faith speaks louder than fear, courage that counts is born and victory begins in the heart long before it appears in reality.

This courage is anchored deep in trust, conviction, and unwavering confidence in God's character. It does not charge ahead trying to force doors open, nor does it shrink back in fear waiting for perfect conditions. Instead, it moves with holy alignment, attentive to the whisper of divine direction. Rooted courage listens before it steps, prays before it speaks, and trusts before it acts. It understands that true strength is in walking steadily in rhythm with the One who orders every step. This kind of courage also recognizes the seriousness of obedience. It knows that delayed obedience is still disobedience, and partial obedience is still compromise. Rooted courage does not negotiate with conviction or edit God's instructions to fit comfort zones. It responds fully, faithfully, and promptly because when courage is rooted in God, it does not have to strive to be bold - it simply stands firm, moves when He says move, and remains when He says remain, confident that obedience is the truest expression of faith.

There will be moments when courage demands that you stand alone, trusting that even in solitude you are anchored in conviction and strengthened by faith. In those seasons, the applause may fade and the crowd may thin. Friends may misunderstand your obedience. Critics may question your direction. Doubt may whisper in the quiet hours, trying to convince you to compromise or retreat. Yet true courage is not the absence of opposition - it is the resolve to remain faithful when standing feels lonely. It is choosing conviction over comfort and obedience over approval. When your foundation is secure in God's truth, you are not easily shaken by shifting opinions or passing storms. The voices around you may rise and fall, but His Word remains steady and unchanging. A life anchored in Him is not built on popularity, but on purpose. So stand firm. Stand faithful. Stand confident. For when God is your foundation, you may stand alone in the eyes of men, but you are never standing alone at all.

Courage that counts chooses character over comfort. It refuses the easy road when that road leads away from integrity. It stands firm when compromise would be convenient and silence would be safer. This kind of courage is not loud or boastful; it is steady and rooted. It chooses integrity over image, knowing that reputation may impress people, but character honors God. When the pressure rises and the spotlight burns bright, true courage remains unmoved, anchored in conviction rather than applause. Courage that counts also chooses long-term reward over short-term relief. It resists the temptation to escape discomfort through quick fixes or shallow decisions. It understands that the greatest victories are not over external enemies but over internal weaknesses. The battlefield of the heart is where real strength is forged. When a person conquers themselves, they become unstoppable in purpose, disciplined in spirit, and powerful in influence. That is the courage that lasts.

Often, the greatest act of courage is forgiveness. It does not always look bold or dramatic, yet it requires a strength deeper than retaliation. It takes courage to release an offense when every emotion demands justice. It takes courage to bless those who misunderstand you, misjudge you, or even wound you. Forgiveness is not weakness; it is spiritual authority under control. It is choosing peace over pride, healing over hurt, and freedom over resentment. True courage is not proven in how hard we fight back, but in how freely we let go. It takes courage to lay down bitterness and embrace freedom. Bitterness chains the heart to the past, but forgiveness unlocks the future. When you forgive, you refuse to allow someone else's actions to define your destiny. You step out of the prison of offense and into the liberty of grace. Forgiveness restores joy and makes room for new beginnings.

And in that release, you discover that the bravest thing you can do is trust God enough to let it go.

Courage is not always loud. It does not always raise its voice, pound its chest, or rush into every confrontation. Real courage has discernment. It knows when to speak and when to remain silent. Not every battle requires your response, and not every accusation deserves your energy. Some fights are distractions sent to drain your focus and pull you away from your purpose. Wisdom-filled courage understands that strength is not proven by reacting to everything but by responding only when God directs. Sometimes the bravest thing you can do is stand still and trust God to defend you. While others argue, you remain faithful. While others accuse, you stay anchored. Silence, when led by faith, is not weakness - it is confidence in divine justice. Courage that trusts God does not feel the need to win every argument, because it knows the Lord fights for those who remain steadfast. Stay faithful. Stay obedient. Let God handle what you cannot, and He will vindicate you in His perfect time.

There is courage in humility. In a world that celebrates image, power, and performance, it takes uncommon strength to lower your guard and admit you don't have it all together. Pretending to be strong is easy - it's a mask anyone can wear. But admitting weakness requires a deeper, steadier kind of strength. It means you are secure enough in who you are - and whose you are - to stop striving for approval. Confessing your need is not a sign of failure; it is a declaration of faith. That kind of honesty takes boldness. The courage that truly counts is the courage to be honest before God and authentic before others. It is the bravery to kneel when pride tells you to stand tall, to ask for help when ego says stay silent, and to confess when hiding seems safer. Real courage is not loud or boastful; it is quiet, surrendered, and grounded in truth. When you choose humility, you step into freedom. When you admit your need, you make room for God's strength to be revealed.

This courage refuses to quit. It does not fold when the wind rises or retreat when the pruning begins. It understands that growth is rarely comfortable and that pressure is often the proof that something valuable is being formed. This courage knows that endurance is not passive suffering but active persistence - a steady decision to remain faithful when results are not yet visible. It trusts that every season of pruning is shaping deeper roots, stronger character, and unshakable resolve. This courage understands that endurance produces maturity, and maturity produces fruit. It recognizes that hardship is not punishment but preparation for greater responsibility, greater influence, and greater impact. Instead of asking, "Why is this happening to me?" it asks, "What is this producing in me?" And because of that perspective, it keeps moving forward. It perseveres, it grows, and in time, it bears fruit that could only have been cultivated through seasons of pruning and pressure.

Courage that counts does not measure success by applause but by obedience. It refuses to bow to the noise of the crowd or the pressure of popular opinion. The world celebrates what is seen, shared, and praised, but heaven honors what is faithful, surrendered, and aligned with God's will. Courage that counts is anchored in conviction, not compliments. It stands firm even when misunderstood, criticized, or ignored, because its reward is not earthly validation but divine affirmation. To live for an audience of One is to walk in steady confidence, knowing that obedience outweighs recognition. It means choosing integrity when compromise would be easier and righteousness when applause would be louder. This kind of courage is quiet but powerful, unseen but eternal. It finds peace not in approval ratings but in the presence of God. When the day is done, the only evaluation that truly matters is not the cheers of people, but the pleasure of the Father. That is courage that counts.

When storms arise, courage anchors itself in truth. It does not drift with fear or bend with every gust of uncertainty. Instead, it steadies the heart by remembering what God has already done. It recalls past victories - those moments when the odds were heavy, the night seemed long and yet dawn still came. Courage draws strength from testimony. It whispers, "If He did it before, He will do it again." In the middle of chaos, it chooses to stand on what is eternal rather than what is temporary. Courage also recalls God's faithfulness. It plants its feet on promises that outlast circumstances and refuses to be shaken by changing winds. The storm may roar, the rain may fall, and the ground may tremble, but the foundation remains secure. Truth does not erode under pressure. It holds firm because it is rooted in the character of God. And when everything around you feels unstable, courage reminds you that you are not standing on the storm - you are standing on the Rock.

Every generation needs men who embody courage that counts. Real courage is not loud, flashy, or self-promoting - it is steady, sacrificial, and steadfast. It shows up early, stays late, keeps its word, and refuses to bow when conviction is tested. It anchors families, strengthens churches, and stabilizes communities because it is built on character rather than charisma. Courage that counts is forged in private long before it is revealed in public. It is cultivated in prayer, refined in obedience, and proven through consistency. These men are not driven by ego but by eternal purpose. They love boldly, lead humbly, and serve faithfully, understanding that true strength is measured by what they build in others. When storms rise, they don't fall apart - they rise above and become the shelter. When confusion spreads, they do not retreat - they become clarity. Every generation rises or falls on the depth of its men, and the call remains the same: stand firm, live true, and embody a courage that leaves a legacy.

Courage will always demand a price. It will cost you comfort when you choose conviction over ease. It will cost you popularity when you stand firm while others compromise. It will cost you convenience when you obey what is right instead of what is simple. The courageous path often feels lonely in the moment, but it is never wasted. Every bold decision to do what is right, every refusal to bow to pressure, and every step taken in faith rather than fear builds an inner strength that cannot be shaken. It produces peace because you know you honored your convictions. It produces strength because resistance builds resilience. And it produces lasting impact because brave obedience leaves a legacy others can follow. The sacrifices made in courage today become the testimonies of tomorrow. What feels like loss now becomes a story of breakthrough later. Courage may cost you something in the present, but it will reward you with purpose, influence, and a life marked by integrity that echoes far beyond the moment.

In the end, the courage that truly counts is the steady courage to trust God completely. It is faith in action when the outcome is uncertain. It is obedience under pressure when compromise would be easier. It is choosing righteousness when no one is watching and standing firm when everyone else is bending. This kind of courage does not depend on applause or approval; it is rooted in conviction. It believes that God is faithful, that His promises are sure, and that His ways are higher even when the path is difficult. It is also steadfast love in a shifting world. While culture changes and opinions fluctuate, godly courage remains anchored in truth. It forgives when offended, serves when unrecognized, and perseveres when misunderstood. May you walk in this courage quietly in humility, faithfully in devotion, and boldly in conviction. May your life reflect not just moments of bravery, but a consistent trust in God that shapes your words, guides your decisions, and leaves a legacy of courage that truly counts.

| 29 |

"THE LEGACY OF COURAGE"

Courage is never accidental. It does not appear by chance, nor does it grow in the soft soil of ease. It is forged in the private places where pride is surrendered and faith is chosen. It is shaped in the fires of adversity, where pressure refines character and trials strip away every false strength. When fear demands silence but faith commands movement, courage rises not because fear is absent, but because conviction is greater. The legacy of courage is not built in comfort; it is established in conviction. It is anchored in the unwavering belief that obedience matters more than approval and purpose outweighs popularity. True courage leaves footprints for others to follow, not because it sought recognition, but because it chose righteousness. It stands when standing costs something. It speaks when silence would be safer. And long after the moment has passed, the impact remains - proof that a surrendered heart, tested by fire and led by faith, can build a legacy that outlives the fear that once tried to silence it.

Every generation inherits something. Some inherit wealth. Some inherit wounds. But the greatest inheritance a person can leave is courage. Courage is more than a moment of bravery; it is a pattern of faithfulness etched into the soul. It is the quiet decision to stand for truth when compromise would be easier, to forgive when bitterness feels justified, and to trust God when outcomes are uncertain. Courage plants something eternal in the hearts of those who witness it. It becomes a living testimony that obedience is worth the cost and that faith is stronger than fear. Courage plants seeds in the hearts of those who watch us stand when it would have been easier to bow. When people see steadfast faith in the face of adversity, a legacy is formed that cannot be erased by time. Long after applause has quieted and accomplishments have been forgotten, the imprint of courage remains - calling the next generation to rise, to believe, and to stand firm in their own hour of testing.

Courage begins with identity. When you know who you are in Christ, fear loses its authority. The enemy thrives on confusion, but courage thrives on clarity. A man who knows he belongs to God cannot be easily intimidated by circumstances. Identity anchors the soul when storms rise and voices of doubt attempt to speak louder than truth. When you understand that you are chosen, redeemed, and empowered by the Spirit of God, you stop reacting out of insecurity and start responding out of conviction. That revelation silences fear because fear feeds on uncertainty, but faith stands firm on what God has already declared about you. Challenges may still come but they no longer define you. Your confidence is rooted in Christ, not in comfort, applause, or outcomes. The enemy may attempt to intimidate, but intimidation only works on those unsure of their authority. When you know you are a child of God, called and commissioned, you stand steady with uncommon courage that refuses to bow to fear.

The legacy of courage is the steady decision to walk in righteousness when compromise would be convenient and applause would be easier to win. True courage is formed in the unseen moments when no crowd is watching, no reward is guaranteed, and no recognition is promised. It is choosing integrity over influence, character over comfort, and conviction over convenience. It is telling the truth when deception would be profitable and honoring God when dishonor seems more advantageous. This kind of courage does not always draw attention, but it draws heaven. It is standing alone if necessary because you know heaven stands with you. It is the confidence that obedience matters more than popularity and that faithfulness outlives fame. A courageous life leaves a quiet but powerful imprint - children learn from it, communities are strengthened by it, and generations are shaped because of it. The legacy of courage is a life that whispers, "I will obey," and in that whisper shakes eternity.

Throughout scripture, courage was always connected to calling. Joshua was told to "be strong and courageous" not as a motivational slogan, but because he had an assignment that demanded it. The promise of the land required the bravery to step into it. The presence of giants required the resolve to face them. When heaven assigns destiny, it also supplies the strength to pursue it. Courage is not random boldness - it is the backbone of obedience when the stakes are high and the path is unfamiliar. Courage is required wherever destiny is involved. If your calling is great, your courage must grow to match it. The size of your assignment will stretch the limits of your comfort, your confidence, and sometimes even your reputation. But destiny does not bow to fear. It responds to faith-filled action. As God enlarges your vision, He simultaneously enlarges your capacity to stand firm. The greater the calling, the deeper the dependence and the stronger the courage He develops within you.

Fear whispers in the quiet places of the heart, painting pictures of defeat before a single step is taken. It magnifies the giants and rehearses the pain of a loss that has not yet happened. Fear imagines the battle already lost and convinces the soul to retreat before the first stone is ever thrown. But fear is a storyteller, not a prophet. It speaks possibilities rooted in doubt, not promises grounded in truth. Courage does not pretend the giants aren't standing in your path. It looks them in the eyes and refuses to back down and surrender the ground that faith has already claimed. Courage steps forward not because the path is easy, but because God has already gone ahead. It trusts that obedience is greater than outcome and that faithfulness matters more than applause. Courage understands that victory is not the absence of struggle - it is the decision to move forward despite it. And when a believer chooses courage over fear, heaven backs the step that faith is bold enough to take.

The legacy of courage is not forged in a single dramatic moment; it is built decision by decision. It is built when you pray instead of panic, anchoring your heart in God's promises rather than the noise of fear. It is built when you forgive instead of retaliating, choosing freedom over bitterness and grace over pride. It is built when you believe instead of doubt, standing on what God has spoken even when circumstances try to preach a different sermon. These daily choices accumulate into something far greater than you realize. They become an example your children and your spiritual sons and daughters will one day lean upon when their own storms arise. They may not remember every word you preached, but they will remember the life you lived. They will recall how you handled pressure, how you carried disappointment, how you responded when the battle intensified. And when their moment of testing comes, your courage will speak for them, reminding them that faith works and that God is faithful.

Courage always costs something. It may cost your comfort, calling you out of familiar surroundings into uncertain territory. It may cost relationships when others misunderstand your convictions or resist your growth. It may even cost your reputation when you choose integrity over popularity. But whatever courage costs, cowardice costs more. Courage demands a temporary sacrifice; cowardice demands a lifelong payment plan of compromise. Every bold step forward requires surrendering ease, approval, and sometimes applause but it positions you to walk in purpose, truth, and freedom. The price of fear is regret, and regret is a burden far heavier than temporary sacrifice. Courage may wound your pride or stretch your faith but regret slowly drains your spirit with missed opportunities and unrealized potential. Temporary discomfort refines you; prolonged fear confines you.

When you choose courage, you may feel the sting of the moment, but you will never carry the weight of wishing you had tried.

A courageous life teaches others how to live because courage is never private. Your family is watching how you respond to pressure - whether you panic or pray, whether you react in anger or stand in steady faith. Your community is watching how you handle injustice - whether you remain silent to protect comfort or speak truth with humility and conviction. Your church is watching how you endure trials - whether you retreat when faith is tested or remain planted when the winds rise. In every arena of life, your response becomes someone else's lesson. One bold act may inspire, but a pattern of bold living transforms atmospheres. When you stand firm in adversity, you give others permission to do the same. When you choose integrity over ease, you raise the standard for everyone around you. A courageous life does not merely survive difficulty - it models faith, resilience, and trust in God through it. And in doing so, it leaves behind a blueprint for bravery that others can follow.

The legacy of courage requires endurance. It is not enough to start strong; you must finish strong. Many begin with passion but retreat when resistance intensifies, mistaking early enthusiasm for lasting strength. But true courage is proven over time. Anyone can surge forward when inspiration is fresh, but legacy is built by those who remain when the road grows steep. Endurance transforms a bold beginning into a faithful finish. Courage presses forward when enthusiasm fades and discipline must take its place. It chooses commitment over convenience and conviction over comfort. The world celebrates quick victories, but heaven honors steadfast hearts. Finishing strong requires grit anchored in purpose and faith rooted deeper than circumstances. Those who endure become pillars for the next generation, proving that courage is not a moment - it is a lifelong decision to stand, to persevere, and to complete what God has called you to begin.

Spiritual courage is rooted in trust. It is not self-confidence; it is God-confidence. It does not rise from your own strength, talent, or resolve, but from an unwavering assurance in who God is. It declares with bold conviction, "The Lord is my helper; I will not fear." This kind of courage is steady because its foundation is steady. When your heart is anchored in God's faithfulness, His promises become your security. You are no longer driven by circumstance or intimidated by opposition, because your trust is not in what you see - it is in the One who sees all. When your confidence is anchored in God's character, storms may shake you, but they will not move you. Trials may test you, but they will not define you. Fear may whisper, but faith will speak louder. Spiritual courage stands firm not because life is easy, but because God is unchanging. The winds may howl and the waves may rise, yet the soul that trusts in the Lord remains planted and unshaken.

Courage transforms pain into purpose. What the enemy meant to break you becomes the very testimony that builds others. The wounds you once tried to hide become windows through which God's glory shines. The nights you cried, the battles you fought in silence, and the valleys you thought would bury you were actually shaping you. God was building strength in your struggle, wisdom in your waiting, and faith in your fire. Your scars become sermons. Your trials become training grounds. Your endurance becomes evidence of God's sustaining power. The very places where you were stretched are the places from which you now speak with authority and compassion. Because you endured, you can encourage. Because you survived, you can strengthen others. What once felt like devastation has become divine development. Courage does not deny the pain - it redeems it. And when you stand and testify, you prove that what was meant for harm has been transformed into holy purpose.

The legacy of courage refuses to be silent in the face of darkness. It does not whisper when truth must be declared, nor does it retreat when conviction is challenged. True courage defends the weak when they have no voice, stands in the gap when others step back, and protects what is sacred even when the cost is high. Courage understands that silence in moments of moral crisis is agreement with injustice. A lasting legacy of courage refuses to allow culture to dictate conviction. While the world bends to pressure and applause, courage remains steady, grounded in principle and guided by faith. It does not conform to popular opinion, nor does it trade integrity for acceptance. Courage stands firm when standing alone becomes necessary. It holds the line when compromise seems easier. And long after the noise of culture fades, the echo of courageous lives continues to inspire generations because when courage stands firm, it builds a legacy that darkness cannot overcome.

True courage is humble. It does not step forward to be seen; it steps forward because it must. It does not wait for applause, nor does it measure its obedience by recognition. It moves quietly, confidently, anchored in conviction rather than praise. The courageous heart understands that doing what is right is its own reward, for integrity before God and faithfulness to truth produce a peace and strength no applause or recognition could ever equal. It chooses integrity over image, obedience over opportunity, and faithfulness over fame. While others chase validation, true courage remains steady, content to stand firm even when no one is watching. Heaven records what earth may overlook. God honors what the world ignores. The humble act of courage offered in secret carries eternal weight. When no spotlight shines and no crowd applauds, heaven still takes notice. And in the end, it is not the noise of men but the approval of God that defines a life of true courage.

Courage also knows when to kneel. There is bravery in battle, but there is also bravery in surrender. It takes courage to repent, to lay pride down at the altar and confess that you were wrong. It takes courage to admit weakness in a world that rewards image over integrity. It takes courage to ask for help when your heart is weary and your strength feels spent. Kneeling is not quitting; it is choosing humility over ego and truth over pretense. The strongest warriors are not those who never bow, but those who bow before God and rise transformed. Strength is not the absence of vulnerability; it is the refusal to let vulnerability define you. True strength faces its frailties and still moves forward. It acknowledges the wound yet refuses to live as a victim. It accepts correction without collapsing into shame. There is power in the man who can still stand firm in faith. Courage does not hide scars; it redeems them. It does not deny weakness; it surrenders weakness to God and walks on in renewed resolve.

The legacy of courage is generational. When one person chooses to stand in truth, integrity, and faith, it creates a ripple that reaches far beyond the moment. Courage echoes through families, churches, communities, and nations. When you refuse to bow to fear, you silently give others permission to rise above theirs. Your stand becomes a standard. Your faith becomes a foundation. The seeds of bravery you plant today may bloom in the hearts of those who watched you trust God when it would have been easier to retreat. You may never fully see the impact of your yes, but heaven records it and generations benefit from it. Every act of faithful courage shifts spiritual atmospheres and opens doors others were too weary or too wounded to push through alone. When you step forward in obedience, chains break from those connected to you. The legacy of courage is not about personal recognition; it is about generational transformation. Stand firm. Someone is rising because you did.

You are writing your legacy every single day long before it is ever carved into stone or remembered in stories. It is written in the integrity you choose when compromise would be easier. It is written in the quiet acts of service, the unseen sacrifices, and the steady decision to fight the good fight of faith when doubt whispers and pressure mounts. Legacy is not built in one grand moment; it is formed in daily obedience. Every conversation, every response to adversity, every act of courage or kindness becomes a sentence in the story your life is telling. The question is not whether you will leave a legacy but what kind it will be. Will it be a legacy of bitterness or belief? Of fear or faith? Of self-preservation or selfless service? Your choices today echo into tomorrow. Live deliberately. Speak life. Stand firm. Because the legacy you are building is not just about how you will be remembered - it is about how others will be strengthened because you chose to live boldly, faithfully, and with purpose.

Every day presents a crossroads and every decision shapes the story you are writing with your life. When you choose faith over fear, you align your heart with God's promises instead of your circumstances. When you choose obedience over comfort, you declare that His will matters more than your ease. When you choose purpose over popularity, you build something eternal rather than something temporary. Live in such a way that when your life is finished, it can be said that you stood firm in the storm, trusted God fully in uncertainty, and refused to bow to pressure or applause. Let your faith be louder than your fear and your obedience stronger than your desire for approval. May your life preach long after your lips grow silent. May your choices carve a testimony that inspires generations. And when history tells your story, may it be said that you chose courage, you trusted God, and you left behind a legacy that still calls others to stand, believe, and move forward in bold, unwavering faith.

| 30 |

"LIVING WITH UNCOMMON COURAGE"

Living with uncommon courage is not about one heroic moment that earns applause; it is about a lifetime of faithful decisions made when no one is watching. It is forged in the quiet places of the heart, where conviction outweighs convenience and obedience matters more than ease. True courage is not proven in seasons of comfort but revealed in times of conflict. It shows up when pressure mounts, when fear whispers, and when compromise seems easier than commitment, yet you stand firm anyway. Uncommon courage is formed when ordinary men choose purpose over popularity and faithfulness over fleeting approval. It is the daily decision to honor your values, to walk in integrity, and to remain steadfast when the road narrows. It is not loud, but it is powerful. Not flashy, but enduring. And over time, those consistent, courageous choices shape a life that leaves a legacy - one defined not by a single bold act, but by steadfast devotion to what is right.

Uncommon courage begins where fear ends its rule. Fear will always knock at the door of destiny, whispering doubt, magnifying risk, and urging retreat. Yet it is not fear that determines your future - it is your response to it. Courage decides who answers that knock. The brave are not those who never tremble; they are those who move forward while trembling. They feel the weight of uncertainty, the pressure of opposition, and the vulnerability of risk, yet they refuse to surrender their calling to intimidation. Uncommon courage is born in the moment you choose obedience over anxiety, conviction over comfort, and purpose over panic. It is the quiet, resolute decision to step forward when every part of you wants to step back. Fear may speak loudly, but courage speaks with authority. Fear is a feeling that comes and goes; courage is a decision that defines who you become. When you decide to act despite the trembling, you break fear's rule and step into destiny.

To live with uncommon courage is to reject mediocrity, complacency, and spiritual passivity, choosing instead to rise into the fullness of who God created you to be. Uncommon courage dares to believe that you were not designed for the sidelines but for significance. It boldly declares, "I was made for more," and then backs that declaration with relentless faith and decisive action. It understands that potential is a gift, but fulfillment requires pursuit. Those who live this way refuse to settle for comfort when they are called to growth, and they will not trade eternal purpose for temporary ease. When adversity tightens its grip and fear whispers retreat, uncommon courage stands firm and presses forward. The courageous may feel the weight of the moment, but they will not bow to it. They grow through resistance, sharpened by opposition and strengthened by trials. They know that pressure does not come to crush them but to reveal the strength that was within them all along.

True courage is steady confidence rooted in truth. It is quiet but unshakable, humble yet immovable. When values are challenged and convictions are tested, courage does not panic or posture - it stands firm. It holds its ground without hostility and speaks with clarity without compromise. Courage understands that volume is not power; consistency is. It is the calm resolve to remain anchored when the pressure to drift feels overwhelming. Courage does not bend to cultural winds or bow to temporary trends. It is guided by principle, not popularity. While others may chase approval or shift with the moment, courage remains faithful to what is right. It recognizes that integrity today builds legacy tomorrow. Every decision made in truth lays a foundation for influence that outlives the present season. Courage sees beyond immediate comfort and chooses lasting character over fleeting applause, knowing that a life built on conviction will stand long after the noise fades.

Uncommon courage requires uncommon discipline. You cannot drift into bravery; you must decide to pursue it long before the moment demands it. Courage is not a spontaneous reaction but a cultivated response. It is forged in quiet places where habits are built, convictions are clarified, and weaknesses are confronted. When you strengthen your mind with truth, anchor your spirit in unwavering faith, and sharpen your character through daily obedience, you are preparing for battles you may not yet see. The battles of life are won by preparation. When pressure rises and opposition appears, you will not rise to the level of your hopes - you will fall to the level of your training. Every act of integrity, every choice to stand firm when compromise would be easier, and every moment of perseverance when quitting seems justified is building unseen strength. Uncommon courage is the result of consistent commitment. It is the reward of those who prepare in private so they can prevail in public.

Living courageously means speaking truth when silence would be easier. It means choosing conviction over comfort and integrity over approval. Courage does not wait for consensus; it rises from character. When the pressure mounts and the room grows quiet, the courageous heart refuses to compromise what it knows is right. It understands that silence in the face of wrong is not neutrality - it is surrender. To live with courage is to value truth more than popularity and principle more than peace. History has always been shaped by those willing to stand when others sit, to speak when others stay quiet, to act when others hesitate. Every turning point began with someone who refused to bow to fear. They stood alone if necessary, anchored by belief and driven by purpose. Courageous living is rarely applauded in the moment, but it is always honored in the long run. The legacy of the bold is not built in comfort - it is forged in conviction.

Courage will cost you. It may cost you approval from those who prefer convenience over conviction. It may even strain relationships or close doors that once seemed promising. Courage rarely travels the path of least resistance; it walks the narrow road of integrity. When you choose what is right over what is popular, what is true over what is trending, and what is eternal over what is temporary, there is often a price to pay. But that price is an investment, not a loss. What courage gives in return is far greater than what it takes. It gives you peace of conscience - the quiet confidence of knowing you stood firm. It forges strength of character that cannot be shaken by opinion or opposition. It aligns your life with purpose, anchoring your steps in meaning rather than impulse. There is no regret in bravery, only growth. Every courageous decision stretches you, strengthens you, and shapes you into the person you were created to become. In the end, courage does not diminish your life - it defines it.

Uncommon courage transforms adversity into advantage. It refuses to be paralyzed by pain or defined by difficulty. While others ask, "Why is this happening to me?" the courageous dare to ask, "What is this shaping within me?" That single shift in perspective changes everything. Instead of becoming victims of circumstance, they become students of it. Adversity becomes the classroom where endurance is forged and purpose is clarified. Pressure does not destroy the brave - it develops them. Just as fire refines gold and resistance strengthens muscle, life's challenges reveal what is truly inside a person. Courage under pressure exposes integrity, awakens resilience, and cultivates unshakable confidence. The brave do not deny the weight of the moment; they grow beneath it. They rise from storms wiser, steadier, and more equipped than before. What was meant to test them ultimately trains them, and what once felt like opposition becomes the very tool that propels them forward.

Courage builds resilience. It is the steady force within that refuses to surrender when life pushes back. When setbacks come, the courageous rise again because they have decided the fall will not define them. When doors close, they search for new doors to knock on, new paths to pioneer, new opportunities to grow. When storms rage, they anchor deeper, fastening their hope to something stronger than the wind. The courageous understand that endurance is strength under control. It is power disciplined by patience. It is emotion mastered by purpose. Resilience is forged in repetition choosing faith over fear again and again, choosing effort over excuses, choosing perseverance over retreat. Every trial becomes training. Every delay becomes development. Every challenge becomes conditioning. And in time, what once threatened to break them becomes the very weight that strengthened them. Courage does not eliminate hardship; it transforms it into the foundation of unshakable strength.

Living with uncommon courage means choosing to lead by example when it would be easier to blend in. It is the daily decision to stand firm in your convictions, to act with integrity when no one is applauding, and to speak truth when silence would be more comfortable. Your family is watching how you handle pressure. Your community is observing how you respond to adversity. Your generation is taking cues from the standard you set. Courage is not merely a private virtue; it is a public witness. The way you live either raises the bar or lowers it for those who follow behind you. Your courage gives others permission to be brave. When you take the first step, others find the strength to move forward. Boldness is contagious. One act of faith can spark a chain reaction of confidence, conviction, and character in an entire circle of influence. When you live with uncommon courage, you don't just change your own story - you ignite bravery in others and help shape the spirit of your time.

Courage is deeply connected to faith because it dares to trust beyond what is visible. It does not wait for perfect clarity or guaranteed outcomes before taking a step. Faith-filled courage moves forward even when the path is partially hidden, believing that God is already present in the unknown. It understands that not every detail will be explained in advance, yet it chooses to walk anyway. Courage rooted in faith is not reckless - it is confident that the One who calls you forward has already prepared the way. When courage and faith work together, obedience becomes the bridge to breakthrough. Fear will always argue for caution, comfort, and delay, but faith whispers, "Step forward." Courage listens to that whisper. It believes that obedience opens doors that fear would keep closed and that blessings often wait on the other side of a bold decision. When you trust beyond what you see and obey beyond what you fully understand, you position yourself for doors that only faith-filled courage can unlock.

The courageous do not wait for perfect timing; they move when conviction calls. They understand that if they wait for every variable to align and every doubt to disappear, they may never move at all. Purpose rarely announces itself with ideal conditions - it calls in the middle of uncertainty, risk, and incomplete information. Yet when conviction is clear, the courageous choose action over comfort. They step forward not because the path is fully visible, but because their calling is undeniable. They also recognize that hesitation, if left unchecked, can quietly become a habit. The longer a decision is delayed, the heavier it feels. Courage interrupts that cycle. It acts decisively when purpose is clear, understanding that momentum builds confidence. Each bold step strengthens resolve and sharpens discernment. The courageous know that destiny often hinges on timely action. They move when it matters most - before fear has the chance to take root and before opportunity slips quietly away.

To live courageously is to embrace responsibility. Courage does not run from accountability; it steps toward it. It understands that growth begins the moment excuses end. When you choose ownership, you stop surrendering your power to circumstances, critics, or past failures. You recognize that your decisions shape your direction, and your discipline determines your destiny. Blame may feel easier in the moment, but it slowly erodes strength. Ownership, however, builds resolve. It forges character. It transforms obstacles into opportunities for maturity and refinement. Courage understands that influence is not a platform for comfort but a calling to serve. Leaders who live courageously model integrity, humility, and consistency. They own their mistakes, correct their course, and keep moving forward. Responsibility is heavy, but it produces strength in those willing to carry it. When you embrace the weight instead of resisting it, you grow into the very leader you were created to be.

Uncommon courage is sustained by vision. When you can see clearly where you are going, you gain the strength to endure what you are facing. Vision anchors the soul when circumstances try to shake it. It reminds you that today's discomfort is not your final destination. When your eyes are fixed on purpose, pain becomes temporary, obstacles become stepping stones, and opposition becomes confirmation that you are moving in the right direction. Clarity about the future produces confidence in the present. Vision fuels perseverance, and perseverance builds victory. When you know the promise ahead, you refuse to quit in the process. Every setback becomes a lesson, every delay becomes preparation, and every challenge becomes training. Uncommon courage rises from a deep assurance that what lies ahead is worth pressing toward. Stay focused. Keep seeing beyond the struggle. The clearer your vision, the stronger your endurance, and the stronger your endurance, the greater your victory.

Courage also requires humility. The strongest leaders are those who remain teachable in every season. It takes real strength to admit you don't have all the answers, to listen when correction comes, and to grow when growth is uncomfortable. Pride resists instruction, but courage embraces it. The bravest hearts are surrendered - submitted to purpose, accountable to wisdom, and anchored in something greater than themselves. Humility does not weaken courage; it refines it, directing its power toward what truly matters. True courage does not boast; it builds. It does not dominate; it serves. It lifts others instead of proving itself superior. Courage rooted in humility seeks impact, not applause. It steps forward when necessary, but it also kneels when appropriate. It protects without parading, leads without lording, and speaks with conviction without crushing others. The kind of courage that changes lives is the kind that is strong enough to serve and secure enough to stay humble.

Living with uncommon courage means finishing what you start. Many people begin with excitement, full of vision and passion, but only a few press on to completion with excellence. The difference is not talent, opportunity, or even initial zeal - it is courage. Courage keeps showing up when progress feels slow and results seem distant. Uncommon courage understands that the true measure of character is not how boldly you begin, but how faithfully you endure. Courage pushes through when enthusiasm fades and remains steady when motivation fluctuates. It does not depend on feelings; it is anchored in commitment. When obstacles arise, courage chooses discipline over distraction and perseverance over excuses. It understands that greatness is built in the unseen moments when no one is watching and quitting would be easy. To live with uncommon courage is to decide that finishing strong matters more than starting fast, and that excellence at the end is worth every challenge faced along the way.

Let your life be marked by conviction instead of convenience. Refuse to shrink back when pressure rises or when the crowd chooses comfort over calling. Courage is not loud arrogance; it is steady obedience to what is right, even when the cost is high. It is choosing integrity over applause, faith over fear, and purpose over popularity. Every day you are given opportunities to step back or step up - and greatness is built in the moments when you decide to step forward. And when your story is told, let it be said that you did not live safely - you lived courageously. That you did not hide from challenge - you rose to it. That you did not drift with the current - you set a standard. And that you did not settle for common - you chose uncommon courage. May your legacy reflect a life fully lived, a heart fully surrendered, and a spirit that refused to bow to fear. In the end, it will not be comfort that defines you, but conviction - not ease, but endurance - not safety, but strength.

Uncommon courage is a decision - a daily, deliberate choice to stand when it would be easier to sit, to speak when silence feels safer, to trust when doubt whispers louder. Courage is built in quiet moments long before it is displayed in public victories. It is formed in prayer, in perseverance, in discipline, and in the unwavering belief that what God has placed inside you is greater than the pressure around you. You do not have to be extraordinary to live courageously but living courageously will make your life extraordinary. Every time you choose faith over fear, obedience over comfort, and conviction over compromise, you step into a higher version of who you were created to be. Courage stretches you, refines you, and positions you for impact beyond your imagination. So walk forward boldly. Choose courage again tomorrow. And the next day. Because uncommon courage is not about who you are today - it is about the man you are becoming.

SUMMARY

"Uncommon Courage" has shown us that courage is not a personality trait reserved for the fearless, but a daily decision made by those who choose purpose over comfort. Every meaningful step in life - success, growth, obedience, leadership, and legacy - demands the willingness to move forward despite uncertainty and resistance.

Courage is the key that unlocks potential, activates faith, and turns calling into destiny. When fear says retreat, courage says advance; when doubt whispers limitations, courage declares possibility. To live an uncommon life, you must practice uncommon courage choosing to stand, to act, and to believe even when the cost is high.

As you close this book, remember this truth: destiny is never fulfilled by intention alone, but by courageous action. May you rise with resolve, walk boldly into your purpose, and live a life marked not by what you avoided, but by what you had the courage to pursue.